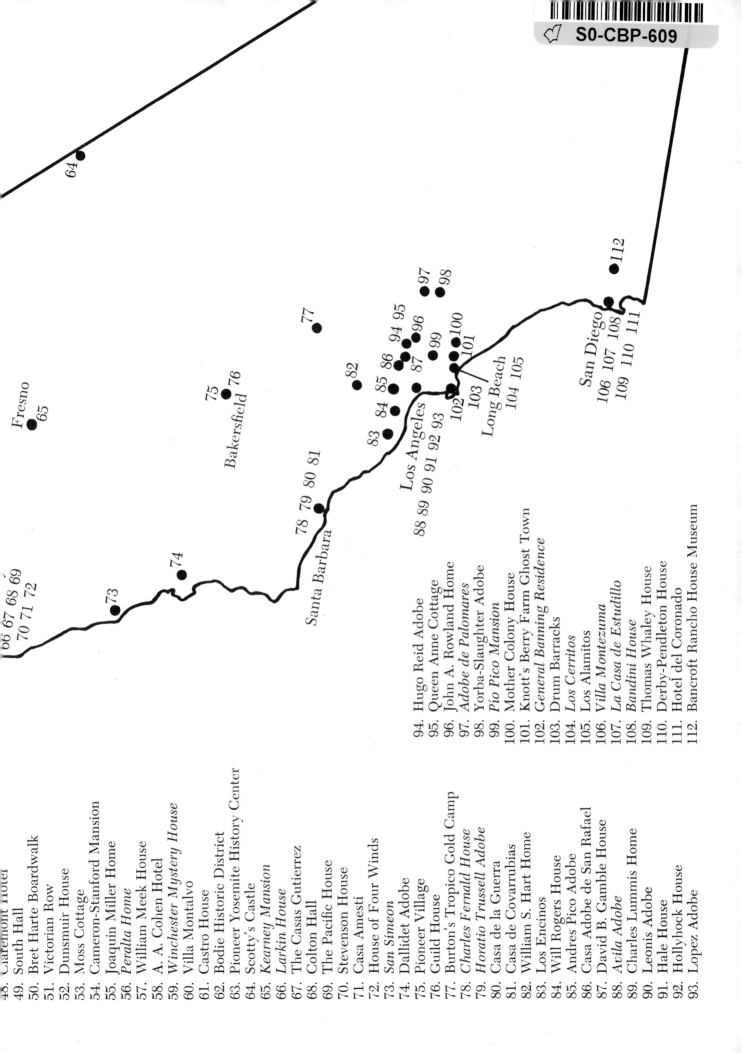

64

Fresno
65

Bakersfield
75   76

77

78 79 80 81

Santa Barbara

73

74

66 67 68 69
70 71 72

82

83 84 85 86 87
88 89 90 91 92 93

94 95
96
97
98
99 100
101
102
103
104 105

Los Angeles

Long Beach

112

San Diego
106 107 108
109 110 111

48. Claremont Hotel
49. South Hall
50. Bret Harte Boardwalk
51. Victorian Row
52. Dunsmuir House
53. Moss Cottage
54. Cameron-Stanford Mansion
55. Joaquin Miller Home
56. *Peralta Home*
57. William Meek House
58. A. A. Cohen Hotel
59. *Winchester Mystery House*
60. Villa Montalvo
61. Castro House
62. Bodie Historic District
63. Pioneer Yosemite History Center
64. Scotty's Castle
65. *Kearney Mansion*
66. *Larkin House*
67. The Casas Gutierrez
68. Colton Hall
69. The Pacific House
70. Stevenson House
71. Casa Amesti
72. House of Four Winds
73. *San Simeon*
74. Dallidet Adobe
75. Pioneer Village
76. Guild House
77. Burton's Tropico Gold Camp
78. *Charles Fernald House*
79. *Horatio Trussell Adobe*
80. Casa de la Guerra
81. Casa de Covarrubias
82. William S. Hart Home
83. Los Encinos
84. Will Rogers House
85. Andres Pico Adobe
86. Casa Adobe de San Rafael
87. David B. Gamble House
88. *Avila Adobe*
89. Charles Lummis Home
90. Leonis Adobe
91. Hale House
92. Hollyhock House
93. Lopez Adobe

94. Hugo Reid Adobe
95. Queen Anne Cottage
96. John A. Rowland Home
97. *Adobe de Palomares*
98. Yorba-Slaughter Adobe
99. *Pio Pico Mansion*
100. Mother Colony House
101. Knott's Berry Farm Ghost Town
102. *General Banning Residence*
103. Drum Barracks
104. *Los Cerritos*
105. Los Alamitos
106. *Villa Montezuma*
107. *La Casa de Estudillo*
108. *Bandini House*
109. Thomas Whaley House
110. Derby-Pendleton House
111. Hotel del Coronado
112. Bancroft Rancho House Museum

REMAIN To Be SEEN

Representing the Italian Villa style at its purest in California, the Bidwell mansion in Chico is a medley of color at early evening. (*—Tom Tracy photograph*)

REMAIN To Be SEEN

 Historic California Houses
Open to the Public

by Elinor Richey

Santa Clara County
LIBRARY

BERKELEY   Howell
-North
Books   CALIFORNIA

Renewals:
(800) 471-0991
www.santaclaracountylib.org

REMAIN TO BE SEEN
Historic California Houses Open to the Public

Printed and bound in the United States of America

Library of Congress Catalog Card No. 7-77694

ISBN 0-8310-7097-8

Published by Howell-North Books
1050 Parker Street, Berkeley, California 94710

CONTENTS

Contents continued . . .

The Gallery

(Alphabetically arranged)

Acknowledgments

ALAMEDA COUNTY HISTORICAL SOCIETY
THE BANCROFT LIBRARY
BERKELEY CHAMBER OF COMMERCE
THE BERKELEY DAILY GAZETTE
THE BERKELEY PUBLIC LIBRARY
CALIFORNIA HISTORICAL SOCIETY
CITY OF OAKLAND
THE CHICO ENTERPRISE-RECORD
EL PUEBLO DE LOS ANGELES
THE FRESNO BEE
FRESNO CHAMBER OF COMMERCE
HISTORIC AMERICAN BUILDINGS SURVEY
LONG BEACH PUBLIC LIBRARY
LOS ANGELES CHAMBER OF COMMERCE
LOS ANGELES PUBLIC LIBRARY
OAKLAND CHAMBER OF COMMERCE
THE OAKLAND MUSEUM
THE OAKLAND PUBLIC LIBRARY
PACIFIC TELELPHONE AND TELEGRAPH CO.
THE OAKLAND TRIBUNE
THE SAN FRANCISCO CHRONICLE

THE SAN FRANCISCO PUBLIC LIBRARY
SANTA BARBARA HISTORICAL SOCIETY
SERRA MUSEUM AND LIBRARY
STATE OF CALIFORNIA LIBRARY
WELLS FARGO BANK HISTORY ROOM
MRS. MARY ELLEN BAILEY
MRS. FRANCES BUXTON
MR. MARTIN COLE
MR. ROBERT DeVELBISS
MR. AND MRS. ALFONSO FAGES
MRS. VIVIENNE L. GEORGE
MR. AND MRS. EDWIN GLEDHILL
MR. LOUIS KOUE
MRS. JACQUES MARX
MRS. CELESTE McCLOUD
MR. TED MOULTON
MISS IRENE MORAN
MR. JAMES E. MOSS
MR. LOREN NICHOLSON
MRS. MILLIE ROBBINS
MR. AND MRS. LOUIS STEIN

MR. LEONARD VERBARG

DEDICATION

TO HILL
who found the right roads

Distinguished by its meticulous classic detailing, the elegant E. B. Crocker house exemplifies the height of Victorian taste. Today it houses Sacramento's Crocker Art Gallery. (*—Pope Studios*)

INTRODUCTION

Concern for our environment is a prime preoccupation in California nowadays. We're alarmed over what we're losing — clean air, green space, the California crab. And our familiar landmarks. The disappearance of a favorite vintage house or building makes us feel bereft, uneasy. We don't know precisely why this is, but psychologists say the old and familiar in our environment satisfies our animal sense of territory; a structure that "has always been there" tells us we're on friendly ground — we're *safe*. Moreover, our older buildings place us in *time*. They suggest an orderly progress from the past into the future, thus lending a comforting sense of permanence and continuity. Amidst them, we can better understand our present situation. And those Victorian structures still among us answer a human need for ornamentation, an element conspicuously missing in the stark lines of modern architecture. A passing glimpse at a *fin de siècle* lunette can be as sustaining as bread. In short, our older structures give us a sense of identity and belonging, thus we want to keep them and our anger rises — fear even — when they are snatched away.

Californians have long been fascinated by their colorful past with its overlays of Indian, Spanish, Mexican and American history. And they are jealously protective of their landmarks that recall that past. Despite its relatively short history, California is one of the most history-minded states in the nation; having come from somewhere else, its citizens hastened to establish something familiar around them and to guard it. Historical societies abound in every hamlet; historical sites multiply almost daily. What is different today — what has spread alarm — is the enormous pressure

for land clearance generated by the population explosion on the Pacific Slope. Change has been so whirlwind fast, so overpowering. Often, despite all we can do, a distinguished house or building falls to make way for a freeway, a shopping center, an apartment development, even a mere parking lot.

But historical preservation has never been easy. One of the most salient findings in researching this book was that of the 110 recognized landmarks herein depicted almost half came near to being demolished. Now officially preserved, protected and, barring catastrophe, safe for posterity, they once but narrowly escaped oblivion. Reflecting upon this caused me to decide that in writing about the 22 houses selected for major attention I would not merely chronicle the story of the homes and their occupants but would report how each came to be saved — what individuals or groups rescued it, what methods they used. The first of them to be rescued was Governor Pío Pico's old adobe near Whittier, which in 1906 was on the brink of being hacked up and dumped into the river for bridge fill when its admirers intervened; the latest reprieve was a gem of a Victorian in San Diego.

However, the preservation movement in California long predates the Whittier rescue. It began in the 1870s with a mood of apology for past mistakes. After conquering the *Californios*, the *Yanquis*, in their zeal to make their new state seem familiarly American, obliterated many of the reminders of the Spanish and Mexican eras. Spanish structures were scornfully effaced and vandalized; missions and casas were turned into cattle barns and chicken runs. Then, almost suddenly, the Americans had a change of heart. Awakening romantically to their Spanish heritage, they decided it was part of California after all, and they began to restore what they had mutilated or destroyed.

The first projects were launched in Southern California, which inherited more Spanish structures than any other part of the West. There historical societies and church orders joined hands in 1876 to save the moldering San Luis Obispo de Tolsa Mission. Confusing restoration with repair, these novice preservationists displayed more earnestness than expertise. Recapturing the original appearance of the 1772 structure seems not to have occurred to them. They roofed it with shingles, enveloped the crumbling walls with utilitarian clapboard and, instead of returning the noble bells to a proper tower, hung them in a Victorian wooden cupola. The mission's appearance today is the result of extensive re-restoration in the 1930s.

The next restoration, at the less abused Mission San Miguel Arcangel, achieved happier results. Then, after the tomb of Father Junípero Serra, the founder of the missions, was discovered in 1882 under the debris of the collapsed roof of the mission at Carmel, a fund-raising drive among wealthy San Franciscans financed work that returned the mission's handsome contours, although altering some exterior and interior details. At several missions the restorers' zeal to give the inside a thorough cleaning dealt disastrous results to the original decorations.

When, in the 1890s, preservationists focused on the San Juan Capistrano and San Fernando missions, Los Angeles author-editor Charles Lummis organized the Landmarks Club to guide those and similar undertakings in the area. Lummis pointedly observed of the work in progress, "These two missions are being protected, not spoiled." The improved standards maintained there were largely due to his watchful group. By then, adobe restoration techniques incorporated such refinements as tinting plaster with oxblood and walnut stain and patting into place with rawhide mittens. Later, San Francisco's Mission Dolores was skillfully restored under the meticulous eye of architect Willis Polk.

After rehabilitation, most missions were deeded to the Catholic church, which returned them to parish use. Some priests who assumed charge became studied preservationists, but others were inclined to whitewash away original Indian stencils and to replace the simple, hand-wrought Indian furnishings with French Gothic imports. Still, out of these early experiments came the skillful mission restoration techniques of the present century. Yet as late as the 1930s Mission San Diego was given a most incorrect reconstruction.

The new ardor also embraced Spanish dwellings. The writings of Helen Hunt Jackson excited interest in them, but unfortunately her architectural depictions were most unrealistic, being a panorama of elegant, pastel-tinted *casas*, all tile-roofed, all multibalconied. Her misinformation and the fact that restorers worked singly or in small groups contributed some glaring inaccuracies. In their eagerness to recapture Ramona's time, the restorers were inclined to seize upon a rude two or three-room adobe and endow it with spacious additions and trappings more suited to the Escorial Palace than the humble, dirt-floored frame house it originally had been. The restorers of Pío Pico's house fell into this error, and later a state grant was necessary to remove inappropriate expansions and ornament.

But the game of landmarking continued apace. In 1903, William Randolph Hearst conducted a spirited preservation campaign in the *San Francisco Examiner* to save Fort Ross and the mission at Sonoma and present them to the state. Joseph R. Knowland also gave preservation a strong boost through the columns of his *Oakland Tribune*. Knowland, who was also a member of the California Assembly, spoke up and down the state stressing the need for historical restorations, emphasizing his points with stereopticon slides. Then, in 1906, California clubwomen co-operated in an ambitious project to name, preserve, and mark El Camino Real, the route of the mission founders. Along the highway, from San Diego to Sonoma, was hung the famous chain of mission bells. The picturesque bell replicas, suspended from iron poles and set a mile apart, spurred further beautification of the route.

Toward the end of the 19th century California's American history was getting old enough to inspire reverence and landmarking. In 1888 the Native Sons of the Golden West began the reclamation of long-neglected Sutter's Fort in Sacramento, the port of entry for so many American settlers. They raised $20,000 ($15,000 donated by Charles Crocker, the railroad millionaire) and purchased the one remaining fort structure and presented it to the state. In 1891 the legislature appropriated a like sum and purchased the surrounding property, paving the way for a complete rebuilding of the rambling compound. The Native Sons followed that feat by helping preserve Monterey's old Custom House and Colton Hall, the meeting place of California's Constitutional Convention. Another vigorous preservation force was the Society of California Pioneers, an organization composed of persons who arrived in California before 1850 and their wives and descendants.

Some historical societies undertook to operate landmarks themselves, but most preferred to restore and then find another caretaker. Municipal government was sometimes the recipient, but more often the landmark was deeded to the state. In enlisting the state government in their projects, California preservation groups differed from their eastern counterparts. In the East, both restoration and operation of historic houses has traditionally been the province of private organizations. These range in size from small-town societies to state, regional and national ones, such as the Association for the Preservation of New England Antiquities, the National Trust for Historic Preservation and Colonial Dames of America. (Although the two latter organizations have few properties in the West, each has one in California. Casa Amesti in Monterey is a National Trust property; Octagon House in San Francisco is owned by the Colonial Dames.) But acquiring a landmark and restoring it are only half the battle; maintaining it through the years is an equally expensive undertaking. Many house museums in the East are run down because they must live on entrance fees and donations. Wisely, California historical societies, being new and far from affluent, early trained their state government to the habit of maintaining landmarks. Few historic houses are profitable — which, of course, isn't their purpose; but when a government agency operates multiple properties it can balance the houses that lose money against the ones that are money-makers.

The state parks unit, today called the Department of Parks and Recreation, has long been the chief custodian of state-owned landmarks. Currently it maintains and operates several dozen structures classified as state monuments. Nearly half are from the Spanish and Mexican eras, the rest an assortment ranging from the humble home of Bear Flag President William B. Ide near Red Bluff to William Randolph Hearst's magnificent castle in the Santa Lucia Mountains. In recent years, faced with rising maintenance costs, the state has become wary of white elephants and is quite selective in the properties it acquires. Moreover, it has a program of encouraging citizen participation in maintaining and furnishing its properties. The reconstruction of Sutter's Mill, the Coloma sawmill where John Marshall discovered gold, was financed half by public subscription, half by the state. With the assistance of the California State Historical Landmarks Advisory Committee, the parks department has designated and marked with plaques nearly 900 "State Historical Landmarks" and "Points of Historic Significance." Many of these landmarks are house museums operated by municipalities and private historical societies, while some are privately owned residences.

Increasingly, a favored means of exhibiting historic houses is to restore an entire village as a "living museum," as was done early at Old Sturbridge Village in Massachusetts and Greenfield Village in Michigan. The California Department of Parks and Recreation has developed two excellent such museums. One is the Columbia Historic District in the Mother Lode town of Columbia, where the state has spent $1,000,000 since 1945 in acquiring some forty structures and restoring them to their appearance at the height of Gold Rush prosperity. The other is the mining ghost town of Bodie in Mono County, where 168 structures have been preserved in a state of "arrested disintegration." In 1952 the state joined with the City and County of Los Angeles in its long-continuing restoration of the original forty-acre Pueblo de Los Angeles, second of the pueblos to be established in Alta California. Several million dollars have been spent in re-creating the atmospheric plaza district at the foot of Olvera Street, which lies in the shadow of the Los Angeles

Civic Center. Numerous history-rich buildings have been purchased and restored for public exhibit. These restorations are being done with a fidelity that didn't mark earlier efforts.

This era of nostalgia has also made popular the invented historic district, the so-called "Pioneer Village" and "Street of Yesteryear." These vivid exhibits, which are copied after the outdoor architectural museums the Swedes have been enjoying since the 19th century, are created by moving period structures onto a plotted site or by building such structures anew. California's first was the "Ghost Town" at Knott's Berry Farm in Buena Park, to which Walter Knott moved old buildings from towns all over the West and created replicas of others to form "a gold mining community of the mid-1800s." The Kern County Museum at Bakersfield developed its Pioneer Village on twelve acres behind the museum by bringing pioneer structures from various parts of Kern County. Other pioneer villages, in varying stages of development, have been established at San Jose, Visalia, Santa Cruz and Fresno.

Alongside these methods of preservation, in recent decades another approach has operated: landmark protection by means of local ordinances. While Californians did not invent this method, they have been among its prime users and innovators. In the late 1950s a Santa Barbara historian, W. Edwin Gledhill, became concerned at the condition of El Pueblo Viejo, Santa Barbara's original Spanish district, long the top tourist attraction in a city whose chief income derives from tourist trade. The cluster of adobe houses and buildings that border the commercial district were suffering a variety of afflictions — deterioration, improper alterations, and incompatible neighboring development. Pricked by modernity and shabbiness, the Old World atmosphere was rapidly dissipating.

At his own expense Gledhill went to New Orleans to investigate how that city had retained the French flavor and substance of its 18th-century Vieux Carré. He returned with a plan for preserving El Pueblo Viejo via a local ordinance that would declare it a historic district and place it under controls. Learning this would first require a state enabling act, Gledhill enlisted help of the Santa Barbara Historical Society in pressing for the necessary legislation. Their efforts brought passage in 1959 of a California law enabling cities to create historic areas for the protection and perpetuation of buildings and other objects having a special character or special historic or aesthetic interest or value.

Soon after, in 1960, followed a Santa Barbara ordinance establishing legal protection for 16 square blocks of its oldest district, an area containing 15 adobes and other historic buildings, as well as the city's later public buildings designed in Spanish style. Among the latter was the handsome county courthouse with its sunken gardens and colorful murals. All buildings of Spanish origin and design were to be preserved and any alterations were to follow the original style; all later construction was to follow an approved compatible design. Building and alteration plans had to be approved by an architectural board of review with power to enforce its decision by denying a city construction permit.

As a result, El Pueblo Viejo made a glowing comeback. Handsomer than ever, today it is one of the most photographed historic areas in the country. Moreover, business and property values have risen both in and around the controlled area. Not surprisingly, it has inspired a train of imitating ordinances and districts all over California. They include Sonoma's Old Sonoma Historic Area, which protects those remaining Spanish buildings of the old pueblo that sprang up around the northernmost of the missions, and the fifty-acre historic area around the Mission of San Juan Capistrano. The Gold Rush towns of Nevada City and Murphys have established controlled districts to protect their old brick and frame buildings remaining from prospecting days. The cities of Los Angeles, San Diego, and San Francisco have also passed such districting ordinances. The newest district is San Francisco's Jackson Square Historical District, which contains two square blocks of commercial buildings dating from the 1850s, 1860s and 1870s. The handsome brick and granite buildings, which comprised the city's first retail and office district, miraculously escaped the earthquake-fire of 1906.

Districting was a handy tool, but it didn't cover the whole problem. It didn't protect scattered historical landmarks, only those standing in groups. While urban redevelopers could more easily be steered away from areas of concentrated historical structures, they swept unheeding over the historical house or building that stood singly. A new kind of preservation enthusiasm was approaching from the Eastern Seaboard. It offered an aesthetic argument, calling for saving structures for architectural reasons: houses and buildings that represented some significant style or building innovation or the work of a distinguished architect. This kind of structure, too, almost always stood alone, vulnerable to the wrecking ball. By the time the public learned a quality building was in danger, the owner was usually set on accepting some developer's tempting offer. There wasn't enough time to find another buyer, or to try to meet the selling price. Even San Francisco's famous Montgomery Block, which had the highest architectural *and* historical credentials, fell to the ax despite anguished local protest and the pleas of architectural experts all over the world.

Especially menaced in the early 1960s was Los Angeles. Historians and architecture lovers saw danger lurking in every corner. Not only was the city beset by an overwhelming immigration (more than 1,000 newcomers a day), but it was in the throes of rampant freeway building. As the cement octopus reached in all directions, as housing developments spread like a tidal wave, whole districts — landmarks and all — were being bulldozed and the chunks and splinters hauled to fill canyons on which to build still more housing developments. The city was about to become *Lost Angeles*, so far as its traditions were concerned.

Fortunately, Los Angeles was also experiencing a "culture boom," acquiring a new art museum and music pavilion. When some of the city's favorite houses and buildings began to disappear, public indignation began rising. One alarmed group was the Southern California chapter of the American Institute of Architects. The chapter formed a Preservation of Historic Buildings Committee to pinpoint the city's worthy period architecture and to study how it might be given legal protection. The committee carefully tailored an ordinance proposal that skirted opposition by committing neither city nor property owner to expen-

diture. Then it began rallying support among civic, educational, historical and business organizations.

In May 1962 the Los Angeles City Council passed a so-called "spot protection" ordinance. It created a five-member Cultural Heritage Board, an arm of the Municipal Arts Commission, and empowered it to designate as monuments those structures, sites and monumental trees which it deemed to have historical or cultural significance. Enforcement was through the board's power to withhold as long as a year any alteration or demolition of which it did not approve. During the year's "grace period" the board was to encourage and assist local citizens and organizations in saving the endangered monument. The ordinance was hailed as a first in the national press, which recalled that Los Angeles also had been the first major city to enact (in 1909) a zoning ordinance that separated residential and industrial areas.

During its first exhilarated year the board selected 16 Cultural Heritage Monuments. Some were self-evident, having been previously designated by another government or private group; some were recommended by the A.I.A.'s committee. But several were "discovered" by interested citizens. Indeed, the board was inundated with landmark suggestions. Even two burlesque houses felt their structures deserved landmark status. A fourth of the selections were Spanish; the others included Victorian mansions, churches, an office building, a public building, and a 150-foot-high stone formation shaped like an eagle. There must have been chagrin in certain quarters of City Hall at two of the designations: Frank Lloyd Wright's Hollyhock House, built for the oil heiress Aileen Barnsdall, and The Towers of Simon Rodia, the so-called Watts Towers, hand-sculptured of steel, broken bottles and sea shells. The city, after being presented Hollyhock House, had been ready to demolish it in 1942 when an admirer purchased and saved the residence. And in 1959 the city condemned the Watts Towers but was dissuaded by an aesthetic furor that echoed around the world.

If the city awaited a test of its ordinance, it soon was given two. In its second year, the board conferred monument status upon the Hyde Park Congregational Church, a diminutive 1901 frame structure that was the last remaining landmark of the former community of Hyde Park. The church promptly informed the board it had already made plans to raze and rebuild on the site. The board delayed the demolition but couldn't persuade the church to change its mind, and an effort to find another buyer who would move the landmark to another location failed when the structure proved too infirm to be moved.

Soon after came a threat to a monument in the Calabasas community, the circa 1840 Leonis Adobe, once the seat of a prominent ranchero. The adobe was found to be crumbling badly in the winter rain and its owner, who hadn't welcomed the restricting monument designation, declined to rehabilitate it. The board raised a flag of distress. Interested Angelenos quickly organized a Leonis Adobe Association and launched a vigorous fund-raising campaign. Their success permitted them to purchase the adobe, restore it, and furnish it with period furnishings, including some of the original furniture. In May 1966 the association opened the attractive landmark to the public free of charge.

Thus the Los Angeles ordinance revealed certain weaknesses. In the end, it could not stop demolition if the owner were adamantly set on razing; nor could it force an owner to maintain the landmark. Moreover the ordinance did not solve the financial problem of preservation; the burden of purchase and restoration still fell on private groups or individuals. In short, the ordinance could only buy time by delaying demolition. But since fund raising nearly always requires time, the "grace period" could make all the difference between losing a landmark and saving it.

During the board's decade of creating landmarks, success and failure have rhythmically alternated. Several new monuments are added each year; the count at this writing is exactly 100. Besides Frank Lloyd Wright designs, the monument roster includes works by Joseph Cather Newsome, Bertram Grosvenor Goodhue, Robert David Farquahar and George H. Wyman. The motion picture industry has been memorialized by designating Charlie Chaplin's old studio and Grauman's Chinese Theater. Several venerable oaks and fig trees have been chosen, as well as whole groves of deodar cedars and olive trees.

Cities across the country have adopted ordinances patterned after the Los Angeles method, as have several California towns and cities, including San Francisco. San Francisco's landmarks had been almost as hard-hit as Los Angeles', victims of large-scale redevelopment in the downtown district and neighborhood urban renewal projects. The Montgomery Block was but one of a train of distressing losses. Columnist Herb Caen warned that the city was swapping its character for "look alikes" and "ice-trays-in-the-sky." To educate the city on the value of its architecture and the need to save it, the San Francisco Junior League undertook to survey all pre-1920 structures and rate their significance. Meanwhile, a group of concerned citizens had formed the California Heritage Council to lend state-wide assistance in landmark campaigns and to advise in restorations. These groups, together with the local A.I.A. chapter, sought as an additional tool a preservation law.

In 1966 the San Francisco Board of Supervisors passed an ordinance that incorporated Los Angeles' "spot protection" and Santa Barbara's districting. The board it created was larger than Los Angeles', being an 11-member body attached to the City Planning Commission; moreover it seemed to possess stronger enforcement power. While giving the board power to delay demolition and alterations, the ordinance also contained a punitive clause: violators could be fined $500 and/or jailed six months for each violation.

To date, the San Francisco board has designated some 46 landmarks and one historical district, the afore-mentioned pioneer commercial block. Unlike its Los Angeles counterpart, the board in its first selections exhibited an overriding fear of controversy, choosing obvious landmarks such as Mission Dolores and the San Francisco Opera House, both presumably as safe as the White House. In most instances when property owners opposed landmark designation, the board backed down. A salient example was the 1887 James Flood house, the last remaining Nob Hill mansion of the Comstock and railroad tycoons. The Pacific Union Club, the present owner, feared the designation might draw sight-seers. Controversy also caused the board to withhold designation from the eminently eligible Seawall Warehouse and the Kong Chow Chinese Temple, both since claimed by the bulldozers.

More recently, however, the board has shown more courage. Over the protests of owners it conferred landmark status on Willis Polk's 1918 iron and glass Hallidie Building and on the so-called House of the Flag on Russian Hill. And it certainly braved opposition, not only from owners but from other business interests, in creating the Jackson Square Historical District with its tight controls over roughly 100 buildings in a high-rent commercial district. However, the board has yet to test its punitive power. Some observers predict the punitive provision will prove unconstitutional when tested in court. "Spot protection" ordinances have also been passed in Lompoc and in San Diego, which also has a districting provision. In Berkeley, the Architectural Heritage Committee of Urban Care is seeking passage of an ordinance in some ways similar to San Francisco's.

At this writing a proposal is pending in the legislature that would remove the major objection to landmark preservation ordinances. Under present tax policy a privately owned landmark must be evaluated by the standard of the "highest and best" possible use of the land, and property owners argue that landmark designation with its accompanying restrictions against alterations and demolition prevents them from realizing the financial gain that would ensue from converting to the most profitable use. The proposal would direct tax assessors to evaluate designated landmarks on their present use, not their maximum potential, thereby lowering taxes on such structures and, in effect, compensating owners for preserving a landmark.

Still another kind of preservation has been operating in the gold country, the one-mile-wide, 100-mile-long strip through the Sierra foothills that yielded $87,000,000 in bullion during the Gold Rush. Excepting the missions, no other areas in California are so rich in historical fact and fiction as these communities dating from the 1850s. Fortunately for history, economic stagnation long kept the gold country snoozing in a state of near-hibernation. Remaining virtually unchanged for decades were the false-fronted stores, iron-shuttered buildings and gingerbread frame houses and

hotels with swinging-door saloons. Then, suddenly, new freeways made the semighost towns easily accessible to tourists and week-enders from coastal cities. With them came a flood of gas stations, drive-ins and slablike motels with revolving neon signs.

Some local residents, cheering the end of economic stagnation, began remodeling their houses and business structures to match the new motels. But others preferred the way their towns had looked before, as did history-minded admirers of the area. Together they sought to stop the alterations and halt sales of older buildings to newcomers who desired only the land underneath. The state, too, became concerned; realizing that it was exactly what the crowbars and hammers were ripping away that had attracted the lucrative tourist trade, it stepped in with grants to help save the threatened landmarks.

The preservationists soon realized some sort of controls were needed. Consideration was given to the Santa Barbara-type districting ordinance. But small-town residents were reluctant to pass a law that told them what to do with their homes and businesses. Also, they had observed the tight controls the parks department had instituted in Columbia, where owners were permitted to keep their businesses in the exhibit area only if they conformed with myriad regulations and dressed in 49er costumes. Fearing stringent regulations, the townsmen opted instead for voluntary controls.

Local historical societies and preservation groups, aided by outside experts, including Ted Moulton of the California Heritage Council, worked out guidelines for maintaining the historical appearance of the Gold Rush towns. Optimistically, they set out to win co-operation by gentle persuasion. In some towns prizes and certificates were offered to citizens and businesses that met the prescribed standards. One recipient was the Mother Lode Bank of Sonora, which after losing its early structure to a fire, constructed a handsome brick building reminiscent of the period. In Nevada City, James Schaar carefully restored the Red Castle, an 1860 three-story, Gothic Revival brick house, and opened it as a tourist home; in the same town the Nevada County Landmark Association was successful in saving the old Assay

Office. Neil Stark refurbished his atmospheric National Hotel in Jackson. The City of Auburn guided its old district through a successful restoration. There have been other noteworthy feats of preservation — but not enough. These examples have attracted more admiration than imitation.

As the gold county becomes increasingly popular as a site for week-end homes, the value of land keeps spiraling upward, posing a threat to what stands upon it. With land offers growing more tempting, the cultural worth of every period structure is on a collision course with its commercial value. Some of the towns are beginning to concede that voluntary controls are not enough. As previously mentioned, Nevada City and Murphys have passed districting ordinances. Neighboring towns are watching the results.

More recently, another aid to preservation has entered the picture: federal money. Bitter criticism directed at federal urban renewal projects for sweeping out worthy architecture instead of incorporating it into project plans moved Congress to seek to make amends by aiding remaining city landmarks. Both the National Historic Preservation Act and the Model Cities Act provide for matching grants for acquiring and restoring structures of historic or architectural significance. In Los Angeles a Victorian apartment building was saved with a federal grant, while in Monterey urban renewal funds were used to revitalize the historic area which once served as the seat of government for Alta California. Historic buildings were restored and a tunnel built to divert heavy vehicular traffic from the vicinity of some of California's most cherished landmarks. The City of San Diego obtained federal money through its Model Cities Program to purchase and restore Villa Montezuma, a handsome Queen Anne-style mansion, which will be used as a combined historic house and culture center. Restoration of the old octagon-shaped Hall of Records in Santa Cruz has been partly underwritten with federal money.

Federal Urban Renewal funds are assisting the impressive effort to re-create pioneer Sacramento along the banks of the Sacramento River, a continuing joint project of the Sacramento Redevelopment Agency and the California Department of Parks and Recreation. Plans call for eventually restoring or rebuilding some forty historic buildings of the era 1849-1870 and selling most to private buyers for commercial use. The parks department will operate as museums several buildings that were connected with the building of the first transcontinental railroad. The Morse Building, a double-verandaed brick office building, was restored as a Federal Urban Renewal historic demonstration project, one of the first in the country. In the same vicinity the B.H. Hastings bank building, which served as the western terminus of the Pony Express, is being stabilized with a federal grant. Federal funds were assigned to San Diego to stabilize three Spanish adobes in the Old Town historic area.

Looking to our national government for preservation assistance is new to Americans; our tradition, which we inherited from England, has been to regard preservation as a local matter. But in most European countries it is long-established practice for the central government to foster and oversee local historical and cultural monuments, which constitute the Continent's prime tourist assets. Even the Romans were enthusiastic preservationists.

Preservation methods change, but there is nothing new about our attachment to our landmarks, a preoccupation basic to mankind through the ages. Historical preservation is even older than civilization. In fact, preservation of the past is precisely what brought civilization about.

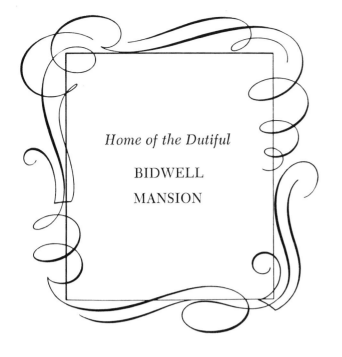

Home of the Dutiful

BIDWELL
MANSION

So ECLECTIC WAS DOMESTIC ARCHITECTURE during the Victorian Era, so wide and varied the possible choices, that a man of means might express his personality through his house as easily as with his tie and waistcoat. In 1864 when John Bidwell, one of California's most honored and affluent pioneers, then newly elected to Congress, decided to build a mansion on his Chico ranch, he might appropriately have opted for Gothic. Gothic was thought to suggest loftiness and piety, characteristics widely attributed to the bachelor farmer. Or he might have expressed another side of his nature by insisting upon the tried-and-trusted traditionalism of waning Greek Revival. Instead, Bidwell, possibly the most saintly nonclerical figure in western history, surprisingly chose a romantic, even sensual, Italian Villa.

To build it he commissioned the fashionable San Francisco architect Henry Cleaveland, who later would design the elegant first Palace Hotel. The design the two men settled on for a site on the banks of rustling Chico Creek was in the height of the Victorian escapist mood, and in it Cleaveland tried out much of the rich detailing that he later would use in the Palace.

This un-Bidwell-like house came about because, for the first time in his life, Bidwell was feeling matrimonially inclined. For years he had side-stepped the conjugal net, no easy feat, since his handsome face with its broad, high forehead and slender nose, his tall figure, and his shy, silent

air were as attractive to pubescent young women as his industriousness and clean living were to their fathers. Reposing in the California State Library is Bidwell's diplomatic letter refusing John Sutter's offer of his pretty daughter Eliza's hand in marriage. It was like him to decide on matrimony before he had shopped for a bride.

Bidwell, who came west at 21 in 1841 with the first overland party to reach California, and who served as right-hand man to the flamboyant Sutter, was the most deliberate of men. Most men came west to get rich but he came planning to farm, like his New England ancestors. He intended to work for Sutter only long enough to buy some land, and three years after arriving, while pursuing horse thieves, he spotted the land he wanted. Everybody trusted the earnest young man, and both Indians and Spaniards confided where gold might be found, but he was too intent on earning a farm to go looking. As historian Bancroft sardonically put it, Bidwell "had many narrow escapes from making the grand discovery of gold."

By 1848, having left Sutter, Bidwell was clearing his newly bought acres when he paused to make a trip to buy fruit trees and heard of John Marshall's discovery of gold. He didn't delay his mission, but after he had returned and planted his trees he decided to pursue some of his gold tips — he could use more land. Panning on the Feather River he found color and reasoned there would be more color in the riffles upstream. There

Bidwell Mansion detail. (*—Uncredited photographs in this chapter: Ward S. George*)

Exterior, built 1854, Belmont Mansion

was. He made the second biggest strike of the Gold Rush, and the riffles soon were overrun with prospectors and became known as Bidwell's Bar.

For two years he divided his time between farming and panning, quitting the latter before his claim ran dry. His gold take is said to have amounted to several hundred thousand dollars. Bidwell bought adjoining lands, enlarging his tract to 26,000 acres, which he called Rancho Chico. His grain and fruit farm, his store and his hotel for Oregon-bound travelers made him, without ever having to hurry his pace, a millionaire.

The stylish villa that began rising to replace Bidwell's Spartan adobe farmhouse was a three-story, 26-room house of plaster-coated brick. Its dominant feature was a lofty, front-centered square tower with arched windows and surmounted by a balustrade. Balustrades appeared also atop the wide, pilastered veranda, and these, together with the slender consoles supporting the roof, gave the effect from a distance of a delicate fringe. All windows were arched, some flanked by brackets pierced with a floreate pattern. Rooms and halls were on a palatial scale, with a grand mahogany staircase and handsome carved fireplaces of marbleized slate. If all this were not elegance enough, the staid bachelor had the house exterior painted pink with chocolate trim.

Several months after construction was begun, Bidwell met the woman he would marry. He met her in Washington, D.C., where he had gone to sit in Congress, and he knew at once his search had ended, even though she was twenty years his junior and moved in Washington's high society. Her family traced back to Andrew Ellicott, who helped L'Enfant plat the District of Columbia and served as the country's first surveyor general. But Annie Ellicott Kennedy, a petite, animated, blue-eyed brunette, was a society girl with a difference: instead of spending her days delivering calling cards and fitting ball gowns, she toiled in a Presbyterian city mission planting faith in unbelievers. Smitten though he was, Bidwell did not hurry his courtship, and when he proposed at the end of his two-year term he did not press Annie for a decision.

Back in Chico, directing his estate and overseeing completion of his house, Bidwell continued his suit with highly formal letters. He expressed thanks for copies of *The Presbyterian* and praised Annie's "conscientiousness." But he sought to interest her in Rancho Chico with reference to "very pleasant weather" and "many roses in bloom" and with progress reports on the emerging mansion. "The windows are all in. . . . The plumber is nearly through with his part. . . . The bell hanger has been up." He omitted to report the discovery that in his absence his small wine-making operation, intended purely for church communion purposes, had been turned to brandy making. Bidwell ordered all vines destroyed and the brandy spilled.

Annie's replies, while less formal, were in effect sermonettes. She repeatedly pressed for assurances that he had received full justification as a Christian. But the mansion piqued her curiosity — she requested a photograph of it. Finally, in December 1867 she accepted Bidwell's proposal, writing, "I trust it is . . . for our mutual usefulness." Their wedding was set for April and Bidwell hastened off on the long trip by way of the isthmus to fetch her. The wedding of the 29-year-old bride and the 49-year-old groom was a Washington social event; among those attending were President Johnson and Generals Ulysses S. Grant and William T. Sherman.

They arrived home in the full glory of a California spring. Annie was delighted with her fur-belowed pink mansion and plunged into decorating it in the French mode. The pair quickly settled into companionable and affectionate domesticity; "Precious" was his name for her, while she called him "General Dear," after his title in the state militia. The marriage that had seemed so improbable to their friends proved to be an ideal union. Their differences were merely of age and stature; he stood a full six feet to her four feet eight inches. Their minds could scarcely have been more attuned.

Both were piously religious, scrupulously moral and dedicated to doing their duty. Annie had worked among the wretched in the Washington slums; Bidwell very nearly did not reach California with his overland party because his sympathetic overtures to the Indians caused the party leader to try to abandon him upon the plains. Both had been schoolteachers, and both absolutely abhorred alcohol and tobacco. Eliza Griegson, in her pioneer memoir of life at Sutter's Fort, recalled Bidwell as "an honest steady sobber [sic] man using neither liqure [sic] or tobacco." Annie had early associated herself with the temperance movement and such was her aversion to tobacco that when she learned a certain flower in her garden was of the genus *Nicotiana* she ordered it uprooted at once.

Annie found work cut out for her at Rancho Chico. While training the ranch Indians to perform household tasks, she discovered that they were heathen. When Bidwell purchased the ranch, it had contained a village of Indians who went wholly unclad. He had coaxed them into garments by putting them to work in briars, thus demonstrating the advantages of clothing oneself. Once clothed they were taught to perform agricultural work and other ranch tasks and were exhorted to cleanliness, sobriety and thrift. But he had neglected their souls.

Annie presented herself at their village and set about converting them into Presbyterians by means of pictures and charts. Soon she was conducting a Sunday school for Indian children and preaching a weekly sermon to the adults. To broaden their religious understanding she began instructing them in English. Bidwell, delighted with his wife's project, constructed a chapel and school; then he kept on building, for Annie had persuaded the Indians to move out of their half-underground dwellings into frame houses.

The little church grew in both congregation and ritual. Annie taught the Indians gospel songs and organized a brass band for accompaniment; she also conducted weddings and funerals. She

Front parlor with many original furnishings. (*—Lloyd A. Maxon*)

Part of Bidwell's book collection in the parlor.

was distressed to learn that in performing pastoral duties she had exceeded authority, but she rectified this by persuading the Presbyterian church to ordain her as a minister. Then she performed baptisms as well. As the town of Chico began to grow around the square the Bidwells donated, churches sprang up and Annie was sometimes invited to deliver guest sermons. In time her Indian flock came to regard her as a kind of special chief, while she came to view them as her children. After much thought, Annie decided to ask them to give up their tribal dancing, and so great was their devotion to her that they unhesitatingly did.

Meanwhile, Bidwell concentrated on politics and agriculture. He declined a second nomination for Congress, desiring to be near his estate, but he was willing to perform state duties, and his admirers were anxious to see him in the governor's chair. However, a formidable obstacle intervened: his incorruptibility. In his earlier campaigns he had sought to avoid commitments, and now with Annie's encouragement he positively refused to engage in any sort of reciprocity or compromise. Nor would he engage in the universal practice of priming votes with whisky and cigars; lemonade was his standard treat. His disclosure that if elected he would sign no saloon licenses made him anathema to the vineyardists. His opponent made certain everyone heard of Bidwell's assault upon his grapevines and brandy kegs and made hay of the slogan, "Let the grapevines stand!" Further, Bidwell was no public speaker; he issued his earnest pronouncements with ponderous gravity — as one reporter phrased it, "weighing his every word as though it were a nugget of pure gold." He lost the election but won a fantastically loyal following who revered him as their stainless hero and nominated him again and again. Although he never again held office, when nominated for president on the Prohibition ticket, in 1892, he drew the largest number of votes yet garnered by that party.

More successful was Bidwell's career in agriculture. As a public service, he devoted part of his farm to experiments testing the adaptability of plants and trees to California. He laid out orchards for cultivating 400 varieties of fruits, with Annie assisting him by carrying a surveyor's flag. He grew the first oranges in Northern California, experimented with olive and raisin processing, and brought the casaba melon up from Nicaragua. He oversaw his project while riding a huge, sway-back mule named Linda. His products took many prizes, including a gold medal for wheat at the 1878 World's Fair in Paris, but he stopped exhibiting at fairs because of the horse racing, which he felt encouraged gambling.

Annie's family had feared she was cutting herself off from civilized society, but the Bidwells' activities made their pink mansion a mecca for V.I.P.'s. Bidwell's politics prompted visits by Governor Leland Stanford, Horace Greeley, President Grant and, in the 1880s, President and Mrs. Rutherford B. Hayes. His experiments with plants drew naturalists John Muir and Asa Gray and the English horticulturist Sir Thomas Hooker. Annie's work for the Women's Christian Temperance Union and her campaign to place temperance texts in the California public schools brought Frances E. Willard, and none less than Susan B. Anthony came to thank her for her work in women's suffrage. Phoebe Hearst came to discuss their joint work for the National Indian Association. In fact, visitors were so frequent that a servant was stationed in the tower to watch for their appearance on the horizon so that the Bidwells might be freshly dressed and ready to welcome them. In their later years, the couple wore white almost exclusively;

Annie's only adornment was the white ribbon bow that signified having taken "the pledge." Her small figure became plumply rounded, and her white hair encircled her head in short curls. Bidwell with his flowing beard was a dignified saint, she a smiling cherub. They entertained their guests graciously but simply, serving them lemonade on the veranda and cutting casabas under the trees; they took them on botanizing expeditions and picnics in the mountains in a horse-drawn tallyho. Their guests may have valued these visits somewhat as a rest cure, what with total abstinence, early bedding, and abundant exercise in the open air.

Duty spurred Bidwell to the end, and his vigorous seventies were devoted to rounding out his good works. Concerned for the future of the Bidwell Indians, he traveled to Washington to urge legislation that would permit Indians to own land and thereby enable him to deed land to his charges. When this was unavailing, he and Annie decided to will land to the Presbyterian church with a proviso that the church care for the Indians. They also provided for other worthy recipients, assigning gifts to the City of Chico, to temperance and to the church. Bidwell gave up his prized cherry orchards as grounds for a state normal college that later would become Chico State College.

Another project of Bidwell's twilight years was road building. Impatient with governmental delays in opening roads through the mountain district, he undertook to build them himself and Annie enthusiastically assisted. The "mutual usefulness" she had prayed for when joining her life to his by now had melded into a rhythmical unity of purpose and effort. She again carried the surveyor's flag and set up housekeeping in a tent, while Bidwell labored alongside his construction crew. One April day in 1900 he was bending to place a crosscut saw on a fallen tree in the roadbed when he suffered a heart attack. Later in the day he died, at the age of 80.

Annie lived twenty years longer, to the age of 79, continuing her projects, her preaching, her philanthropies. She died believing her beloved Indians were provided for, but her very earnestness had intervened. Her bequest of the mansion and lands to the Presbyterian church was so fraught with stipulations — not merely were the Indians to be looked after but the house was to be devoted to a coeducational school that taught the "evil effects of alcohol and narcotics on the human system, not only physically but in the impairment of all moral, religious and patriotic impulses" — that the church found it unfeasible to accept the trust. The property was placed on the market.

The mansion together with fourteen surrounding acres was purchased by the normal college, which used it successively over the years as a girls' dormitory and for administrative offices. But by the early 1960s the college no longer needed it. Dr. R. Coke Wood of the California Historic Landmarks Commission suggested that it become a state parks property, and Chico townspeople formed the Bidwell Mansion Restoration Association to encourage this step. In 1964 the California legislature assigned jurisdiction over the century-old mansion to the government division that is now the State Department of Parks and Recreation.

When transferred, the monument consisted of the mansion, the carriage house and a few original furnishings. State experts estimated the restoration would cost about $200,000; the work was to be done gradually as appropriations permitted. The division recognized the Chico association as an official state committee for advising and assisting in the restoration and appointed a parks member to work with the group. The initial appropriation of $60,000 was spent on paint, roofing, rewiring and installing police and fire alarm systems. The mansion's exterior, which had been painted white, was returned to its original pink. A subsequent appropriation of $65,000 has made possible a return to the original state many interior changes that had been made. State money has been supplemented by the fund-raising activities of the restoration association and the Chico Women's Club.

New flowered carpets are being financed through a unique project suggested by William Penn Mott, Jr., director of the California Department of Parks and Recreation. The asphalt floor tiles which have covered the floors in recent decades are the key to the fund raising; visitors to the mansion are invited to autograph the tiles for a minimum one-dollar donation per signature. Several Chico organizations have come over in groups to sign. After the tiles are covered with carpets a chart will show the location of donors' signatures. New curtains are being stitched up as a work project of the Chico Women's Club with material being provided by the state.

More and more the mansion is becoming the home the Bidwells knew. A vigorous continuing project of the restoration association is tracking down and returning, through purchase or donation, the original furnishings. Mrs. Bidwell's heirs have made contributions. Not long ago a former Chicoan now residing in San Francisco discovered she owned a Bidwell chair and donated it to the mansion. Presently about forty per cent of the original furnishings are in place. Even the bouquets are authentic: the Chico Horticultural Society keeps the mansion supplied with flowers, the arrangements being made by Mrs. Coin Knotts, a daughter of Bidwell's chief horticulturist, using the Bidwells' favorite cut flowers.

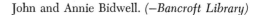

BIDWELL MANSION is located at 252 Esplanade in Chico. Open daily for guided tours from 10 a.m. to 5 p.m., except Thanksgiving, Christmas and New Year's Day. Admission 25 cents for persons 18 years old and over, others admitted free.

John and Annie Bidwell. (*—Bancroft Library*)

From Ugly Duckling
to Swan

THE GOVERNOR'S
MANSION

IN 1924, AT THE HEIGHT of the reaction against everything Victorian, the critic Lytton Strachey observed that the 18th century had returned to favor after being vilified, and it was possible that by year 2000 people might begin to see some good in the 19th century's Victorian Era. He was a half century off the mark. The 1950s saw the budding of a Victorian revival that by the 1970s has reached full flower. Not only is every imaginable Victorian art object being collected, but even Victorian architecture has circled back into esteem. Rococo houses, once neglected and ignored, are being lovingly refurbished, both by speculators alert to real estate trends and by owners surprised to learn their ugly ducklings possess the potential to become glorious swans. Strachey had failed to consider the quickening pace, which has accelerated virtually everything, even taste revivals.

It is due to this lively revival that California's former Governor's Mansion is once again in favor. After decades of being derided as a monstrosity, a torture chamber of physical discomforts, a fire hazard, and finally being abandoned precipitously by Governor Ronald Reagan in mid-office, the high-shouldered mansion on Sacramento's H Street now finds itself surrounded by admirers. Every

thirty minutes capacity-size tour groups enter its portals to gaze upon its features and furnishings in the spirit of visitors to an art gallery. Having served from 1903 until recently as the residence for the state's first family, this Victorian, atypically, has enjoyed the very best of care. Thus the venerable house finds itself, as it approaches its 100th birthday in 1977, not only at the height of its popularity but almost as good as new.

In its youth, of course, it was not called a Victorian. Its style was known as Stick Villa, a design that borrowed shamelessly from several other Victorian styles and because of its exuberance was sometimes called Barbary Coast Gothic. These houses wore the tall, square tower of the Italian Villa, the mansard roof of the French Second Empire style, and the stick framing and floreated lathecut of the Stick-Eastlake, the latter being the only element that owed a debt to Victorian England. But style mixing was then much admired — the more the merrier — and the Stick Villa was the favorite of those who struck it rich in the lush times of the Silver Seventies, which was when the house was built.

In the burnished formal library, largely furnished by the pre-World War I governor, Hiram Johnson, are displayed two books that bear the

Stairway from foyer. (—All photographs: Historic American Buildings Survey)

Albert Gallatin home, 1880s.

initials "A. G." They are the only remaining possessions of the mansion's first owner, Albert Gallatin. A native of New York State, he came west in 1860 and cast his lot with the lusty river town that had sprung up to serve the gold camps. Soon after, he had the good fortune to become associated with the then unknown merchants Mark Hopkins and Collis P. Huntington, joining them as a partner in their hardware business. After his partners became absorbed in building the Central Pacific, Gallatin assumed management of the firm and grew affluent on profits from supplying the railroad project. By 1877 he could afford to build himself a house, employing the services of the most fashionable architect in Sacramento, Nathaniel Goodell. Goodell had come out from Massachusetts during the Gold Rush, and while he had no luck panning, he succeeded as a builder for those who did. In the 1870s Sacramento, straining toward respectability, was experiencing a building boom and Goodell, who was mostly self-taught, was in high demand by the prosperous citizenry to build stylish frame town houses along the wide, tree-lined streets.

Gallatin acquired a prime building site, a half block on coming H Street at the intersection of Sixteenth Street, but at first his building plans seem to have been quite modest. Initially he stipulated that the cost should not exceed $14,500. However, perhaps with Goodell's encouragement, he jettisoned this figure in short order. Their joint concept blossomed into a grand-sized house with three stories, a basement, and a two-story tower. Inside were palatial halls, two 18 x 30-foot reception rooms that could be thrown *en suite,* an elegant winding staircase, and a third-floor ballroom. The full ground-level basement, which gave the house a high-perched look, was a precaution against the river floods that had long plagued Sacramento. (In 1862 Governor Leland Stanford was obliged to board a rowboat to attend his inauguration, and upon his return home had to climb in a second-story window.)

Top-grade building materials went into the construction, mostly acquired at wholesale rates through Gallatin's hardware business. The firm had supplied the materials for the recently completed State Capitol, and Gallatin incorporated

Front parlor.

many of the same items into his mansion. Being in hardware, Gallatin took special pride in the metalwork. The heaviest, most intricate cast-iron cresting and finials went on the roof and tower; inside, the brass hardware was as ornate as could be — even door hinges were richly incised. All interior detailing tended toward the fancy. Italian marble fireplaces were elegantly arched and columned, and over each hung a vast gilt-framed mirror. The paneled woodwork incorporated a variety of life-sized reliefs of heads, animals, fish, fowl and fruit realistically fashioned of molded wood shavings. The molded plaster ceiling had gold-leaf tracery on the raised designs.

At the rear of the mansion was built a two-story carriage house in a matching style and scarcely less rococo. During the two years the house was under construction, costs mounted higher and higher. Gallatin said he stopped counting after expenses hit the $75,000 mark, and this figure would have run appreciably higher had supplies been bought retail.

In 1878 Gallatin moved his family into the finished mansion. It was much admired and imitated and was locally thought to surpass even the Leland Stanford and E. B. Crocker homes. But Gallatin was permitted to enjoy it for less than a decade; a profitable side line to his hardware business drew him away from Sacramento. While his partners branched into railroading, he had dabbled in emerging hydroelectric power and in 1887 the company he was connected with wished him to assume the presidency, which meant moving to San Francisco. There he became a major influence in electric and gas utilities, associating himself with three firms that later would merge into Pacific Gas & Electric Company. In 1895 Gallatin gained national prominence by opening the first long-distance transmission of hydroelectric power in the United States, from Folsom to Sacramento.

The H Street mansion's second owner was another prosperous businessman, Joseph Steffens, the son of Canadian immigrants to Illinois and a partner in a Sacramento paint firm. Steffens was a long-time president of the Sacramento Chamber of Commerce but was best known as the owner of a string of fast race horses. Today, he is best remembered as the father of Lincoln Steffens, the "muckraking" author, who wrote a famous autobiography that chronicled his Sacramento boyhood, spent partly in the H Street mansion.

Meanwhile, the state had long talked of acquiring a governor's mansion, lacking since the capital moved to Sacramento in 1854. Governors had been obliged to provide their own quarters, and while Governor Stanford, a local resident, had lived elegantly in his own house, others had been obliged to rent, some living in modest hotel rooms. This was by no means an unusual circumstance in new capitals; in the early years of Washington, D.C., most high government officials lived in crowded boardinghouses. In 1870 the

Vertical complexity yields visual appeal in the near century-old Governor's Mansion, located in the heart of Sacramento.

state began construction of a house intended for a governor's mansion, only to run out of funds; later the structure became a printing office. But in the atmosphere of pride and optimism at the turn of the century, it was decided California's chief executive deserved an official residence, and a search was launched to find, if possible, a suitable existing one.

After a selection commission began inspecting prospects, Steffens added his mansion to the available list, and amid considerable surprise and controversy it was chosen. Many thought the house too outmoded. During the Victorian Era residential styles came and went like ladies' hats, and by then Stick Villas were several hats behind.

Serving on the commission was Governor-elect George C. Pardee, who influenced the selection. Branding the house old-fashioned, the *Sacramento Union* commented: "The capital commissioners evidently considered comfort more than modern styles. . . . It is known that the governor recognized that the building had not the architectural design of modern construction, but he considered that the palm trees and other sub-tropical growth about the place more than compensated for any imputed shortcomings in other regards." But the governor may also have been swayed subconsciously by the mansion's vague resemblance to the Oakland home he had grown up in, an 1869 Italian Villa with a front-centered square tower.

Formal dining room.

The price paid was $32,500, which, deducted from the $48,750 appropriated by the legislature, left a modest fund for purchasing furniture and making repairs.

In November 1903 the Pardees moved in and became the first official occupants. The family included four lively young daughters, who made frequent use of the large croquet grounds. Several alterations were made during the Pardees' residency. Two rooms, one above the other, were attached at the west, one for a servants' dining room (later used as the family dining room) and a governor's office (later a bedroom). The curious boxlike extension of the master bedroom into a dressing room was also made at that time. By 1907, when the Pardees surrendered the mansion to another Oakland family, the James Gilletts, the state had spent a total of $56,000 on purchasing and improving the house.

The next expenditures were unplanned — for damages resulting from an attempt to assassinate Governor William D. Stephens. It happened during Christmas week in 1917; a dynamite blast, attributed to the Industrial Workers of the World, left the governor and his wife unharmed, but destroyed the kitchen and pantry. The rooms were rebuilt, taking advantage of the opportunity for modernization. Two years later, during the vogue for sleeping in the open air, a sleeping porch was appended at the southeast corner.

Thereafter, attacks on the mansion were confined to verbal and printed ones, made intermittently over the years. The complaints most likely originated among occupants but were articulated by their sympathizers in government and in the press. The gist was that the house was antiquated and the state ought to provide more modern quarters for its first family.

Interestingly, the main attack was on the grounds that the *Sacramento Union* in 1903 had conceded to be the house's one redeeming feature — comfort. Notions of comfort had undergone a change. The big, high-ceilinged rooms were said to be hard to heat or cool and, being ranged along a central hall, were inconvenient. A newspaper's revival of the question sometimes drew a letter from a former occupant who now felt free to speak up, usually a former governor's grown-up

offspring reporting the mother's laments at trying to rear a family in the formal setting.

Further, the advent of simple, squared-off modern architecture made the mansion seem "deplorably over-ornate." The Los Angeles newspapers seemed to vie in taking aesthetic potshots: to the *Los Angeles Times* it resembled "a six-tiered wedding cake," while to the *Mirror* it appeared "the inspiration for a Charles Addams cartoon." The changing environment was likewise deplored. Sixteenth Street had become one of the city's busiest arteries, and the central business district was reaching toward the neighborhood, dotting it with service stations, motels and other commercial establishments. A new freeway was routed near by. When the state fire marshal declared the mansion to be a fire risk and unfit for occupancy, its abandonment seemed only a matter of time.

Then, surprisingly, the mansion's stock seemed to rally. As a concession to modernity, the iron grille and finials were sheared from the roof. Fire precautions were taken in the form of rope fire escapes to supplement the metal ones. Wartime

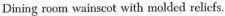

Dining room wainscot with molded reliefs.

exigencies and the accompanying construction freeze quelled new mansion talk, and when it revived again, the Victorian reappraisal had set in to counter aesthetic attacks. Talk of replacing the mansion drew a new sort of letter: "Why must all so-called old buildings be replaced with slabs of brick, cement and glass?" "Isn't 88 years old quite young compared to the 200- and 300-year-old homes in the East?" If the White House could be made livable, it was asked, why couldn't the Governor's Mansion?

Further encouragement came from within the mansion. The energetic Earl Warren family, who occupied the house longer than any other official family (from 1943 to 1955), insisted they found the house quite comfortable. The athletic governor bounded up and down the long staircase to his third-floor office besides walking the nine blocks to his office in the State Capitol. The succeeding Goodwin Knights were delighted with the architectural style. Each Christmas season, Mrs. Knight hung the square tower with colored lights. While the Edmund "Pat" Browns seemed lukewarm about the mansion, they were appeased by the new outdoor swimming pool their admirers had installed on the side lawn.

But it was only a false rally after all, the rally before the end — as the Governor's Mansion, at least. In 1967 Governor Reagan, the former popular movie star, became the thirteenth governor to occupy the mansion. Soon after moving in, he and Mrs. Reagan, a former Hollywood starlet, candidly expressed their displeasure with the period house, which they found in startling contrast to their ultramodern home in Pacific Palisades. At a press conference the governor said he and the first lady were thinking of living elsewhere. Soon after, an accidentally triggered fire alarm at the mansion sent Mrs. Reagan and her eight-year-old son Skipper scurrying out into the front yard. She told reporters the experience had made her more determined than ever to move out of the house. Several weeks later the Reagans moved into a leased residence in the suburbs of Sacramento, and it was tacitly understood that the mansion's official use had ended.

For the remainder of 1967 the fate of the mansion hung in limbo while a California Senate subcommittee studied possible uses suggested by the governor's office: open it for a six-month trial to see if it had attraction as a public monument; move it to another site; turn it over to a private historical group and let them operate it; or sell the mansion to private interests for use or demolition.

Both the press and public rallied strongly behind the first suggestion, and in time the legislature sided with them. The California Department of Parks and Recreation was assigned to operate the mansion during its trial run as an historic house museum. It was to be exhibited furnished as it had been during its final years of use, with reminders of most of its occupants: the huge porcelain bathtub selected by the Pardees, Governor Johnson's library, the front bedroom decorated by Mrs. Knight, the Rose Room furnished by Mrs. Brown and the richly-hued Oriental rugs Mrs. Warren selected. The original cast-iron fence erected by Albert Gallatin still surrounded the premises.

From the beginning, crowds flocked to the box office set up in the rococo carriage house. There was never any doubt the state had a hit on its boards. In 1968 the mansion was officially designated a State Historical Landmark, and the department extended the successful trial run into a permanent showing.

Sixty-five years after the selection commission dissolved following the purchase of the Gallatin mansion, a second group formed to choose another Governor's Mansion. And this time, mindful of experience, sentiment favored new construction. A building site was purchased, an ample plot on a bluff overlooking the American River, but at this writing construction is still awaiting funds and has not gotten underway. Thus it is possible a new governor might assume office before the projected modern mansion is ready for occupancy, possible that he might reverse the trend of events by demanding to live in the old one. But it is expected he would choose not to disturb the old mansion, which finds itself at last playing a role for which it is wholly suited.

The GOVERNOR'S MANSION, located at 16th and H streets in Sacramento, is open to the public daily by guided tour, from 10 a.m. to 5 p.m., except on Thanksgiving, Christmas and New Year's Day. Admission is 50 cents for those 18 and over, free to all others.

Entrance hall displays Oriental rugs and ceiling tracery.

The Houses
General Vallejo Built

PETALUMA ADOBE

AND

LACHRYMA MONTIS

SQUATTING UPON A BARREN KNOLL near the Pacific Coast thirty miles north of San Francisco is a structure so huge and hulking that it startles anyone who comes upon it unawares, yet it is but half the size it was built in the mid-1830s. Once a hive of vital activity, today it broods in a silence broken only by the wind that rattles the dry grasses.

The Petaluma Adobe was the largest adobe structure ever built in Northern California, and it was meant to startle none less than the Czar of Russia. To the fury of California's Mexican rulers, his subjects had been doing some poaching in the district. Mexican procrastination about establishing settlements north of San Francisco had emboldened the Russians to steal down from their Alaskan toe hold and set up a fur post at Fort Ross, only 65 miles north as the crow flies from the inadequate San Francisco Presidio. It looked like a springboard for another southward leap. Spurred to action at last, the Mexicans established a pueblo at Sonoma and then seven miles to the southwest toward Petaluma built the giant adobe as a road block to the feared advance.

The structure has a puzzling neither-fish-nor-fowl aspect because it was multipurpose, designed to serve simultaneously as fortress, headquarters for colonization and residence for the man entrusted with these vital operations. This symbol of Mexican impregnability was given the shape of a rectangle, 250 feet long and two stories high, with a great inner court overlooked by a continuous second-level veranda. (The entire south half of the rectangle was destroyed by fire in 1947, leaving a giant "U.") Walls were laid four feet thick at their base and, for defense, windows were few, those small and protected with both iron grilles and thick shutters. The structural framework was gigantic redwood beams lashed together with rawhide thongs as strong as iron. Lumber for the woodwork was supplied by a steam sawmill an American had erected at Bodega, the first such mill on the Pacific Coast.

For nearly a decade, beginning in 1834, the knoll was a beehive of construction activity, engaging an army of workers including Indians, Hawaiians and Americans. Building two stories was a break with adobe tradition; after building got under way, it was decided to follow the two-story plan recently introduced by the American Consul Thomas Larkin in Monterey and to copy Larkin's shingle roof as well.

Looming high and mighty like his house in California history is the man who masterminded the structure, Mariano Vallejo. The Monterey-born son of a Spanish soldier in the Portolá expedition, Vallejo was only in his mid-twenties when Governor Figueroa dispatched him north to halt the Russians. Bearing the formidable titles of *comandante* of the Northern Frontier and director of

Gazebo at Lachryma Montis. (—*Uncredited photographs: California Dept. of Parks & Recreation*) » 32 «

Wing of Petaluma Adobe.

colonization, he was handed unlimited authority over his territory and thus became California's most powerful administrator, save the governor himself. He had been a soldier since 15, however, and already had proven his valor in Indian campaigns. Besides, he was bright, self-educated from books smuggled in behind the priests, and fairly bursting with ambition. Although stockily built, he was lively and energetic and beamed a perpetual smile above his round, full chin. Further he possessed diplomatic aptitude, being genial, courtly and slightly dandyish; he had sent to Paris for a wedding vest for his recent marriage to a San Diego beauty. These qualities would come in handy for penetrating the Russians' lair and sniffing out their intentions.

While drilling his troops and building a cache of arms, Vallejo paid courteous visits to Russian headquarters at Fort Ross and suavely charmed his way into their confidence. But what he ascertained there was most surprising: the Russians had abandoned plans to establish an American colony and had begun phasing out their California operations. It wasn't the rattle of Mexican sabers that had shied them, however, but inhospitable hints dropped by the United States.

The Mexicans had been so preoccupied with the fur trappers that they had scarcely noticed the Americans rumbling across the Sierra. Now Vallejo, gauging the increasing arrivals of immi-

grant wagons hung with pots and plows, perceived that the annexation of California was imminent — not by Russia, but by the United States. This didn't distress him; he had long admired the *Yanquis*. In 1836, when invited by an American family on Yerba Buena to join them in celebrating the Fourth of July, he had delivered an impassioned oration on George Washington. Further, he had grown disgruntled with Mexico's lax, penny-pinching administration (his salary was far in arrears). Although he publicly joined his government in warning off the gringos, he privately welcomed them.

This shift in foreign policy, so to speak, changed the course of the Petaluma Adobe; it no longer was needed for a showdown with the Russians. Vallejo constructed himself a casa in Sonoma, and the fortress was turned to enterprises connected with his surrounding ranchos. The Mexican government had presented him with lands totaling more than 175,000 acres, mostly territory the Russians had been thought to be eying; the grant doubtless was a calculated incentive to defend it. Now with no necessity for defense, except against a few disgruntled Indians who preferred Russians to Spaniards, these lands were devoted to stock raising and agriculture that proved astonishingly profitable.

In the adobe were stored and processed the ranchos' products, with lower floors serving as

» 33 «

warehouses, upper floors as factories. Trained Indian artisans, who daily answered roll call in the courtyard, worked over looms, weaving blankets, rugs and coarse textiles, and at leatherwork, fashioning boots, shoes, bridles and saddles. Smaller surrounding buildings smoked, clattered and steamed with the processes of meat curing, tanning, blacksmithing and soap making. The wares of this remarkable manufactory, which in full gear employed 600, were marketed to settlers and Indians and exported via ship to coastal communities as far south as San Blas, Mexico. The most satisfied customers were the Fort Ross Russians, who continued to send orders even after they retreated to Alaska in 1841. In a good year, Vallejo grossed more than $100,000.

These once animated workrooms have been restored and re-equipped to demonstrate their original use. Some of their actual products are displayed there in the dim light, which must have strained many Indian eyes. Also restored is the large family apartment, to which the Vallejos retired in summer to catch the breezes the knoll enticed and to which guests were assigned in winter. The rusticated chairs, sofas, beds and candle sconces are of Spanish motif as interpreted by Indians.

The prosperity that radiated around the adobe made Vallejo the most affluent man in Northern California. As his military role diminished, he grew florid and portly, assuming the role of a good-living country squire. His troops, with only an occasional Indian skirmish to quell, mostly drowsed in the Sonoma Plaza, playing the guitar while guns and cannon rusted. Indeed, soldiering seems to have become a kind of play. Vallejo outfitted an Indian chief in his employ with a Mexican officer's uniform and cockade and provided him with an "honor guard" of 44 Indians bedecked with capes and caps. He also indulged the queer notion of training Indians to fence with cattle bones, drilling them in spectator duels in the plaza. These same Indians doubled with war dances to entertain visitors.

Additionally, dozens of Indians were attached to the Vallejo household, which was run on a luxurious scale. The local Indians were of a highly specialized bent and refused to learn but one task; the one assigned to the dusting or churning would disdain to take a turn at the ironing board. It was a division of labor not unlike that of the almoners, cupbearers and carvers at the teeming court of Henry VIII.

Maintaining a sumptuous table and wine cellar, Vallejo exchanged social compliments with the Russian commander, Count Rotcheff, and his exquisite blonde wife, the Princess Helena de Gagarin, the possessor of a stunning Paris wardrobe. Vallejo found her bewitching, describing her in his journal as "a very beautiful lady of twenty Aprils," while he and the commander he had expected to cross swords with toasted each other with brandy and framed business contracts.

Vallejo also enjoyed a happy family life as the doting father of 16 active children, for whom he sought every advantage. For their musical education, he purchased one of the first three pianos to arrive in California; a sea captain brought them around the Horn on speculation from Boston in 1843. It took three years to find a piano teacher, one Andrew Hoeppner, who entered a contract "solemnly to teach M. Vallejo and his immediate family to play the pianoforte, with all the science of the art, giving lessons of music at least during five years, or more should it be necessary." Vallejo, in turn, agreed to cede title to a thousand acres of land "as soon as Mr. Hoeppner shall have fulfilled religiously and entirely the stipulation." Vallejo himself seems to have passed up the opportunity to turn virtuoso, but visitors noted his delight in his young daughters' renditions for company in the parlor. Reportedly, he often was so overcome when the performer executed a thrilling run up the keyboard that he would dash forward and kiss her fingers. A yellowed record in the county recorder's office shows that Mr. Hoeppner received his teaching fee seven months before the five years had elapsed, claiming land which embraces the present town of Glen Ellen.

But Vallejo's life was not all roses of Castile. He brooded about the state of the country, about the many revolutions (which he adroitly managed to avoid) and the increasing brawls between "greasers and gringos." The instability was breeding lawlessness, especially thieving and cattle rustling. Men of property were worried about keeping it, and since Vallejo had more he worried more.

It may have been in the interests of protecting his fortune that Vallejo began surreptitiously to pave the way for American annexation. He seems to have believed that American administration would bring instant law and order. Although Americans, defying an edict forbidding them entry, were multiplying most conspicuously and Vallejo was under orders to expel them, he procrastinated. He didn't merely tolerate the *Yanqui*, he sold him provisions, sheltered many at the Petaluma Adobe and sold some of them land. He even loaned money and gave land to the most promising. Meanwhile, he rejected a shipment of colonists from Mexico, sending them back home.

Most Mexicans were far from sharing Vallejo's affection for Americans; indeed, they bitterly resented their success in business and amour. General José Castro is reported to have said: "A California *caballero* cannot woo a señorita if opposed in his suit by an American sailor. These heretics must be cleared from the land!" Governor Pío Pico was fuming with indignation, but perceiving he couldn't count on Mexico to rout the "perfidious people," he was considering seeking British help in expelling them.

The Americans grew alarmed. There were by now several thousand in California, and among them flew the rumor that "Castro's raisin' an army to run us out!" Hopes rose with the arrival of Captain John Frémont and a troop contingent, but he claimed to be on a geographical expedition and went on to Oregon. Some felt the Americans should seize the initiative.

Ostensively on the spur of the moment — but some believe at Frémont's suggestion — a small group of Americans decided to overthrow the Mexicans, set up a republic and seek union with the United States. They recruited followers by implying that they were under military orders. Ironically, they selected as their target not the American-hating officials but their secret ally, Vallejo, perhaps because he was more accessible.

A shaggy group of 32 buckskinned Americans stormed into his house at dawn on June 12, 1846; Vallejo couldn't believe his ears when told he was under arrest. He hospitably offered them brandy, of which they thirstily partook while still insisting he surrender. Finally, he decided they were offering him some kind of safekeeping and accompanied them trustingly.

The rebels paused at the Sonoma Plaza and ran up a Bear Flag, hastily fashioned of a red petticoat ruffle and a remnant of muslin upon which was sketched a crude star, a bear that looked more like a pig than a bear, and the words "California Republic," with the *i* in "republic" first omitted then inserted above. This handiwork, which burned in the San Francisco earthquake-fire, was generally credited to William Todd, one of the rebels and a nephew of Mrs. Abraham Lincoln. With their colors flying and a Mexican general in custody, the rebels declared California a republic. By this time Vallejo realized the situation, and his outrage was consummate. His docility so reversed itself that his captors had to tie him to a chair.

The upstart republic lasted less than a month. California was annexed by United States forces in an extension of the Mexican War; the Bear Flag was hauled down and the Stars and Stripes run up. Freed from jail, Vallejo toasted the new order, even though the Americans had stripped the contents of the Petaluma Adobe and squatters were camped over much of his land. Confident that his losses would be restored with apology, he announced his eagerness to assist the new American territorial government.

After California became a state, he was pleased to be sent to its Constitutional Convention, and his joy was unbounded when he was elected to the state Senate. In this euphoria at becoming an American he gave real estate developers two valuable tracts of land on the Carquinez Strait, on condition that they be named Vallejo and Benicia after himself and his wife; he also suggested that the former be made the state capital. He hadn't a doubt in the world that he would play a leading role in the new scheme of things.

The affluent new Americans were building residences in the Gothic Revival style, and Vallejo was no longer content with adobe walls. He set his heart on a Gothic house with all the latest American fixtures. His comely daughters were

Trees planted by Vallejo shade the back yard and rear veranda of Lachryma Montis. (—*Dorothy Pingree*)

At left, finialed front gable fringed with lacy bargeboard overhangs an arched Gothic window. Opposite, the Swiss-chalet outbuilding at Lachryma Montis is now a museum. (—*Both, California State Library*)

catching the eyes of American officers at gala balls in Sonoma and San Francisco. The oldest were approaching the betrothal age, and the proud father was anxious to give them a proper setting.

In the spring of 1852, Vallejo began building a ten-room house on a wooded slope on the outskirts of Sonoma, near an abundant artesian spring. Although pinched for cash due to costly litigation to recover his land, he wouldn't hear that anything be less than the best. The Gold Rush had pushed building costs sky-high: bricks were selling for a dollar apiece; carpenters were demanding $17 a day. But Vallejo still considered himself rich and, like the *Yanqui*, had many exciting deals in the wind.

All was tailored to the American taste. The rambling, multigabled, verandaed two-story design was constructed of planed redwood, befringed with lacy Gothic scrollwork and painted white. Adobe brick was considered much too old hat to be exposed to view, but a layer was placed between the walls for insulation. Interior finishings were of the finest imported hardwoods and marble; the walls were hung with ornate French wallpapers. In the Brussels-carpeted drawing room, voluptuous French furniture, all gilded and ormolued, rippled with curvaceous backs and cabriole legs. Upholstery was of the stiffest horsehair.

Opulent too was the landscaping in the Italian formal style then so popular with Americans. Between bordered walks and bowers of myrtle and jasmine, fountains splashed in the sun, and in the foreground a terraced garden rose from a crystal lake. There were costly plantings of exotics — pomegranates, bananas, Oriental grapefruit, figs, nectarines and, beyond the gardens, a large orange orchard. Vallejo christened this storybook setting with the high-flown name of Lachryma Montis, or "tear of the mountain," in reference to the spring. It is said that on a moonlight night, with the scent of honeysuckle and jasmine in the air and a guitar strumming, no more romantic place could be imagined. The setting could scarcely have been more calculated to encourage proposals of marriage. In fact, the five Vallejo daughters all married well and, to Vallejo's satisfaction, all of them to "foreigners."

At Lachryma Montis, Vallejo insisted on a princely style of living and entertaining. He undertook to establish himself as the unofficial host to visiting American dignitaries, and he was ecstatic when he enticed a prize catch to his polished mahogany table. He chalked up quite a guest roster that included Commodore Robert Stockton and the future generals Grant, Sherman, Sheridan and Halleck. At such times he would don his elegant *comandante's* uniform with its dashing epaulets, standing ramrod straight in it and wearing his beard impressively *à la bosca* with a narrow strip running from ear to upper lip.

Sad to relate, Vallejo's best-laid plans for becoming a prominent American somehow went

Museum interior.

He slipped deeper into debt. His once vast domain shrank to the mortgaged land on which Lachryma Montis stood, while his thundering herds dwindled to one milch cow and an old buckskin horse. His wife, once a pampered creature in rustling crinoline and flashing diamonds, took in boarders and dried fruit and chili peppers for the San Francisco market. She talked of converting the family bathroom into a public bath, but there Vallejo proudly drew the line.

In his twilight years, a forgotten figure, ignored by the celebrities he so admired, Vallejo sought satisfaction in past and vicarious glories. He boasted of his proud ancestors, among them the 17th-century Spanish admiral, Alonzo Vallejo, who had had the unhappy task of escorting Columbus back to Spain in chains. He wrote swaggering memoirs, embroidering them with fictitious adventures. He made a religious pilgrimage to Mexico City, making a point to sit in the seats of eminent divines, and when in Washington, D.C., to seek restitution for his losses, he made a celebrity hunt there, even wangling an introduction to Abraham Lincoln. A letter home exulted: "I have sat in the same seats where Washington sat and all the great men of the United States. I have seen it all and touched everything." Up to his death in 1890 his admiration for America never diminished.

The obscurity that closed in on Vallejo seemed final. It wasn't. Twentieth-century historians rediscovered him as the Spanish Californian who did most to pave the way for United States annexation and to ease the difficult transition period. The forgotten hero was eagerly reclaimed by the public, and during the 1920s when California was selecting its candidates for the Hall of Fame in the nation's capital Vallejo rated highest in California newspaper polls, although politicians finally assigned the honors to two religious figures, Father Serra and Starr King.

But Californians erected their own memorials to Vallejo's honor, and in 1933 the state purchased Lachryma Montis and its furnishings from Vallejo's daughter Luisa, his last living offspring. It was opened to the public, together with an adjacent museum of Vallejo relics, including his guns, saddles, spurs and *comandante's* uniform. The famous

astray. One by one his dreams vanished like thistledown. The prestigious positions in the new government went to Americans, and he and the other Spanish gentry were thrust into the background. The state capital went not to his namesake town but to Sacramento. His land empire vanished before his eyes, as lawsuit after lawsuit went against him. One of his granddaughters recalled: "The American lawyers were far better than the Mexican lawyers Grandpa had representing him. The squatters not only stayed, Grandpa had to sell more land to pay the lawyers." And all his fondest business deals fell through. As his situation worsened, Vallejo seems to have fallen for every proposition dangled before him. One in which he plunged money and vain hopes was a scheme to wangle a franchise to plant eucalyptus trees all across Mexico.

Vallejo piano, which had been inherited by an older daughter and strayed to Mexico, was returned to its old place in the parlor. Then, in 1951, the state acquired the Petaluma Adobe, after it had been maintained for a time by the Native Sons of the Golden West.

Historians keep the name of Vallejo burning bright, and honors continue to accrue. Perhaps the old *comandante* would have been most delighted by the one approved in the 1960s by John F. Kennedy and Lyndon Johnson: naming a nuclear-powered Polaris submarine after him. In October 1965 at a shipyard on Mare Island off Vallejo, once part of his domain and named after his horse, one of Vallejo's great-granddaughters in festive ceremonies, of the sort he loved so well, christened the wonder vessel the U.S.S. *Vallejo*.

———

The PETALUMA ADOBE is located three miles east of Petaluma on U. S. 101. LACHRYMA MONTIS is located at West Spain Street and Third Street West in Sonoma. Both are open daily including Sunday from 10 a.m. to 5 p.m. Closed Thanksgiving, Christmas and New Year's Day. Admission 25 cents for persons 18 and older, free to all others. A ticket bought for either the Petaluma Adobe or Lachryma Montis admits at the other on the same day.

Mariano G. Vallejo. (—*Bancroft Library*)

At left below are Vallejo's small hardwood chest and miniature portrait. Veranda at Lachryma Montis is shown below.

Housebound
in the Lowlands

JOHN MUIR

MANSION

PERHAPS A GLACIER or a mountain meadow would better represent John Muir's natural habitat than does the neat, cupolaed Italianate house that has been preserved to memorialize him. For only reluctantly was the wild Scotsman persuaded to come down from his beloved Yosemite and adopt the ways of lowlanders, those "soft succulent people who sleep in downy beds." And even then, until he died he was ever stealing away with his hardtack and bedroll to "climb the mountains and get their good tidings."

But his house at Martinez, behind the Berkeley hills, was for 24 years the base of the indefatigable naturalist, the place he called home, where he hosted the world-famous. And it was there in his modest upstairs study that the author who was first to decry man's despoliation of his environment wrote the angry, eloquent books, articles, speeches and letters that won us our system of national parks and forests — those miracle spots that grow ever more vivid as the green around them fades.

Today a visit to Muir's upstairs study with its mementos of his world travels, his books and photographs, his worn oak desk, brings a shocking revelation. On the windows are neither curtains nor shades, just as when Muir occupied the room; the tour guide explains the author wouldn't permit anything to obscure his view of the green Alhambra Valley. The shock comes when the eye falls upon the view those windows frame now:

an unrelieved panorama of gas stations, motels, drive-ins, oil-storage tanks and tract houses. While there is today a growing body of ecologists chanting "conserve, conserve," there is no burning-eyed John Muir to lead them.

The man who gave the nation a new conscience showed few signs of turning national leader when in the spring of 1868 he debarked in San Francisco, steerage class. At thirty, his credentials were hardly impressive: a college dropout from the University of Wisconsin (following no curriculum he was listed in the college directory among the "Irregular Gents"); a conscientious objector to the Civil War; a sometimes inventor of contrivances that were mostly impractical and all unremunerative; and a frequent wanderer in the wilderness from Canada to the Gulf Coast. His employment experience consisted of brief stints at a Canadian broom and rake factory and an Indianapolis machine shop. He was alienated from his father, a stern Scotsman who had emigrated with his family to a Wisconsin farmstead, and who considered his eldest son a failure. Muir jauntily styled himself a tramp, signing his letters "John Muir, Earth-Planet Universe." He had come west to tramp California.

Muir did not take to San Francisco, nor it to him. His deep-set blue eyes glared out at the city from a tangle of shoulder-length auburn hair and beard above a skinny frame in dingy jeans and a frayed coat. Sauntering up Market Street,

Ceiling medallion in Muir Mansion. (*—Uncredited photographs: Historic American Buildings Survey*)

scowling at what he considered an ugliness of commercialism, he stopped a passer-by and inquired the quickest way out of town. "But where do you want to go?" the man asked. "Anywhere that's wild," Muir dourly replied. Fastening narrowed eyes upon Muir, the man pointed to the ferry dock.

After crossing to Oakland, Muir hiked across the poppy-strewn San Joaquin plain to Yosemite, which he had read about in Indianapolis while recuperating from an injury. Entering between soaring rock walls into the hushed valley then awakening to spring was the critical event of his life. It was the most magnificent place he'd ever seen, beside which the highest achievements of man paled. Its impact upon him was overwhelming and permanent. Thereafter, his life's purpose was to protect Yosemite — later he extended it to include all of nature — from those who would abuse and exploit it.

His experiences at Yosemite formed the foundation of all his future activities. Quickly he became engrossed with two aspects of the natural spectacle, glaciers and the giant redwoods, and decided to remain and study them. To meet his meager expenses he herded sheep, only to become disgusted at the devastating effect their foraging and trampling wreaked upon tender mountain vegetation. "Hooved locusts" he branded them and began a campaign to get sheep barred from the area. Yosemite was then a state park operated largely for the profit of the hotel owners; the lax controls permitted grazing, even timber cutting. Muir worked for a time at a sawmill for the pioneer journalist and hotelkeeper James M. Hutchings, who needed lumber for enlarging his hotel. But Muir would process only fallen timber; he wouldn't touch hewn trees.

No more to his liking was work as a guide for the tourists who increasingly were flocking to *his* Yosemite. The chattering visitors exasperated him with their carelessness, with their lack of reverence, with what he called their "cheap adjectives" — the expressions "so pretty" and "how charming" sent him into a frenzy. Even artists who took liberties with nature in the interests of composition angered him. "Do you think you can compose better than the Almighty?" he demanded.

Fierce conviction was a trait inherited from his father, a religious zealot tireless at spreading evangelism and combating the "work of the Deevil," in which he included his son's interest in studying and sketching botany. Muir had rebelled against his father's unbending attitude without realizing his own uncompromising nature. Now he righteously vented wrath on those who did not reverence Yosemite as he did — on unthinking tourists, on the "tree-killers," on the "wool-and-mutton men" — just as later he turned it on miners, oilmen and utility companies. And his righteousness was his strength; his opponents found his pious certitude not only exasperating but often exhausting to the point of surrender.

Observing, sketching, taking notes, Muir focused on Yosemite closer scrutiny than it had ever received. The state geologist had attributed the formation of the unusual sunken valley to a sudden sinking of the earth floor. Muir soon was detecting evidence of glacial action — boulders of different composition from the mountain granite and parallel scoring on the valley's rock walls. Investigating further, he found remains of small glaciers still melting under the higher snow fields. He rightly concluded that rivers of ice had gouged out the canyons and carved the peaks. Passionately he argued his theories with all who would listen, while preaching against the despoliation of nature's bounty.

Out of his argumentation sprang his writing career. Those weary of listening to his vehement harangues, as well as impressed listeners who desired for him a wider audience, urged him to write instead of talk. Skeptically and reluctantly ("I find this literary business very irksome"), he began writing his nature sermons with an eagle quill on rough notebook pages. In the early 1870s he began sending them to publications his friends recommended, and to his surprise editors took at once to his unique blend of scientific observation, poetic expression and fierce conviction. To the fury of the state geologist, the geology department at the University of California recognized his glacial findings. And his astonishing appeal to "protect the wilderness — it is a necessity," won excited converts. His was a new voice in America. Nobody had ever postulated nature's "rights" or questioned "progress." Soon everybody was discussing California's supersalesman of nature, even the United States president.

His admirers' next step was to coax him down the mountain, specifically to the San Francisco area, where he would have access to libraries and intellectual companionship. It wasn't easy. For a decade he had headquartered in and near Yosemite, during which he had published some forty newspaper and magazine articles that had awakened national interest in conserving California's natural beauties. Famous men had come to seek him out, among them his idol, Ralph Waldo Emerson. Why join the "house-bound" lowlanders? What could the "wastes of civilization" offer him?

Nonetheless, he gave in, calling it an experiment. He moved into a rented room in San Francisco and complainingly but earnestly labored over his writing, accepting the advice of friends in improving his composition. With his articles in demand by top magazines, he began a campaign,

infuriating to many Californians, to persuade the federal government to annex Yosemite and drive out its exploiters.

Muir, markedly shy with women, was indignant to learn his friends had chosen a bride for him. She was Louie Strentzel, the quiet, intelligent daughter of a Polish-born physician and fruit grower who lived across San Francisco Bay near Martinez. When the couple were maneuvered together in a Berkeley living room, Muir was scarcely civil and quickly fled the house. Thereafter he carefully avoided her, until three years later when, unannounced, he presented himself at her home, pretending he had come to see her father. The father invited him to stay for a visit, during which there was an evening stroll with Miss Strentzel and somehow her woolen fascinator found its way into his pocket. Back in San Francisco, he wrote: "Dear Miss Strentzel: The other day I chanced to find in my pocket that slippery, fuzzy mesh you wear over your head." Soon after, he called again,

Martinez Adobe on the Muir estate. (*—Louis Stein*)

John Muir Mansion. (—*National Park Service*)

this time to propose marriage, which she accepted. She was 33, he 42. After their wedding in 1880, they settled down to married life in the home of her parents, not far from the site of the cupolaed house they would later occupy.

Thus the rugged wilderness man was tamed into a regimen of respectability in a cozy setting of needlepoint and antimacassars. The Strentzels soon presented their substantial farmhouse to the new couple and built for themselves a fine Italian villa on the hill. New responsibilities fell on Muir. He undertook management of the fruit ranch and is said to have driven hard Scotch bargains with both buyers and suppliers. Soon he was the father of two young daughters, Wanda and Helen.

Then Dr. Strentzel died and Mrs. Strentzel invited the Muirs to move up the hill with her. Muir protested; he thought the house too fancy. But at his wife's coaxing he relented and thus found himself the master of a mansion. The 17-room house was one of those fool-the-eye structures studiously constructed and painted to look like hewn stone with carved roof brackets and quoins at corners. Inside were such elegant features and luxuries as a mahogany staircase, molded and tinted medallioned ceilings, seven classic fireplaces of colored marble and two porcelain bathtubs. Muir always felt vaguely guilty there.

Fortunately for America, neither domesticity nor success changed him in any basic way. He remained a wilderness man with Spartan tastes, indifferent to man-made possessions, which for him couldn't compare with a Yosemite snowscape. He was ever slipping back for sustenance. But having discovered his pen to be a potent weapon against nature's exploiters, he curbed his craving for action. His wife and daughters soothed his irritations and encouraged his writings, his wife acting as critic, his daughters mastering the complicated new typewriting machine to prepare the manuscripts he tied up scroll-fashion for their attention.

But his greatest writing spur was his victories. On a wave of popular enthusiasm whipped up by his articles came the creation, in 1890, of Yosemite National Park (although he would have

Corner in the library.

Scientific expeditions to far-flung points of the globe in the company of famous men provided respite from writing and ranching. His companions often complained that the hyperenergetic, fearless Muir was a difficult traveling companion. Windswept mountaintops were his realm. There were trips as well to receive honorary degrees from Harvard and Yale Universities and the University of Wisconsin.

But always the specter of a depleted natural heritage drew him back to writing. Adamantly he refused to compromise his goals. He wished not only to save Yosemite, but all the trees in the Sierra; and he cherished all redwoods no matter where they grew. Should not noble giants which had stood 3000 years be shielded from the saws of Lilliputian men? Of course, he made enemies. He was maligned and ridiculed, but it rolled off him like rain off a mountain eagle. And he knew defeats. One of his bitterest was his futile ten-year battle, together with the Sierra Club he founded and headed, to stop the federal government from letting San Francisco convert Yosemite's Hetch-Hetchy Valley into a water-supply reservoir.

His last years were spent alone and in ill health at the house on the hill. His daughters were married (Wanda lived on the ranch in an old Spanish adobe); his wife was dead; most of his friends were dead. Abandoning most of the house to dust and cobwebs, he used only his study and sleeping porch, living much as in his early days at his Yosemite cabin. He wrote in his cluttered, curtainless study by day and at night by a kerosene lamp.

Throughout the year 1914 he labored over his manuscript for the book *Travels in Alaska*. Shortly before Christmas he left to visit his daughter Helen, who lived in the Mojave Desert, carrying his almost finished manuscript. There he caught pneumonia and was taken to a Los Angeles hospital. At his insistence his manuscript was placed beside his bed; he talked of his need to complete it and seemed to rally. Then, suddenly, on Christmas Eve he died at the age of 76.

Over the decades, Muir's popular books and his close identification with our national parks have kept him a national figure and a byword with nature-lovers. In 1938 the National Park

to fight 17 years more to get Yosemite Valley included in it). In swift succession came creation of the General Grant and Sequoia National Parks, for the express purpose of preserving stands of sequoias. In 1891 came the congressional act empowering the president to create forest preserves. Presidents Cleveland and McKinley, both Muir fans, created between them 35,000,000 acres of forest preserves. Muir's first book, *Mountains of California*, exposing timber abuses, aroused a public clamor that resulted in a federal investigation. President Theodore Roosevelt came out to camp with Muir at Yosemite and returned to Washington an aggressive preservationist who would create 150 national forests, five national parks and 25 national monuments.

Service recognized him as "the nation's greatest conservationist" and held a year-long celebration of the centennial of his birth.

Yet his home came very near to being forgotten. Having had a succession of owners, the house was badly deteriorated and had suffered serious vandalization; then in 1955 a history-minded couple, Mr. and Mrs. Henry Sax, bought it for the purpose of rehabilitating it and encouraging its preservation by some appropriate sponsor. Around the same time another concerned pair, Mr. and Mrs. Louis Stein, rescued from a similar predicament the 1849 adobe that Wanda Muir had occupied; it had once been the seat of the historic Martinez family, for which the town was named. The Saxes and Steins, while going forward with exterior restorations, joined forces to persuade some government agency to assume jurisdiction over the structures and exhibit them to the public.

A group of well-wishers organized themselves to assist the project, forming the John Muir Memorial Association, which in turn was aided by the Contra Costa County Historical Society. In 1957 the association launched a campaign to collect public donations for the restorations and that spring held a three-day Muir Memorial Festival as a fund-raiser. As restoration proceeded, the houses were shown by appointment and opened to the public on selected week ends.

The group succeeded in getting most appropriate sponsorship for a Muir memorial, the National Park Service. In 1966 the service acquired both the Muir and Martinez houses, along with the grounds that surrounded and connected them, and soon after designated the property a National Historic Site. While the Muir house was opened as a historic house museum, the Martinez adobe

Stair hall.

was maintained for exterior viewing only. But in the spring of 1972 the adobe was opened for week end showing, its rooms given over to revolving historical exhibits.

The recent surge of concern over the quality of our environment has made John Muir's monument a popular shrine. A tour of the home is preceded by a color slide show of Yosemite scenes of breathtaking beauty, narrated with the writings of the man who dedicated his life to protecting places "where nature may heal and cheer and give strength to body and soul."

JOHN MUIR NATIONAL HISTORIC SITE is located just off Highway 4 at 4202 Alhambra Avenue, Martinez. Open daily except New Year's Day for guided tours at 10 and 11 a.m., 1, 2, 3 and 4 p.m. Fifty-cent admission for persons over 15 (others free) is good for both houses.

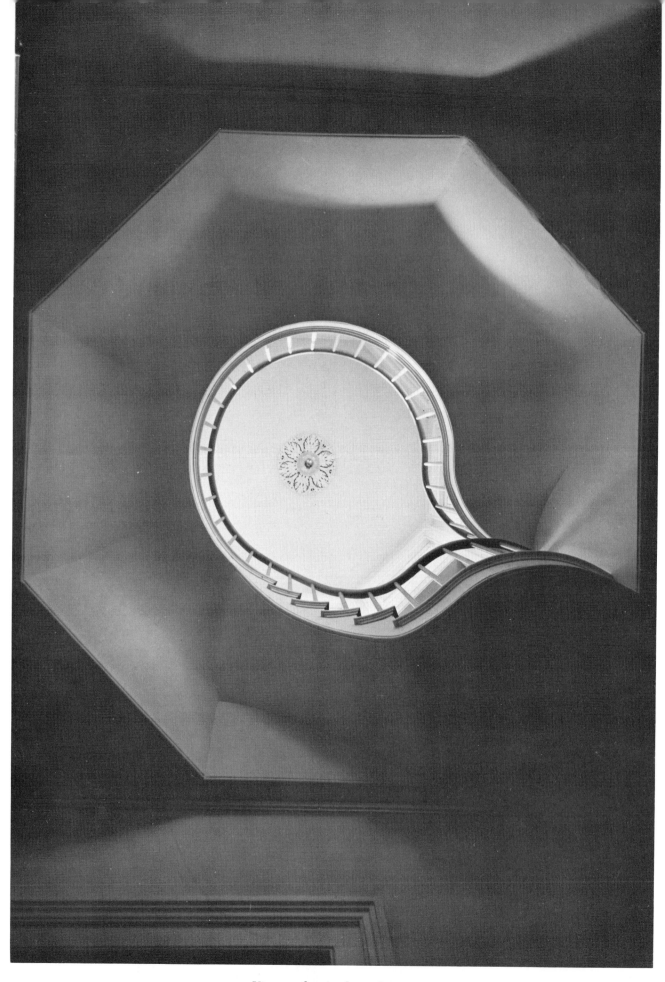

View up the circular stairway.

A Home for All

OCTAGON
HOUSE

SAN FRANCISCO IN THE EARLY 1860s was fairly quivering with expectations. Having fattened off the Gold Rush, it was beginning to taste the bounty of the Comstock Lode. On every side plain, ordinary folk were shinnying up the ladder of success and assuming social airs. The rest were desperately trying to — were reaching for the rung, *any* rung that would put them up there too. There were no employment or investment counselors in those days, but fortunetellers and spiritualists were in brisk demand. Some strivers sought out phrenologists to feel their cranial bumps and tell them wherein their aptitude and opportunity lay while others relied on the trusty American maxims about penny-saving and early-rising.

For some San Franciscans, the golden promise came in a book from the "effete East." Entitled *A Home for All*, it assured the reader he could improve his circumstances by building a certain kind of house and living in it; the house would bring him luck. The author was Orson S. Fowler, an eccentric of fantastically diverse endeavors, all in his earnest view directed toward elevating the common man.

The product of an upstate New York farm, he had worked his way through a seminary by tending the fireplaces of richer students, but by graduation time he had decided on phrenology, instead of preaching, as the more effica-

cious means of uplift. In a short time he was the country's best-known phrenologist with a vast New York practice, but he frequently took time out from profitably feeling heads to explore other routes of human improvement. He enthusiastically conducted studies and experiments in child-rearing, vegetarianism, water cures, corsetry and enhancing sexual vigor for both males and females.

Recently, he had turned his attention to architecture, dedicating himself to designing a house that would assist man's upward climb. Fowler's escalator to higher things took the unlikely shape of an octagon. Throughout history eight-sided structures occasionally were built for public use, but heretofore they had been considered unsuitable for dwellings. Fowler's octagon was constructed of a special mixture of cement called "grout" that was molded into walls, which, according to preference, might or might not be covered with frame. The house was easily constructed, could be built for as low as $1500, and, oh, what it promised!

It would render its occupants healthier, better rested, better tempered and "constitutionally amiable and good." Guaranteed were such specifics as more sunlight, more convenience, easier cleaning, better ventilation, less upkeep, more room for the money, more even heat at less cost and more breeze-catching in the summertime. It

Second-floor stair hall. (*—All photographs: Historic American Buildings Survey*)

was further said to have a beneficial effect upon unborn children and besides which, having no right angles to resist wind, would defy tornadoes. Best of all, the house was said to be "scientific."

The style was enjoying a vogue in New York State and in parts of New England and Wisconsin, but in most places people felt the octagon too queer a shape for living in. Recently it had made a surprising leap across the Rockies into burgeoning San Francisco, whose citizens, having tried a new environment, were open to other experiments.

Several octagon houses had popped up on Russian Hill and Rincon Hill; all were two-story with cupolas and built of the prescribed grout. Most of them, however, deviated from the master's recommendation in one respect; their builders had been unable to resist the Victorian love of ornament. Fowler, a purist, anticipated the International School of architecture in believing that everything about a structure should be strictly functional, scorning such decorative touches as "finefied carvings and cornicings." The geometric walls rising locally wore a wide variety of decorations in the then-current Italianate and Classical Revival styles. All were modest structures. The *San Francisco Bulletin* reported in 1859 that the new houses being built "on the Fowler plan" ranged in cost from $1800 to $3000.

In 1861 William McElroy, one of twenty millers then competing for the San Francisco trade, undertook construction of a small octagon house for his family. His location was in a rural district on the road to the Presidio, later to become fashionable Pacific Heights. The McElroys had made their separate ways west during the Gold Rush, she coming from Pennsylvania in 1849, he from Virginia in 1851. When Mr. McElroy proposed and she accepted, she was employed as a housekeeper for the first St. Francis Hotel on Dupont Street. Now they had a nine-year-old daughter, Emma Eliza; also living as part of their household was a nephew, Samuel Wolfe, an aspiring artist. In addition to their building site, the McElroys had a nest egg in the form of a few town acres on Stockton Street. An existing daguerreotype, made around the time they began construction, shows a stern-looking man with a goatee and a heavy-lidded, thin-lipped woman.

This diligent pair chose as their model the plan presented in the last chapter of Fowler's book and labeled "the best plan of all," and in most respects they followed it faithfully. Unlike some octagon plans which sliced interior space into wedges like a pie, this design offered four almost-square rooms to each floor and four triangular closets. One first-floor triangle accommodated an entrance.

In the core of the McElroy's octagon was a small, square hall containing a winding staircase that led from the first floor to an octagonal cupola. This centered stairwell was the basis of many of Fowler's glowing claims. The closeness of the doors to each other and to the staircase made, he said, for ease of communication between rooms and floors, promoting family togetherness. Further, the central opening was said to generate an even circulation of heat in winter, and in summer to distribute fresh air. Bad air (a 19th-century phobia) was channeled upward and ejected through vents in the cupola. The multiwindowed cupola also admitted sunlight which filtered healthily down the stairwell. It certainly sounded scientific.

The McElroys enclosed their house with the recommended grout wall, which Fowler deemed just as conducive to human well-being as eight-sidedness. What's more, he claimed it to be four times cheaper than wood and six times cheaper than brick. The recipe for grout called for specific measures of sand, gravel, small stones, large stones and lime; if stones were scarce, said Fowler, then substitute oyster shells, slate chips, brick bats or furnace cinders. The ingredients were blended in a mortar bed and poured between wooden molds to form walls, whose thickness might be varied according to the climate. The *San Francisco Bulletin* reported that, locally, ten-inch-thick walls were being poured for lower floors. After the forms were removed, a coat of lime-and-sand plaster was brushed on to repel damp.

Fowler had elatedly discovered grout when on a phrenology lecture tour. He observed that the walls of a Wisconsin inn were composed of an unusual molded material, and he delayed his journey long enough to investigate its character-

Front view of Octagon House.

istics thoroughly. The innkeeper himself was the creator, and he proudly permitted the visitor to test his product by pounding the inside of his parlor walls with a sledge, although charging him six cents per blow. Finding grout to be proof to his assaults, Fowler subsequently hailed it as a great new invention, but in that he was mistaken: the Romans had used something quite similar, as had the English at a somewhat later date.

Several San Francisco octagon builders left their exterior grout exposed, but the McElroys chose to hide theirs with redwood siding. Perhaps encouraged by their artistic nephew, they gave their house some airs in the form of Italianate detailing. The siding was grooved at the edges to suggest stone with wood blocks set at the corners to look like quoins. Both house and cupola had cornices underlined with a dentil course and with scroll-cut brackets at the corners. At the entrance was set a small portico with square Tuscan pillars and pilasters.

In two other respects the McElroys departed from Fowler. He recommended for every house a "gymnastic room" where "females of all ages"

could keep fit. No doubt a woman who had trekked to the Gold Rush alone and toiled in a boom-town hostelry felt no need to court vigor. Nor did they deem his recommended water closet necessary. Fowler, aware of the apprehension at "bringing the privy indoors," conceded it might not appeal to "squeamish maidens," but he strongly adjured "matrons, the aged and the feeble" to ponder "is not such a closet a real household necessity and luxury? . . . it need be used only in cases of *special* need, the one generally used being outside, as usual." He suggested tucking it under the staircase. But indoor plumbing as yet was making little headway in San Francisco, and the McElroys vetoed the notion.

So convinced was Mr. McElroy of the durability of his snug little dwelling that as it neared completion he made a most dramatic gesture. He prepared a time capsule addressed "To Future Ageses [sic] Present," when presumably his house would at last give way and the advanced society would be curious about his own remote times. In a sound tin box he enclosed selected newspapers of 1860 and 1861, together with a framed photo-

Living room.

graph of himself and spouse and a three-page handwritten letter.

Writing in a slanting script with a casual style and casual spelling, he proudly described himself as the builder and first owner of "this Octigon House" which "is intended as our Privet Residence." He was brimming over with optimism for himself and for his adopted city, which he described as "free as free can make us, blessed with a climate and soil unsurpassed" and with immense "traid with China & India," regular steamship service to New York via Panama, two Pony Expresses per week, and downtown real estate that sold for as high as $500 per front foot. In closing he adjured the finders of his time capsule, whom he called "You Young Folks," to be temperate, frugal, industrious and regular church-attenders. Secreting his tin box within the wall of an upstairs room, he consigned it to the abyss of time.

Details are lacking in the affairs of the McElroys over the next several years, except that Emma Eliza took a teaching course and became a primary-school teacher. Less than ten years after completing his house William McElroy died, in the same modest circumstance as when he built it. After Emma Eliza married, Mrs. McElroy went to live with her and her husband, and the octagon was occupied by a long series of renters.

Mr. McElroy had lived long enough to see the style of his "privet residence" go into eclipse. His was one of the last octagons built in San Francisco; elsewhere too the fad faded as fast as it had loomed. A reversal had set in: the good-luck house had turned, by repute, into a bad omen. A Maine man applying the finishing touches to his octagon roof was reported to have fallen to his death. It was said the odd shape attracted ghosts; there were reports of strange lights flashing in their cupolas. In Natchez, Mississippi, what was to have been the grand flowering of octagons, a three-story mansion with Moorish detailing and a Byzantine dome, became an eerie ruin when it was abruptly abandoned by workmen at the outbreak of the Civil War. Paint brushes froze in their buckets; tools rusted where they dropped. And in Kansas an ambitious abolitionist colony, living in octagon houses set on an octagonal street plan, went bankrupt.

Even Mr. Fowler's own octagon, situated in the Hudson River town of Fishkill, New York, failed him. It was his "scientific" grout that gave trouble. He used it to enclose his water closet cesspool, and the porous walls allowed seepage to pollute his well and precipitate an outbreak of typhoid. Fowler sold his house and it rapidly changed hands several times, then was abandoned, becoming known as "Fowler's Folly." Finally, it was dynamited by public authorities as a menace.

The octagon was its own boomerang. It was one of those 19th-century American dreams doomed to failure for promising the millennium. No doubt disappointment fed the bad-luck myth, which was as exaggerated as the glowing claims had been. Most graspers of the octagon were also graspers of other straws, other talismans; they were the frustrated and the slightly odd. The style had been favored by vegetarians, by teetotalers, by nonsmokers, by practitioners of spiritualism. A nature worshiper built an octagon around a tree, to which he affixed a winding staircase. One housing thinker incorporated the octagon with two perfectionist schemes of his own: a corkscrew chimney, designed to catch live sparks, and window shutters that had both vertical and horizontal louvers for exact control of sunshine. A Kentuckian who doted on novelty built an octagon full of pie wedges and then had furniture specially made to fit the corners, quite nullifying any economy the construction method had accomplished. A Massachusetts man who found wind sounds disturbing built an octagon to blunt the wind's force and obviate whistling around corners. One eight-sider was built by a couple who were both deaf-mutes; a man built one for his crippled wife. These yearners, having invested, waited for their stock to rise, and when no change occurred they felt cheated. Moreover, women discovered they had foolishly fallen for a man's promise of easier housekeeping, when in fact the sharp corners invited clutter and were devilishly hard to clean.

Fowler had visualized himself as housing reformer for the masses, or, as he called them, "the million." But the final count of octagon takers was more like 400, although not, to be sure, Mrs. Astor's Four Hundred. In San Francisco eight such houses were constructed. Two were built in the East Bay suburb of Oakland, one on the new Mills College campus. A prominent Oakland financier presented the budding University of California campus with an octagon-shaped gymnasium, which students promptly dubbed "the inkwell." Los Angeles' single octagon house was built by a newcomer from Maine. This was the largest number of octagons produced by any state

west of the Mississippi; elsewhere in the West they were a rarity. Two were built in Minnesota; in Utah a Mormon constructed an eight-sided log house, perhaps as a means of giving equal distinction to each of his wives; and an Oregon farmer constructed an octagon barn.

Only two San Francisco octagons remain today: one the McElroy house, the other a Russian Hill residence built in 1857 by a book salesman for Hubert Bancroft. The bad-luck myth does not seem to have attached to the San Francisco octagons; most were removed routinely to make way for new construction, although the remaining two have experienced several narrow escapes.

The Russian Hill house, which began as a plain two-story with uncovered grout walls, by 1906 had become more pretentious. Its second owner, Louis Feusier, had given it another story and an elegant mansard roof. On that famous April day when the earth shook, the little octagon came

Thomas Chandler grandfather clock.

through the jolts intact, except for a few bricks dislodged from the chimney. But the subsequent fire began raging, and the house was among those ordered to be dynamited to halt the blaze. The Feusiers protested, and at length persuaded the authorities to spare the house and dynamite only the wooden stable in back.

Three cases of explosives, far more than the job required, were placed in the stable and a slow-burning fuse attached. When the blast went off, it blew the stable skyward, and the house that had survived the natural shock rocked perilously on its foundations. Every window blew out, doors flew from their hinges, and chimneys shattered like blown dandelions. But the walls held firm, and the fire never came. The Feusiers were among a small minority of San Franciscans left with a home. Occupied by the Feusier family until 1954, the house is still in residential use.

The McElroy house stood well beyond the fire, but it received a stronger earthquake jolt than the Feusier house. One entire grout wall fell out and part of another; chimneys snapped off at the roof line. Its tenants fled to Oakland for refuge. But since all damage proved reparable, several months later the tenants reoccupied the house.

In 1924 the Pacific Gas and Electric Company acquired the property, intending to build a substation on it, then changed its mind and continued to rent to tenants. Dilapidation crept in; passersby smiled at the odd little house with the peeling paint. The power company didn't even consider it worth wiring for electricity. Then in 1949 the house became vacant and fell prey to vandals; windows were broken, the interior was defaced. Its bleakness repelled both buyers and renters.

P.G.&E. was ready to auction the property for its land when the sale was abruptly postponed. The California branch of the National Society of Colonial Dames had expressed interest in obtaining the house for a combined headquarters and museum. They proposed moving it across the street to a site offered them by the Misses Lucy and Edith Allyne, members of the society who lived on the block and could spare part of their large garden to situate the octagon. The power company sold the house for a token dollar, and

it was moved without mishap to a sixty-foot lot overlooking Gough Street from the other side.

The society's instructions to the restoring architect were to keep the octagon as unchanged as possible while making it serve their purposes. The costs, including moving, would run to $30,000, and their reserve funds totaled only $16,000. They obtained a mortgage while launching a fund-raising drive. Freer space downstairs was a prime need. The house was to serve both as a society meeting place and office, and for displaying colonial-era furniture, manuscripts and artifacts previously on loan to the de Young Museum. First-floor partitions were removed and the four small rooms combined into one. Moved too was the central staircase that Fowler had deemed so important but which many owners found unsuitable for a small house; a new staircase incorporating part of the old one was built in the rear of the room, opening into an ample upstairs hall made from an upper bedroom. Otherwise, the second floor was left unchanged, but for a corner made into a powder room.

Portico entrance.

View of the damaged Octagon House following April 1906 earthquake, one of a famous series of photographs made by Arnold Genthe, now in the Palace of the Legion of Honor.

During the upstairs remodeling Mr. McElroy's time capsule was discovered. The Dames, delighted with their windfall, announced its message to the press and decided to place box and contents on exhibit and have copies of the letter made available to visitors.

Fund-raising activities were successfully completed in 1956, and that year the society's annual meeting featured a gala mortgage-burning celebration. Part of the ceremony included affixing to the newel post an ivory "peace button," which according to an early American custom certified the property to be debt-free.

The house was then opened to visitors who eagerly filed in to peer in the triangular closets and stare up at the glassed cupola, as well as inspect curtained four-posters, Duncan Phyfe sofas, a grandfather clock, a portrait of Daniel Webster, a spoon of George Washington's and a chair belonging to his wife. Fowler, disappointed in his dream that the octagon style would become a lasting tradition, perhaps might be appeased that one of his houses has become a showcase for tradition.

OCTAGON HOUSE is located at 2645 Gough Street, San Francisco. Open to the public from 1 p.m. to 4 p.m. on the first Sunday and the second and fourth Thursdays of each month with the exception of Thanksgiving, Christmas and New Year's Day. No admission charge.

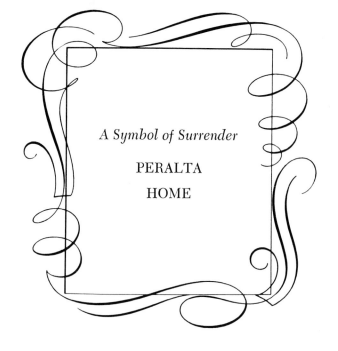

A Symbol of Surrender

PERALTA

HOME

THE EAST BAY CITIES OF Oakland, Berkeley, Alameda and part of San Leandro sprawl over undulating hills and flats that once comprised vast Rancho San Antonio, the most beautiful and fertile of all the California ranchos. But nowhere among them today can be found a single structure remaining from those halcyon days. When the Arabs lost Granada, they had at least the consolation of knowing it was still there, shimmering in the sun. Rancho San Antonio's beleaguered Peralta clan, whose lands were granted by the Spanish crown, saw their paradise vanish before their very eyes.

When a much later generation sought to recapture something of that lost idyl, it was obliged to confer landmark status upon an American-era structure, a San Leandro residence, which since 1926 has housed a women's cultural organization, the Alta Mira Club. While the house (declared a California Historic Landmark in 1937) did once shelter a Peralta, it symbolizes a capitulation to the gringo and his era. True, it has a rather Spanish look, thanks to its plastered sides, iron grillwork and partly tile roof, but these touches were applied in a 1957 renovation given it by the clubwomen — long after Spanish obloquy had waned and the romance had set in. The creamy plaster camouflages red brick.

The clue to the original spirit of the house is the Victorian art glass in the tall front doors. This 1860 home of Ignacio Peralta, one of the four owners of Rancho San Antonio, was built to be as un-adobelike as possible and just as American as could be. At that moment, for the socially ambitious American, Italian detailing outside was in the mode, as French was *de rigueur* within. Thus the classically arched windows, all symmetrically placed, were wedded to rococo chandeliers and voluptuous paneling. These elegant touches seem far more appropriate for the women's cultural organization the house accommodates today than for the unschooled ranchero who was its first master. This house more commemorates victor than vanquished.

The decline of the great Rancho San Antonio didn't date from the 1846 annexation of California during the Mexican War, but from the later Gold Rush or, more precisely, the Gold Rush aftermath. Many men gambled and lost in the frenzied race for gold, but the Peraltas had chosen to stay out of the running. When madness seized the district after discovery of a sparkling nugget in a Coloma millrace, the family patriarch Don Luis, a shrunken, brown gnome of ninety, summoned his four middle-aged sons — Antonio, Domingo, Vicente and Ignacio — and advised them that if

Northeast corner of Peralta Home. (*—All photographs: Historic American Buildings Survey*)   » 54 «

God had wanted the Peraltas to have the gold, He'd have shown it to *them.* "Your gold is here," he adjured. "Stay with the rancho!"

They stayed without murmur. These well-fed rancheros had no craving for gold; they weren't the go-getting sort, as their father well knew. He had handed them the rancho, as he had been handed it in 1820, a grant from the last royal governor under Spanish rule. It was *his* father who had endured the hardships, tramping north through desert and mountain with Anza in 1776. Don Luis won his grant in recognition of forty years' military service, most of it at the San Francisco Presidio, but it was for his sons that he had wanted it. Yet, they had with reluctance departed the family home in the drowsy pueblo of San Jose. He'd had to prod them to drive the family cattle onto the lush grasslands that lay between the silvery Bay and the redwood-fringed mountains and to build their own adobes there in the wilderness. Settlement of the Bay's eastern shore lagged a half century behind San Francisco.

So fertile did they find it, their only problem was keeping the herds a manageable size. The excess they sold as hide and tallow to Yankee trading ships and Russian fur trappers down at their own embarcadero on the Bay, trading them for all the luxuries they and their wives could think of wanting. In their bountiful domain of waving wild flowers and leaping deer, it was only natural they would acquire the *mañana* habit: foresight seemed totally unnecessary.

During Mexican rule, other families acquired East Bay land, and so the Peraltas' smiling present even included pleasant neighbors. Among these rancheros, Rancho San Antonio was the favorite social mecca. Each Peralta brother had his own shining casa in the section of the rancho Don Luis had assigned him. Here were celebrated the gayest fiestas, the grandest wedding feasts. And the envy of the district was the rancho's chapel with its bell cast in Spain and a bull ring with spectator stands; both attracted visitors from miles around, including the padres from Mission San Jose. Only fools would leave all this to go tramping to the mountains to pan gold in icy streams.

At first the Gold Rush influx seemed an added blessing — all those thousands of prospectors swarming off ships at San Francisco seeking provisions to go to the diggings. Slaughtered beef, once left for scavengers after being stripped of hides, brought unheard-of prices, as did wheat, potatoes, vegetables — anything edible. Leather, mules and horses sold high. The only cloud on the horizon was news that even though the Treaty of Guadalupe Hidalgo stipulated that the *Californios'* property rights were to be respected, landowners would have to go to court to prove their titles. But surely that would be quick work; everybody in California knew Peralta land was rightly theirs.

The Peraltas' troubles began when gold seekers' claims petered out and they came sailing back down the Sacramento River, angry because they had come all the way around the Horn for nothing. Many faced the stark fact of being stranded, lacking even passage home. Passing Spanish-owned land along the river, they turned their ill tempers upon the unsuspecting *padrons,* asking what kind of victory it was when the defeated lived off the fat and the victors went without. Those greasers! Why should they have American land?

Galloping about their estate, the Peraltas began to find grubby-looking Americans tenting

Interior vestibule doors with art glass.

under the oaks along the shore. Orders to leave were ignored. Down-and-outers continued to arrive, clustering in brawling camps. One night one of the brothers and a vaquero rode upon a party of men quartering a beef. The squatters swiftly trained their guns on the Spaniards, who retreated in fear of their lives.

Ignacio decided to assert himself. He was the eldest son, and his father had favored him by assigning him the south end of the rancho, nearest the home place at San José. But he was scarcely five feet tall, was slight and pallid and wore an air of pompous dignity gained during terms as a San Jose civic official and provincial legislator at Monterey. The squatters jeered at him as he cantered about in his silver-mounted saddle, imperiously pointing the way off the rancho. They bluffly informed him they didn't recognize grants made by a bygone Spanish king.

Most brazen of all were three squatters named Horace Carpentier, Edson Adams and Andrew Moon, who proceeded as systematically as if they were modern-day developers. After staking themselves off 480 acres, they felled Peralta timber, built themselves a house, and erected a wharf at what is now the foot of Oakland's Broadway. They had occupied land owned by the younger brother Vicente, but they paid his objections no more heed than if he were a Pomeranian yapping at lions. At his brothers' urging, Vicente hastened to the district court to obtain a writ of ejectment.

But when a posse, Vicente galloping in the lead, bore down upon the shameless squatters, they were so meek and smiling he was disarmed. Especially charming was Carpentier, a suave, slender New Yorker with fathomless blue eyes and a thin aristocratic nose; he recently had taken a law degree from Columbia University. What's more, he spoke fluent Spanish. The Peraltas were secretly bedazzled by Americans, and Vicente succumbed completely. He let himself be talked out of the ejectment and into leasing the staked-out acreage to the genial trio.

It was pure dodge. Carpentier and his cohorts hired a surveyor to plat out a town and began selling lots to other squatters, representing themselves as the new owners. The only hitch in their racket was that other opportunists grew envious and sought to muscle in. A "jumpers and squatters war" ensued, the jumpers trying to seize the stolen toe holds. The original squatters organized themselves for mutual protection, even acquiring a cannon, which at one juncture was seized by jumpers who, neglecting to purloin ammunition, promptly lost it back again.

It was on this inauspicious plane of activity that Oakland had its beginnings. The squatters were not all ruffians; some of them were respectable men who acted in the frenzied, licensed way as they'd never have acted back home. Among them was Bret Harte's stepfather, Colonel Williams, later an Oakland civic leader, and the Reverend Dr. Henry Durant, who used his squatter's plot to start a school for three squatter children. That school would evolve into the University of California.

Trespassers — more than a thousand — deployed over every corner of the rancho. The swiftness and audacity of the invasion left the Peraltas as confused as stampeded cattle. Squatters camped noisily all along the creek on which Ignacio's adobe fronted and spread over Domingo's sector, the future site of Berkeley. At one point the stocky Domingo in a fit of rage tried physically to eject some squatters and found himself clapped in jail in violation of the new "squatters' rights" law that had been pushed through the legislature. It invited "settlers" to claim land which appeared "unused" and forbade their ejection. Squatters and squatter-minded courts interpreted "unused" to mean "unused for agriculture," contending that the rancheros, in turning land to pasture, were wasting it and therefore didn't deserve it. Squatters were a growing political power; there was even a gubernatorial candidate running on the "squatters' ticket." Every rancho within a day's march of San Francisco Bay was plagued with its contingent of obstreperous, nonpaying guests, but Rancho San Antonio, being closest, was the prime attraction.

In 1851, at the height of the pandemonium, old Don Luis died, and his wealth in land and cattle was appraised at more than $1,383,500. His four sons now owned Rancho San Antonio, but they hardly felt rich, hemmed in as they were by squatters' fences that prevented their stock from

Peralta Home is now the Alta Mira Club.

grazing or even watering at the creeks. Indeed, the brothers were made to feel like squatters themselves; the trespassers had had the audacity to inform them the government allowed but 160 acres per claimant and suggested they claim their share. It wasn't enough that they were made to feel like squatters, their tormentors wished them also to feel like sinners. They criticized their bullfights, their spurs, their "lascivious dances," their showy clothes, even their courtly manners. To the bewildered Peraltas it seemed that, what with thieves and rogues passing judgment on the innocent and persecuted, the forces of darkness had descended and heaven and hell had been upsided.

A most unexpected source of comfort in their trials was Horace Carpentier, and it is a measure of the Peraltas' desperation that they again trusted him. After the brothers inherited the rancho, he visited Vicente's casa and, feigning sympathy for his plight, offered free legal assistance. Further, with a crucifix dangling from his neck, he represented himself as a former priest and knelt to say a rosary for the abused family. Between prayers Vicente found himself signing a paper he believed was designed to ease his plight, when in fact it was a mortgage to a large part of Oakland. Later,

when the mortgage fell due, he was nonplused and refused to pay; Carpentier secured the title at a sheriff's sale.

Carpentier's next move was to get the legislature to incorporate Oakland. Thereupon he got himself elected Oakland's first mayor and installed his own trustees, who obligingly deeded him the Oakland water front, the franchise to provide ferry service, and the right to operate a toll bridge across a slough that divided the town. Carpentier was almost as successful at hoodwinking Americans as Spaniards.

The Peraltas had filed to establish their land title, but land cases moved slowly. Ignacio, his father's executor, was impotent to halt the squatter advance and pinned his hopes on persuading the courts to oust the malefactors. But since he was unable to understand English, much less technical court language, he was at the mercy of attorneys, and history has branded the California land lawyers of the 1850s as being mostly shysters. As the case creaked on, legal costs drained the family of all ready cash and the lawyers demanded more; there was nothing to do but sell land. Some land went to lawyers in lieu of legal fees, some to the hated squatters.

After several years of baffling litigation, a favorable land title at last was confirmed — but only to be contested by an organization of squatters. Their lawyers appealed, unleashing a barrage of injunctions and counterclaims, to meet which the Peraltas, who understood money no more than legalese, fell prey to loan sharks. The going rate was 12 per cent *weekly*. When the extortionate lenders pressed for payment, the brothers were forced to sell off more land, and at less than market value because of the challenged title. Between them the lenders and lawyers probably picked off more spoils than the squatters sniping from behind trees.

During all this time the Peraltas had to pay high taxes on land that no longer yielded income. Except for the roistering squatters' town of Oakland, the rancho had become a ghostly wasteland of dry forage grass crisscrossed by rude fences enclosing shanties and tree stumps. Conspicuously missing were the honest farms the squatters had so extolled; they preferred the sweatless role of speculator. So menacing was the atmosphere during the protracted squatter suit that the brothers were obliged to move their wives and children to places of safety. The brothers were not even permitted the comfort of family solidarity, for another set of greedy land lawyers had persuaded the Peralta sisters to sue their brothers for a share of the rancho, even though their father had provided separately for them. Lawyers for the brothers and the sisters, each standing to gain large tracts of land if the case went his way, fought one another without quarter.

In the end the Peraltas' title withstood all tests of its soundness and the patents were duly issued — but not until the mid-1870s, by which time two of the brothers were dead, nearly all of the land gone and all their cattle. The main effect of the termination was to set off a hectic unscrambling of land titles in the budding cities of Oakland and Berkeley. It had taken three decades and a vast family fortune to clear a title that was one of the most impeccable in California. The Peraltas came out of their grueling ordeal with little more than their honor, like the old man in Hemingway's tale, who fought with all his might to keep his great, shining fish from getting

East parlor, showing French wallpaper.

away, but by the time he reached shore the sharks had picked it clean.

In later years a Peralta descendant assessed the effects of the squatter invasion upon her family in terms of wrecked and blighted lives. Vicente, the most harassed of all, died insane at 59. Domingo saw his embittered sons turn criminal and outlaw; one died in prison. Antonio, whose rancho was largest, encompassing the present city of Alameda and part of Oakland, died penniless and lies buried in an unmarked grave in an Oakland cemetery where numerous other Peraltas were consigned to the "poor plot." Horace Carpentier, by dramatic contrast, died worth more than $4,000,000, the fruits of his machinations in the Oakland mud flats.

The only Peralta son to be permitted a measure of comfort in his old age was Ignacio. Despite all, he had retained a certain admiration for Americans, and in 1853 had proudly welcomed an American son-in-law when his pretty daughter Maria married Lt. William Toler. The young Navy lieutenant was a Virginian and West Point graduate who had been with Commodore Sloat when he seized Monterey and whom history credits with raising the first American flag after annexation. Toler carried his petite, dark-eyed bride off to the Eastern Seaboard, but in time they returned to California to live. Finding his father-in-law helplessly submerged in debt and litigation, he helped him retrieve a remnant of his estate.

Further, Toler in 1860 built his in-laws a new house. The Americans' derision of their old adobe had made them ashamed of it. He let them choose whatever style they liked, and of course they chose American, or the imported style the Americans had embraced for the moment, which was modified Italian. Windows and doors were given tall arches and classic moldings, but to satisfy the Victorian taste for ornateness, doors were fitted with panels of leaded and tinted art glass. The selected building material was something of a status symbol: the red burnt brick that was being used in some of San Francisco's more impressive new houses and buildings. It was the first brick house on the east side of the Bay. In front of this stylish house was a stylish garden: a formal arrangement of clipped borders, gravel paths, romantic statuary and a playing fountain. Surrounding all was an ornate wrought-iron fence.

Inside, interior décor reached exuberantly toward French, with molded ceiling medallions surrounded by painted frescos and flanked by walls of florid French wallpaper. Furniture was in the curvate lines of Louis Quatorze, the fireplaces of carved white marble. Still, for all these grand touches, the house did not attain real significance due to its small size: it had only four rooms on the main level (the rear extension was added by a later owner), four more in the half-basement. The floor plan was strictly New England, with foursquare rooms opening off a central hallway.

In his plush little villa, Ignacio lived out his remaining days. His American house and American clothes did not, as he had hoped, gain him social acceptance in the new society; the more the ratio of *Californios* to Americans diminished, the more they were looked upon as "foreigners." But among his family and friends his stylish house gave him distinction; it was the favorite setting for their gatherings, mostly devoted to mapping strategy to meet the latest Yankee thrust. As the only possession which conferred a measure of status upon him, Ignacio's house was his most cherished possession, and he was obsessed with protecting it. In 1874, when a frail, tiny figure in his mid-eighties, he became disturbed because some Indians had camped on the fringe of his small acreage. Perhaps he visualized another invasion. He tottered down to order them away and such was his vehemence that he provoked the Indians — a people even more scarred than the Spanish — into attacking him. He died from the injuries, lying in the great carved bed of his spacious Victorian bedroom, which today serves the culture club as a ladies' powder room.

———————

The PERALTA HOME is located at the corner of Leo Avenue and Lafayette Avenue in San Leandro. It may be viewed 10 a.m. to 3:30 p.m. weekdays by telephoning the Alta Mira Club and making an appointment. No admission charge.

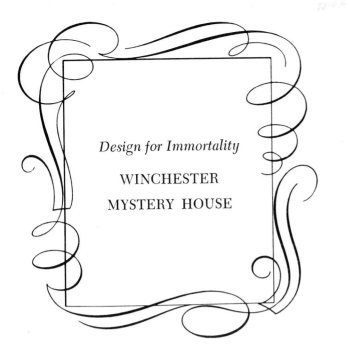

Design for Immortality

WINCHESTER

MYSTERY HOUSE

WHAT EXPLAINS A HOUSE that has closets full of stairsteps, stairs leading to blank walls, chimneys that stop at the ceiling, doors opening into space, interior balconies set an inch above the floor, and an intricate system of bells and gongs having no discernible purpose? Was there ever rhyme or reason to a structure that swelled and elled so aimlessly over six acres that when its owner died and movers sought to collect the furnishings from the interminable maze, they got lost and had to be rescued by a search party? What brought about the structural phenomenon called Winchester Mystery House?

One necessity, of course, was money — large quantities of it. Connecticut-born Sarah Winchester was heir to the fortune piled up by the innovative repeating rifle used in the Civil War and in the opening of the West. When William Wirt Winchester, son of the company's founder, died prematurely he left her $20,000,000 and company stock that earned an income of nearly $1000 a day. Deciding to make her home in San Jose, she undertook to build there an appropriate residence; being childless she could give the project her undivided attention, and being rich she could follow wherever fancy led.

Free-flowing money accounts for many gargantuan, preposterous houses built during the Victorian Era, houses built to some transcendental point far beyond mere comfort or need. Today many are white elephants, burdening their inheritors with the problem of what in the world to do with them. But those monuments to swollen social ambition, no matter how grotesque they appear today, once had their heyday, however brief, before fashion passed them by. Sarah Winchester's house, for all its lavish cost and elegant fixtures, never really had a fling. Her ballroom, with its imported silver chandelier, on which she spend $10,000 for flooring and paneling never witnessed a ball. Her house was always set apart, marked by — what was it?

Some say madness. They say Sarah Winchester was driven insane by the deaths of her husband and of her only child, and by her belief God was wreaking vengeance on the Winchester family for causing the death of so many of His creatures; she feared she might be next. These people say she sought to atone by building a house big enough to accommodate the spirits of all who had fallen before the rifle, and she continued building to keep up with the continuing toll.

But that theory comes from those who never made her acquaintance — from those who knew only her irrational house and created an explanation to fit. Those who knew Mrs. Winchester vehemently contradicted that theory. Servants, workmen and the professionals she dealt with knew her as a highly intelligent, cultured woman,

Herringbone pattern parquet floor. *(—All photographs: Winchester Mystery House)*
At left, front view of the home of Sarah Winchester.

Corner of the intricately paneled ballroom.

an omnivorous reader in four languages and highly knowledgeable about her complicated business affairs. Her attorney termed her "as sane as any woman I have ever known" and attested to her astuteness in business dealings, in selecting recipients for her many philanthropies, and in directing preparation of her complicated will. She assisted in the reorganization of the gun company after World War I. The workmen and domestics she employed defended her fiercely, insisting they found her neither eccentric nor unbalanced. "She was a sweet person and not at all crazy," insisted one servant who served her for years. Her long-time chauffeur said the only time he thought her peculiar was when she ordered her wine cellar smashed after the passage of Prohibition; he saw no sense in wasting good liquor.

Still, there is no denying the irrationality of her house. What, then, would prompt a rational woman to build such a huge and wildly improbable dwelling?

The advice of two persons, offered at a most impressionable time, seems to have propelled her toward her singular project. In the 1870s, in New Haven, Sarah Winchester was inconsolable, after first seeming to be the luckiest girl in town. Blonde, plump and pretty, she had moved up the social ladder by marrying a Winchester and becoming mistress of a mansion on aristocratic Prospect Street. But her happiness was fleeting. First, her infant daughter died; then her husband succumbed to tuberculosis. Desolate, she herself became ill and believed she would die.

Although an Episcopalian, she had never been religious. She sought consolation in spiritualism, and during a séance a voice counseled her to build and continue building; that good health would attend her so long as she was building. It pricked her apathy, then aroused hope. Her credulity was hardly remarkable in view of the then rampant vogue for the occult, with many of the rich and famous up to their eyes in it. Whether Sarah confided her stimulating experience to her physician is unestablished, but it is known that he too made suggestions. A warmer climate, he said, might prove beneficial, and why didn't she pursue her talent for design?

The year 1884 found her in the sunny Santa Clara Valley near San Jose cheerfully directing the construction of a house. She had purchased a building project already under way, having been attracted by the warm, protected site in view of peaceful mountains. Interpreting the ethereal message to mean she should build without benefit of architect, she hired workmen by the day. Undeterred by inexperience, she confidently gave them directions, sketching on paper what she wanted done. During the day she puttered in the adjoining orchard, keeping an eye on the carpenters. Many noted in her appearance a resemblance to Queen Victoria: the small rounded figure (she was less than five feet tall), the tiny chin and slightly curving nose. The resemblance would increase with time. She resided in the completed portion of the house. By night, she pored through a stack of building manuals, planning the next day's work. Her health improved rapidly.

Originally, she had planned to present that residence to her sister and build another for herself. But when her sister did not come west, she decided to keep it for her own use and to expand it. She gave it the name of Llanda Villa. Its architectural style was Queen Anne, a cluttery style that rode in on the craze for quaintness and which permitted an almost endless variety of towers, gables, balconies, overhangs, insets and surface treatments. Even the best examples of Queen Anne gave an impression of having grown

Main entrance viewed from interior.

in segments. Mrs. Winchester was fortunate that it was a Queen Anne onto which she began hanging her architectural whimsies, for a considerable time elapsed before notice was taken that something had gone awry — that no ordinary house was taking shape. At first, the neighbors congratulated her on her house and she accepted their compliments with blushing pleasure and pampered their children with French ice cream. Those were the happy years before the ostracism set in.

By the time the outside began to look odd, the interior was considerably more so. The visitor who wandered past the parlor was likely to stumble into a room devoid of windows, or one whose windows were set in interior partitions, or to open an imposing carved double door that uncovered a blank wall, or to find a room decorated in one scheme on one side and in another on

Parquet floor and decorative stairway.

the opposite. Reactions varied from titters to grave concern. Nobody knew quite what to make of it.

Mrs. Winchester's Connecticut physician had rightly recognized in her a talent for design, but it was a talent solely for *small* design, dainty assemblage or intricate mechanism. She had a decided knack for designing charming panels, window treatments, archways, wainscoting, dadoes and fireplaces. She used the finest imported tiles, marble and metals and ordered Tiffany art glass and Belgium optical glass that cost as much as

$1500 a panel. But she also made creative use of modest lathecut from the planing mills. She could plan an exquisitely patterned parquet floor, incorporating six hardwoods cut in one-inch squares. One artisan who worked under her direction recalled, "We'd work for days or weeks on perhaps one small installation."

And at fashioning mechanical devices she was truly ingenious. She invented a window catch patterned after the Winchester rifle trigger and trip hammer. She installed laundry tubs with molded-in washboards, and set curved plates in stair corners to prevent dust pockets. She devised hinged iron drops in fireplaces for disposal of ashes and a hairdo-saving shower that sprayed only from the sides. She set her window screens inside and used a crank to operate casement windows. Many of her practical innovations were later adopted by the building trades.

But, alas, she had no aptitude whatever for large design, for planning architectural space or even simple carpentry. For such tasks she had neither interest nor patience — only the planted compulsion. She seems to have considered rooms mere frames on which to attach her enjoyable little schemes, inside and out; carpentry was a prosaic necessity to be dealt with as briefly and as absently as possible. Likely as not, a new wing would be set on a direct collision course with the last. Twice new additions collided with already existing structures, a barn and a tank house; she simply built around and over them and went merrily onward.

Quite possibly some of the foolish construction errors can be laid to demoralized workmen who became slipshod and neglectful for want of supervision. The carpenters, jealous of the attention lavished on the artisans, may even have avenged their frustration by setting doors in larger frames, by fitting windows over smaller frames with sashes overlapping, laying a floor six inches lower than the adjoining level, and cutting Mutt and Jeff doors — a five-foot door alongside an eight-foot one. Myopically focused upon her latest design, the mistress never noticed such things.

At times she seems to have questioned her course. She was angered and humiliated by a

San Francisco newspaper's scoffing report of her prolonged construction project and her belief it would confer immortality. This criticism caused her to stop and look at herself as others saw her. Abruptly dismissing her building crews, she fled to Monterey and established residence at the Del Monte Hotel. But after tarrying there nearly a year she began to brood. Perhaps afraid that bad health was descending again, she returned to Llanda Villa, recruited workmen and resumed building.

But there was a change in her: she felt persecuted; while reconciled to her obsession, she now perceived its social liability. She drew more and more into herself and into her multistoried shell. She spent long hours in her private séance room, a windowless chamber draped luxuriously with blue satin. Upon entering it she always turned the key. To thwart prying, she surrounded the estate with a thick hedge and shunned the neighbors. Callers were not admitted. When San Jose was anticipating the visit of President Theodore Roosevelt, the local chamber of commerce asked permission to show her house to the president and received a curt "No."

To reduce the outward signs of her activity, she now divided her efforts between new construction and rebuilding. She found she could keep hammers pounding by revamping her creations, ripping out partitions, subdividing rooms, laying new floors, cutting new stairs. She may have been seeking to demonstrate her freedom from superstition by flaunting the "unlucky" number 13. Frequently, her designs incorporated 13 stairs in a flight, 13 panels in a ceiling, 13 windows in a room. She even had art-glass windows made in a design that featured 13 variously colored circles.

The 1906 earthquake brought another pause in construction. The jolt severely damaged a front section of the house, collapsing three floors and toppling a seven-story tower. Mrs. Winchester was trapped in the wreckage and had to be rescued. Although uninjured, she was badly frightened and moved quickly into a houseboat in San Francisco Bay. There she pondered the psychic meaning of the catastrophe. At length she decided that since the damage had been confined to the more elegant rooms, it signified she had been building too pretentiously. After several months, she returned and resumed construction on a more modest plane, but as inexplicably as ever. Curiously, instead of rebuilding the mutilated rooms, she simply sealed them off and ignored them.

Inevitably boredom set in, even for fashioning small designs. After creating scores of parquets and panels and fireplaces, she lost zest for it. It must have overwhelmed her at times to realize she must continue designing and building day after day, month on end, year on end, with no rest in sight — except death. That thought made her recall her blessings: hadn't the course she had followed brought her continued good health? Then she would throw herself into planning yet another wing, ordering materials, sketching designs.

Even after good health deserted her, she would not change her life. The din of hammers and saws did not shield her from the onset of painful arthritis; she was also afflicted with obesity. To enable her to oversee her employees working at far-flung points among the labyrinth of rooms, she installed three elevators, one costing more than $10,000 that served only one floor. In order to visit her attic storeroom where she kept her favorite materials, the art glass, tiles and lighting fixtures, she designed what is surely the strangest staircase in the world: body-width stairs each two inches high and eighteen inches deep that make seven turns to rise only nine feet.

In her later years she rarely left the house, even though she kept a chauffeur in livery and maintained three elegant automobiles, a Buick, a Renault and a lavender Pierce-Arrow. She now found her greatest pleasure in cultivating indoor plants and flowers. She acquired many rare and spectacular specimens and built a greenhouse and an upstairs conservatory. For the conservatory she devised a unique system for watering the plants and channeling off drainage, as well as a small elevator for hoisting plants up and down from ground level.

Her infirmity became crippling, but she continued to follow her toiling workmen via her elevators, the two-inch-high stairs, on crutches and finally in a wheelchair. She never curtailed the work schedule; she never complained. But it is significant that two of her cleverest innovations, the use of rock wool within walls and sand insulation between floors, were directed toward soundproofing to muffle the din of construction. At length, the never-ceasing clatter must have seemed like an orchestra that kept on playing nonstop, requiring her to swing the conductor's baton long after she had come to loathe the music.

When she died in September 1922, the house contained 160 rooms. It had more than a mile of twisting corridors, 40 stairways, 47 fireplaces, 13 bathrooms, nine kitchens, five different heating systems, both gas and electric lighting fixtures, and thousands of windows and doors. More than $25,000 worth of building materials stood in warehouses awaiting use.

She had devoted 38 years to her strange project, had spent more than $5,000,000 on it — and it had not brought her immortality. But it had carried her, active and spirited, to the age of 85, proving perhaps the efficacy of purpose. Her example seems to tell us that possessing purpose, whatever it may be, no matter how burdensome, is infinitely more life-charging than possessing none.

Her will provided that numerous family connections would draw income from trust funds during their lifetime, after which the trusts would revert to her favorite charities, among them the New Haven tuberculosis hospital she had endowed. An exception, however, was Llanda Villa; it went outright to a niece, Frances Mirriam of Palo Alto, who had served for a time as her secretary. The niece promptly moved out the furnishings and had them auctioned off; then she placed the house on the market.

Few buyers were interested, and in 1923 Miss Mirriam was obliged to sell at a sacrifice — reportedly, for $20,000. The buyers were Mr. and Mrs. John H. Brown, who had operated boardwalk concessions at a Southern California beach. That same year they opened the property to the public as Winchester Mystery House, and it was an instantly popular attraction. The tall hedges and the rumors had been building a clientele for years. The overnight stay of the magician Houdini in the house further spread its fame, even though Houdini failed to reveal whether he had succeeded in his efforts to "contact" the former mistress.

In recent years the house has been under the management of a private corporation. Instead of diminishing, visitor ranks continue to swell. Every few minutes small, guided tour groups (long, trailing ones might get lost) depart from the waiting room down a corridor to gasp at the curiosities and admire Mrs. Winchester's charming little designs, which during her day, like desert flowers, were but rarely seen. Her house, belatedly, is having its fling.

———

WINCHESTER MYSTERY HOUSE is located four miles west of San Jose via the Santa Clara-Los Gatos Highway at 525 South Winchester Blvd. Open daily except Christmas from 9 a.m. to 5 p.m. (later during summer months). Admission is $1.75 for persons 12 years and older, 50 cents for children 6 to 11.

View from one of the many cupolas of the 160-room house shows a maze of roofs and gables.

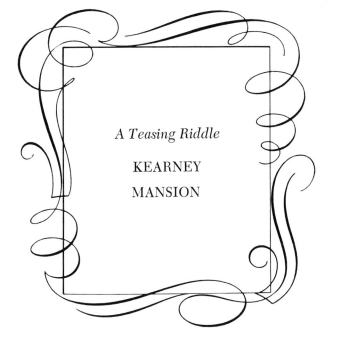

A Teasing Riddle

KEARNEY
MANSION

IT IS A STRANGE, surprising, puzzling house that thrusts out of the flat monotonous fields of the San Joaquin Valley near Fresno, teasing the mind, defying style identification, refusing to be categorized. What *does* it evoke? Soaring yet spreading, exotic yet homey, elegant yet drab...

Inside, bafflement is no less. There you seek clues to M. Theodore Kearney, even more enigmatic than his house, whose nature remains as locked to today's historian as it did to his mystified contemporaries. Of course, there are theories aplenty and unsubstantiated rumors, and if you have briefed yourself for your visit, you carry them up the wide stone steps and through the fan-lit doorway, hoping to fit them against the contents of the rooms and find enlightenment. Indeed, some objects do bear out a certain theory, but others contradict it; still others throw quite a different light on the man. In a framed photograph a stiff-collared, short-bearded man stares out with pale, unfathomable eyes, mocking your efforts.

Kearney's imperious, aristocratic mien concealed him from his fellow men, isolated him as with an antiseptic spray. His princely airs, some said, were ersatz, every bit as copied as the design for his projected Chateau Fresno. He had intended the house today called Kearney Mansion to shelter him only until completion of his grand French chateau, which he envisioned as the grandest residence in the West, but its construction would be thwarted, like his other grand designs.

Despite their lack of rapport, the affairs of Kearney and Fresno were as entwined as the grapevines in which they both specialized, and they appeared on the scene almost simultaneously. Today one of the most important food-producing regions in the world, the San Joaquin Valley was decidedly a late bloomer. The *Californios* had called the dry back country *tierra incognita* and ventured there only to pursue runaway mission Indians or on exploring expeditions (it was Spanish explorers who called the district Fresno after its abundant ash trees and named the valley for the father of the Virgin Mary). Americans ignored it too until the Gold Rush, and then they merely hurried through, bound for the Sierra.

But by the 1870s the miners were scraping rock bottom and began drifting down the slopes and trying their luck at stock raising, letting their cattle run on unfenced government land. They founded the village called Millerton, then decided to abandon it when the Central Pacific Railroad ran its line 25 miles west. Millerton residents moved to a railroad whistle stop called Fresno, pulling their houses behind them like turtles, and the town of Fresno sprang up faster than a present-day suburb.

At this juncture, in 1874, Kearney descended on the helter-skelter town by swinging off a southbound train. A handsome, slender, debonair man in his early thirties, he was an agent for San Francisco land promoter W. S. Chapman. Chapman

Facade of mansion with reflecting pool. (*—Fresno Bee*)

was a prosperous lawyer who had bought up hundreds of thousands of valley acres from the government at from ten to fifty cents per acre, having shrewdly foreseen that the new transcontinental railroad would bring west hordes of land-hungry settlers. Chapman's glowing advertisements and free rail excursions from San Francisco delivered prospects by the trainload to Fresno, where they alighted to blink in dismay at the desolate, sun-baked tracts flourishing with nothing but jack rabbits and tumbleweed. It was Kearney's task to convince them they were gazing upon promising acres and set them reaching for their pocketbooks.

This the authoritative, smooth-voiced man readily accomplished. He was even able to make good his promises, at least to a remarkable degree, via a brilliant subdivision scheme. Because of local conditions, a farmer would not have had the chance of a city mouse against a desert jack rabbit of succeeding alone, but by closely co-operating with a group he could prosper. The extreme aridity made irrigation imperative, and no small farmer could afford his own system; further, expensive wire fencing was required against the free-roaming cattle. Kearney subdivided Chapman lands into tight-knit colonies — composed of 21 sections of twenty acres each — whose members co-operatively financed irrigation and fencing and, moreover, were able to present a united front to harassing cattlemen angered by the plowmen's invasion. To ease co-operation, colonies oftentimes were organized around such common denominators as religion and nationality; one was even composed of sworn teetotalers.

M. Theodore Kearney. (*—Bancroft Library*)

Soon Kearney branched out on his own. While earning a small fortune in fees from those who answered Chapman's siren call, he applied shrewd judgment of land values to investing in the pick of Chapman acres and other tracts. His largest purchases were 4000 acres northeast of Fresno and nearly 8000 acres west of the town.

Suddenly he was a land baron himself, plotting his own subdivisions, and an important figure in the booming town. Important but not popular. While the humble immigrants were awed by him, his fellow businessmen were irritated. Who did he think he was, snubbing them and acting so high-toned? All anybody could learn was that he had come from Boston. But Kearney himself called England home, and his demeanor was that of an English aristocrat — his elegant phrasing and intonations, his London-cut clothes, his buttoned-up arrogance. Indeed, it was noticed that he bore a close resemblance to the playboy Prince of Wales who would become Edward VII. He seems to have noticed it too, for he trimmed his beard and mustache in precise imitation of the royal heir.

Kearney's elegance contrasted sharply with his Spartan quarters above a commissary on his west-side tract. There an astonishing project was under way. An army of workmen labored at earthworks that Kearney announced would become "one of the finest avenues in the world." Rudolph Ulrich, the eminent New York landscape architect, later to design the setting for Chicago's Columbian Exposition, was in charge of creating an 11-mile-long, 140-foot-wide parkway that bisected the tract and led to Fresno. A wide center lane was reserved for pleasure carriages with two side lanes for lesser traffic. Separating the lanes were plantings of pampas grass, flowering oleander, royal palm and Australian eucalypti.

Why, Fresnans wondered, build one of the finest avenues in the world for twenty-acre farms? They learned that the grand parkway augured more. It was to serve a country seat for Kearney that would surpass anything yet seen in California, a magnificent stone castle with dozens of rooms — salons and libraries and ballrooms. Fresno was dumbfounded! Could it be that the solitary man who had never so much as dined with anyone planned to entertain guests? It had been as-

Home of Kearney, Fresno land baron, built 1898-1900. (—*Boruszak*)

sumed that he planned to make his pile and then hie to the hedgerows of his precious England.

Kearney planned to finance his grand estate with the proceeds of the surrounding acres. All previous California land promotion paled beside the slick brochures he created for circulation in the East and abroad. They were more like parlor albums with their flowery prose depicting the tract called Fruit Vale a veritable Eden and illustrated with etchings of the grand parkway and Ulrich's landscaping. A skillful juxtaposition of plantings made the unrelieved plain look like gently rolling acres. Most impressive of all were etchings of a vast "Chateau Fresno," with towers and cresting, surrounded by hedged terraces and playing fountains. Fine print informed that while the latter wasn't yet built it soon would occupy the center of the lush paradise. The happy ending of the charming story was that the reader might live amidst this splendor for a rather modest price, even for a mere down payment and monthly terms.

Eden-seekers flocked in, cash in pocket. If initially taken aback by the barren acreage, they were appeased by the boulevard and the stylish promoter, and they bought lots in Fruit Vale or at one of the other Kearney tracts.

Now that the promotion built around his nonexistent chateau had made him rich, Kearney could afford to begin making his chateau reality. His construction procedure was as perverse as his personality. Upon completing his avenue of approach, he installed mammoth ornamental iron entry gates swung from huge concrete pillars. Next he constructed a two-story, cylindrical-towered gate lodge, modeled after medieval bridge guard towers in France.

Having given his estate a proper front, he then leaped to the rear and began constructing the outbuildings. Just as impressive as the gate lodge were the crested and cupolaed stables, carriage houses and barns. Next rose a large two-story servants' quarters constructed of thick adobe brick made on the estate.

Meanwhile, the surrounding settlers' plots began blossoming into wheat farms, dairylands and vineyards. For while Kearney allowed easy payment terms, on one point his installment contracts were exacting: improvements must be accomplished quickly. This not only created an air of prosperity that enhanced his real estate operations, but proved profitable in another way. Just around the corner waited the depression of the early 1890s, aggravated locally by a prolonged drought. The pinch proved too tight for many installment buyers, and when they defaulted, Kearney quickly reclaimed their property. He had sold barren plains and recovered established farms.

These foreclosures not only enriched him but launched him on another successful career, that of agriculturist. Already he had begun cultivating a small vineyard, marketing its yield to the budding raisin-processing operation that had sprung up with the invention of a mechanical raisin seeder and washer. Many of the reclaimed farms grew raisin grapes, and suddenly Kearney was the leading vineyardist and leader of the raisin industry. He applied his drive and intelligence to improving both growing and processing, while devoting his advertising ability to promoting the raisin market. Largely through his effort, Fresno quickly became the valley's raisin center and top supplier to the nation.

What's more, he ensured that growers got their share of raisin profits. When prices fell in 1897, he organized the vineyardists into a marketing co-operative that demanded and won better prices. Business interests and the newspapers accused Kearney of manipulating the farmers for his own purposes. But the farmers saw that what was good for Kearney was good for them; they made him president of the co-operative and let him run it. Inevitably Kearney's temperament bred resentment, and the farmers split into pro and anti-Kearney factions. Kearney resigned but when the co-operative teetered on bankruptcy, he was persuaded to return. He stayed for a time, then once more washed his hands of it. The raisin co-operative movement limped on without him, eventually evolving into the highly successful, and still thriving, Sun Maid Raisin Growers of California.

Liked or not, Kearney had become the biggest name in the valley, and speculating about him and his past was a popular Fresno pastime. Variously it was said he was a remittance man,

Kearney's desk. (—*All interior views: Bancroft Library*)

supported in exile by an aristocratic family; that an early marriage to an unfaithful wife had embittered him toward the female sex; that he had suffered the tragic loss of a beautiful young wife to whom he remained true; and that he had a deep aversion to all women, his all-male staff of servants being cited as proof. The most dramatic theory painted him the illegitimate son of the Prince of Wales, whom he so greatly resembled. His comings and goings were observed with fascination: his treks to San Francisco, where he had a suite in the Palace Hotel, and his trips to Europe, where he was said to frequent spas favored by royalty and where he selected furniture and art objects, shipping them back to be stored in a warehouse awaiting installation in his chateau.

Scarcely less interesting were the construction activities at Fruit Vale. When the final touches were made on an ornamental tea house, work then began on a residence. It wasn't the chateau, however; rather it was the "manager's cottage." But such a cottage! The big two-and-a-half-story house was built of adobe bricks laid two feet thick, and like the servants' quarters it incorporated modified features of the chateau. It had a high-pitched roof, large arches made of lathecut wood, and sharp-gabled dormers that rather suggested towers. Inside, there were a wide entrance hall, custom-made French wallpaper depicting scenic views of the valley, and elegant *art nouveau* lamp globes from Austria. Three large bedrooms on the second floor each had their own bathrooms, with both bathtub and a shower that sprayed from both top and sides. If this was the manager's abode, what would the master's be!

Pending erection of the chateau, Kearney planned to live in the manager's cottage, and he moved in and surrounded himself with the contents of his warehouse. There were piece after piece of carved furniture of heavy German make, highly-colored fireplaces of Italian tile, vast porcelain jardinieres from Italy and the Orient, flowered Brussels carpets and paintings of stern Rhine castles and brooding scenery in massive gold-leaf frames. The house was kitchenless; food was brought to a butler's pantry from the servants' quarters. Where the kitchen might have been was located the estate office with an adjoining office for Kearney.

Fresnans thought, now, surely, the grand man would invite some guests. But he continued as solitary as before, although it was whispered he always dined opposite an empty plate, a detail which pleased those who subscribed to the "tragic bride" theory. One day all Fresno was set agog when the celebrated English actress Lily Langtry arrived in town for a theatrical performance and was invited to lunch at Fruit Vale. But her visit was brief and not repeated. As well as assiduous Kearney-watchers could determine, his only overnight guest was an architect who came to discuss plans for the chateau.

In the opening years of the new century Kearney's prime preoccupation was perfecting plans for erecting his chateau on a slight rise not far from the manager's cottage. The soaring, round-towered design closely copied that of Francis I's Chateau Chenonceaux on the Loire River. Fashionable New Yorkers were then favoring the style for mansions at Newport and along Fifth Avenue. While final details were being worked out, Kearney began creating the chateau park, an intricate scheme that included gardens in the Italian, French and English styles. More than 500 rose settings of scores of varieties were planted on graduated terraces.

Kearney took time out in April 1906 for a trip to San Francisco. He was asleep at the St. Francis Hotel when the earthquake struck. With great effort he and his chauffeur reached his car, a $14,500 custom-built Mercedes, and fled the city unscathed. But while en route home he suffered a mild heart attack.

By May he had recovered sufficiently to set out on his annual trip to Europe. On his way to the railroad station, he drove to the chateau site and thoughtfully watched the laborers at work. The chateau was to begin rising in his absence.

The men were still at work when a cablegram arrived announcing Kearney's death; he had succumbed to a heart attack in a ship's stateroom midway across the ocean. Work on the chateau ended at once.

His will was a startling revelation to Fresnans. The man they had believed a misanthrope and a hater of California had bequeathed all he possessed, appraised at more than a million dollars, to the University of California. He stipulated that his estate be used for agricultural experimentation and his projected chateau for a school. In a separate document he expressed the wish that the school be called Kearney Agricultural College.

Guest bedroom.

Above, corner fireplace with *art nouveau* lamps.

Below, Victorian Era drawing room.

The will disappointed those who expected it to open a window to his past. Indeed, it heightened the mystery with a strange provision that, should a court of competent jurisdiction decide he had a wife, that person should receive $50, and the same amount was to be awarded to "each and every person who shall in like manner be found to be my child." Also tantalizingly inconclusive was a photograph found among his effects, of a youthful Kearney seated beside a blonde young woman; inscribed on the back was "Lizzie — 1867 — M. Theo Kearney." Some thought the ring on Kearney's finger looked like a wedding band. Papers in his office revealed he had a brother he had aided financially and who had died in Los Angeles. Publicity of Kearney's death turned up a man in San Francisco who said he had known Kearney as a youth when they had worked together in a Boston box factory.

A Fresno newspaper editor who had tilted with Kearney sought vainly to uncover the mystery of Kearney's early years, although he did establish that Kearney's father had not been Edward VII but a Liverpool stevedore who had emigrated to Boston. Observed the editor rather acerbicly of his former adversary: "The dread secret of his life was apparently that his parents were ordinary Irish people, who may even have worked for a living. This he regarded as a disgrace and devoted his life and his death to concealing it."

Kearney's dreams were all ill-fated. Like his chateau, neither the agricultural experiment station nor the college were destined to be. The university found the soil too alkaline for experimental purposes, and a decision had already been made to locate its agricultural college at Davis. The property instead was operated for its revenue, with Kearney's own superintendent remaining in charge and occupying the Kearney house. In time, the university began selling off land, channeling the proceeds (a total of $2,268,000) into the M. Theodore Kearney Foundation of Soil Science.

Fresno did not forget its colorful early citizen. It christened Kearney's scenic parkway Kearney Boulevard and pridefully maintained it. Further, it made known its wishes to obtain the central, landscaped portion of the estate for use as a park to be named for him. In 1949 the university presented Fresno County a fifty-year free lease to 147 acres containing the house, service buildings and gardens (the gate lodge had burned). The county purchased eighty additional acres.

The park was put to immediate public use, but the future of the dilapidated house remained undecided for a decade. Because it needed extensive renovation and a new heating unit, some tax-conscious officials felt it should be demolished. But history-minded citizens urged that it be preserved.

Finally, spurred by public opinion, in 1959 the county undertook restoration, making partial use of prison labor. The aging house received foundation reinforcement, a new boiler, new paint and plaster, and miscellaneous repairs. Subsequently the county entered into a contract with the Fresno County Historical Society whereby the society would furnish the house and operate it as a public museum, turning over admission fees to the county treasurer. The county was to pay utility bills and the salary of a museum administrator.

Furnishing the house proved easy. Kearney's superintendent, Ralph Frisselle, and his descendants had occupied the house up until its transfer to the county. When the family vacated, the university gave them part of the furnishings, donating the rest to the county. When the Frisselle family learned the house was being refurnished, it returned many Kearney items — furniture, clocks, rugs, pictures. Most of the subjects of the latter, to the surprise of some, were beautiful women. The gaps were filled with appropriate items donated by the public. Even a century-old Steinway grand piano similar to Kearney's was given. Beside it was placed the mechanical player attachment with which he had whiled away solitary evenings.

Since the opening of Kearney Mansion to the public in July 1962, additional Kearney items have been discovered. The detailed drawings of the projected chateau were found, rolled up and

Kearney's bedroom.

dusty, in the back of an abandoned garage. These now hang on an upstairs wall. The carriage house has been returned to its original appearance; the big servants' house is currently being refurbished for a history museum.

One effect of the creation of the park and of the restorations has been to make Kearney a household name in Fresno County and beyond. The society's volunteer guides emphasize his role as a key figure in developing the valley and shaping its economy. Kearney and Fresno may have quarreled once, but today, a century after he dropped off that southbound train, they are on the very best of terms.

KEARNEY MANSION is located eight miles west of Fresno at 7160 W. Kearney Boulevard. Open Wednesday through Sunday from 2 p.m. to 5 p.m. Closed on Christmas and New Year's Day. Admission 50 cents for adults, 25 cents for children (6 to 18), others free.

Home of Thomas Oliver Larkin, 1830s. Dining room
below. (*—California Dept. of Parks & Recreation*)

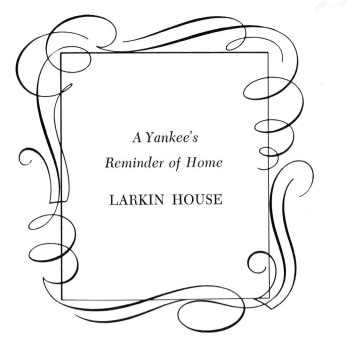

A Yankee's
Reminder of Home

LARKIN HOUSE

PROBABLY THE MOST INFLUENTIAL house ever built in California was Larkin House, constructed in the 1830s in Monterey. Although simple and modest-sized, it did what no other California house had done: it set a style. After settlement a half century before, California in some respects had remained arrested in time; its colonists complacently had changed neither their dwellings nor their dress. Visitors from Spain marveled that the pueblos looked like Spanish villages of the previous century and dismayed señoritas by saying they reminded them of their mothers.

The construction of this two-story, double-verandaed, high-windowed adobe precipitated a rush to construct or remodel in imitation, and such was its proliferation that late-comers in California took it for the original Spanish style. Later translated into wood, the style spread throughout the Gold Rush towns. Twentieth-century architects, finding it in the modern mood, revived it throughout the country; the so-called Monterey Style is still thriving.

But Larkin House precipitated much more than an architectural style. What happened within its walls over a period of three decades exerted a most powerful influence over the course of both commerce and politics in California. California, to an astonishing degree, was shaped by forces emanating from this house.

Starting a style — or exerting influence of any sort — was far from the thoughts of Thomas Oliver

Larkin when in 1835 he undertook to build the residence today called Larkin House. Only four years out of Boston and stuck in an obscure Mexican outpost on the wild Pacific Coast, he sought when combining American building practices with Spanish, not to create something new but to recapture the old and familiar. He wanted a reminder of home.

Larkin had come to California most reluctantly. A slight, lively man with dark, penetrating eyes, he was a member of an old Charlestown, Massachusetts, family that traced back to the *Mayflower*. But it was his bad luck to be left a penniless orphan with no prospects except working for others, which he quickly decided was not for him. At 19 he migrated south, planning to work as a trader until he had earned enough to establish a business in Boston. In North Carolina he launched a succession of ventures, working doggedly at them, but bad luck and poor health stalked him until, at 29, in debt and despair, he could see but three possibilities. He could importune a Washington relative to get him a government job, coax a well-fixed Massachusetts cousin to marry him, or, last choice, join a half-brother in the remote Mexican province of California. As it turned out, he was left with the latter. Instead of returning to Boston in triumph, he went there in 1831 to seek the cheapest passage to what seemed to him "the jumping off place of the world."

Decorative andirons. (*—Uncredited photographs: Historic American Buildings Survey*)

Four years later he was a prosperous Monterey merchant importantly overseeing construction of a substantial house for a wife and two children. Later that year he would tot up his wealth at nearly $5000. The luck that had eluded him in the East had smiled on him in this improbable little settlement of a score or so adobes scattered helter-skelter about a bare peninsula. That it was the capital of California and port of entry for foreign vessels only bespoke the state of the rest of the province. The benign climate had boosted his health, and while working as a bookkeeper for his half-brother he had courted and married Rachel Holmes, a Boston widow who had voyaged out to join her sea captain husband, only to learn he had died of fever. Soon after their marriage, Larkin had opened a combined grog shop and general store. Whether or not his wife put up the money is unrecorded, but she probably had come into a small inheritance. As a bachelor Larkin often had said the woman he married would have to have a nest egg. "All love and no capital will never do for me," he had emphatically declared.

He couldn't have gone into business at a better time. The missions were breaking up into ranchos, bringing economic change. The padres had bartered their mission products directly with the trading ships, but now merchants were needed as middlemen between the ships and rancheros. The merchants bought kitchenwares, textiles and Chinese luxuries from the ships and bartered them for the products of the ranchos, in turn swapping these for more cutlery and calico when the next ship docked. Larkin's Yankee shrewdness, together with those hard knocks gained in agrarian North Carolina, gave him an inside track on this lucrative mercantile cycle.

The 14-room house Larkin set about building in the spring of 1835 on a level site near the Custom House reflected his state of mind. That he built unstintingly denoted an almost cocky confidence in his late-found course, but that his design stopped short of grandness evidenced his intent to tarry but long enough to fill his coffers and then go sailing back in glory to the only place that counted, Massachusetts. Unlike most of the Americans who had come fishing for opportunity, he had

Thomas Oliver Larkin. (*—Bancroft Library*)

declined to "turn papist" or Mexican, settling for a renewable *carta;* and he had taken pains to be married in a Protestant ceremony aboard an American ship offshore. But for the time being, since his pockets were jingling, he wanted his family to live in solid comfort in just as American a house as local materials would permit.

Quite unwittingly he set a style. He would have preferred a traditional New England two-story frame, but the scarcity of timber ruled out such a structure. The Spanish building material, heavy adobe brick, restricted houses to one floor. Larkin scoured up enough timber to build a house that was part wood, part adobe. He constructed a wood frame stout enough to support a second story of adobe, but which permitted a much thinner adobe cover, as well as larger windows.

His floor plan followed the American Colonial precedent of rooms opening off a central stair hall, and he put in fireplaces, a local novelty since the Spanish did their cooking outdoors and coaxed indoor heat from pans of coals. The Spanish had depended on wide eaves as a rain shield for their adobe walls. Remembering the double verandas of North Carolina, Larkin protected his walls by wrapping a double veranda around three sides of his house. The symmetrical arrangement of his doors and double-sashed windows was traditional American Colonial. So was his shingled hip roof

Chippendale chest of drawers and ornate Chinese furniture in living room corner.

— the first in California — built by the New Englander George Yount. Pure practicality, all of it, yet it was quite a departure from the slab-sided, one-story Spanish dwellings. One of the first to copy it was Governor Juan Alvarado.

Work on the house continued into 1838, although the family had moved in long before. After completing it, Larkin totaled up the cost at $4927.60. The most nominal expenditure was for the 85 x 30-yard lot: only $12.40. The adobe walls cost but $203 (the bricks cost $15 a thousand), while the roof of hand-hewn shingles came to $581. An outlay of $126 went for stone for the 60 x 40-foot foundation on which seven men worked seven days, together earning $38.50. Four locks came to $12 and a like amount went for hinges and screws. Larkin splurged $72 more on wallpaper, also rare in Monterey.

One large downstairs room (now the dining room) accommodated Larkin's general store, and adjoining it was his office, for which he procured a commodious $40 desk that is still in place. Installed in another lower room was a large oven for baking ship's biscuits.

Larkin's self-confidence was well placed; he was on his way, indeed. Along the coast from San Diego to San Francisco other Yankee merchants were operating similar establishments; some, like John Temple of Los Angeles, were go-getters,

while others had relaxed into a *poco tiempo* outlook. Larkin quickly became their leader and pacemaker, thereby stimulating commerce throughout the province. *Poco tiempo* was not for this man, whose nature combined a hummingbird's darting energy with a bloodhound's scent for hidden possibilities.

Formerly, trading ships had taken only hides and tallow; he coaxed them into buying provisions — potatoes, beans, butter, dried beef and the aforementioned ship's biscuit. To supply the latter he set up the first double-geared flour mill in California, having made a model for ship's carpenters to follow. He also went into the country and set up soap-making operations. Initiating redwood cutting near Santa Cruz, he was the first to tap the untouched timber resources of the Pacific Coast. This gave him entry into erecting wharves and public and private buildings.

To widen his stock he traded with merchants all over California and in Mexico and Hawaii. His store took on the air of an international bazaar, with Hawaiian sugar, Chinese tea, Mexican serapes and Boston bonnets. When business slowed he went after it, placing ads in American and Hawaiian journals and circulating letters to whalers, inviting provision stops. As a retail stimulant he added the service of wrapping purchases, even though he had to send away as far as Hawaii for wrapping paper. Shipping him a bale of old newspapers for this purpose, his Hawaiian supplier sniffed at this frill: "We are not in the habit of wrapping up goods — yet."

Larkin's voluminous business correspondence discloses his secret of success. The most salient characteristic of this small-statured man was meticulousness. No order was too trivial to fill, no profit too narrow to pursue, no debt too small or too old to dun relentlessly. His enterprises had thousands of ramifications; his mercantile business alone involved countless small contracts, of which this one is typical: "Blair will hand you a small box containing 7500 needles and 4 papers of pins which please sell and ship proceeds in soap." He was able to integrate these multifarious transactions and keep it all sorted out in his head because he kept his mind clear of virtually everything else. He once wrote down as a guide of conduct: "Think not of others, only while with them. . . . Think of what is before you — and no more." His mind uncluttered by sentiment, he was able to concentrate on stretching the margin of profit on those needles and pins.

Above all, he hated to leave an order unfilled, and this sometimes led him to make dubious substitutions. Among his correspondence we find complaints of "soured wine," "weevly flour," "rotten handkerchiefs," of being shipped "old casks and other trash." Soap customers grumbled of short count, "such little cakes," and "mostly tallow." Lumber shipments were criticized for being rotten or "burnt and decayed"; one customer averred he had been sent "the most miserable trash ever taken out of Santa Cruz." Larkin, in turn, castigated his suppliers for sending him short measures of brandy and "indifferent looking soap." Although very insistent that his debtors pay promptly, he was not always quick to pay himself, preferring to keep his capital in action as long as possible. All this haggling, often amounting to accusations of swindling, seems to have been taken cheerfully in stride all around, for their transactions continued undiminished: they needed each other.

Thanks to such single-minded dedication to profit, Larkin by 1842 was able to appraise his wealth at $37,948. He was acknowledged to be the top merchant on the coast, and reports of his affluence attracted admiring letters from his New England relatives. But they worried about his living amidst an alien creed and were pleased that he planned to stay only until he had "accumulated a certain amount of property." They had another count on which to congratulate him — his expanding family. "Nine children in 10½ years!" marveled his stepbrother Ebenezer in an 1844 letter. "This beats any of your Yankee connections."

What with increasing arrivals of both Yankee clipper ships and American immigrants, the United States decided it needed a consul in California.

Larkin's wall safe opens over a table in the master bedroom.

It is unclear why the consummate businessman Larkin was so anxious to obtain the time-consuming, unremunerative office. Some historians believe he was motivated by a desire to steer California into the American fold, thus carrying on a family patriotic tradition (one Larkin forebear supplied the horse for Paul Revere's midnight ride). Others say he knew that whoever got the post would reap valuable trade advantages and it must on no account go to a rival. Undoubtedly the office did enhance his business, but historians agree that he diligently, even brilliantly, performed the duties of consul and went beyond his official duties in assisting annexation.

Larkin became consul in the spring of 1843, having had strings pulled for him by the same Washington kinsman who had been unable to turn up anything for a destitute Larkin in 1831 but who came through admirably for his prospering California relative (and so reminded Larkin later, in asking him for a loan). The office behind Larkin's store now became the United States consulate, into which filed a procession of ship captains and naval officers, along with down-and-out seamen and immigrants.

Those in a position to throw business his way were installed as house guests and entertained lavishly. Himself a man of moderate habits, Larkin could ply the sybaritic taste with as much divination as any present-day Madison Avenue executive. In a letter to a friend he reported himself very busy supplying the frigate *United States* and "making a dance to the officer." With the genteel Mrs. Larkin as hostess, he set a gourmet table, poured the best brandy and threw the most elegant balls in the territory. Much vied for were invitations to his so-called cascarone balls in the upstairs sala, at which guests were supplied tinted eggs filled with confetti for the dancers to crack over each other's heads at unguarded moments. Equally famous were his Fourth of July fêtes, which alone cost him more than a year's consul fees.

Larkin more than quadrupled his wealth during the first half of the 1840s, despite the most unsettled conditions imaginable. One governor after another was deposed in almost nonstop revolution. No sooner had Larkin established a work-

ing arrangement with one than he was shipped back to Mexico. But by carefully avoiding politics, except to put in a cooling word wherever possible, Larkin kept his stock rising.

By this time he had conceived of his plan to guide California toward willing annexation with the United States. Larkin envisioned a peaceful, orderly, business-as-usual transfer with the United States graciously offering, the Californians gratefully accepting. He saw the political turbulence as an opening to further this. Many Spanish-Californians were growing weary of riding into battles that brought only more instability. Larkin recognized their malaise as fertile ground in which to plant the idea of an American California. He made it known that Americans didn't have their governors handed down, but elected them from among themselves; furthermore, the United States hadn't had a revolution since 1776. Under his tutelage the influential General Mariano Vallejo came to yearn for American annexation.

At the same time Larkin encouraged the United States to covet California by making exaggerated assessments of possible interference by France and England, both in his official communiqués and in his letters to New York newspapers. Having excited envy, he blandly promised "the pear is ripe for falling." His journalistic reports also encouraged emigrants to hurry westward, not to the "jumping off place," but to a golden paradise. As in his earlier ads inveigling ships to provision with him, his facts were liberally laced with fiction.

Under prodding by Larkin the powers in Washington awakened to California's possibilities, but to his exasperation American conduct in California often was not the sort to aid his plan for a genial transfer. Especially embarrassing was the behavior of John Frémont. The young captain had come to California with a force of sixty men, claiming to be on a scientific expedition, and Larkin had wrung permission from the *Californios* for the Americans to make a brief swing through the interior. But Frémont defiantly had marched his men, all swinging dreaded carbines, toward the coast, alarming the whole province and setting the military to sharpening their lances. Larkin had to exert his utmost powers of persuasion to induce Frémont to turn back, and even then the headstrong captain, as he boasted in a letter home, retired "slowly and growlingly."

But what dealt the final blow to any chance for peaceful annexation was the raucous Bear Flag Rebellion. North of San Francisco, a group of disgruntled American emigrants, possibly encouraged by Frémont, took it into their heads to declare an independent republic. For a hostage they seized, of all people, General Vallejo, Larkin's convert to Americanization. Larkin's initial disbelief dissolved into a sad relinquishment of his hopes for a voluntary changeover. When soon afterwards Commodore John Sloat sailed into Monterey harbor with news that the United States and Mexico were fighting over Texas, Larkin was resigned, even anxious, for annexation by seizure, as preferable to the obstreperous Bears. The Larkin expert George Hammond believes Larkin influenced Sloat to make his historic decision, five days after landing, to declare California part of the United States.

Monterey uttered not a murmur. There wasn't even a Mexican flag to haul down — the old flag had worn out and there had been no funds to replace it. During this time the commodore enjoyed Larkin's hospitality, and when the Stars and Stripes went up, on July 7, 1846 — the first time they legitimately were raised over California — they flew over Larkin House.

During the months ahead, Larkin House witnessed much exciting drama. Frémont used it as his command headquarters until ordered to the Los Angeles uprising. Commodore Sloat appointed his chaplain, Walter Colton, to be Monterey's first mayor, and he set up offices there until a city hall could be built. When General Stephen Kearny arrived to rule California as military governor, he too was given offices in Larkin House, which thus became the temporary state capitol. Kearny's aide, young Lieutenant William T. Sherman, later to win fame as the scourge of Georgia, occupied a small adobe in the Larkin garden. During the Constitutional Convention of 1849, at which Larkin was a delegate, the house served as the social center for delegates and the site of official dinners and the gala celebration ball.

Larkin was in the very center of the Americanization process, and high office might have been his for the nodding. For whatever reason, he made the decision to decline political life. Perhaps he wanted to be free to capitalize on the commercial expansion predicted to follow annexation. He began buying up real estate in Monterey; then, sensing the promise of San Francisco, he focused attention there, acquiring large tracts near the water front.

He didn't foresee the Gold Rush, but he was ready when it came. He quickly threw up housing on his lots and named his own price. To provision the prospectors he invested in shipping to Mexico, Hawaii and China, buying interest in four vessels. He opened general stores in the mining camps; he even staked claims and hired Indians to work them. He was ever buying up lots in San Francisco and Sacramento. No wild gambler, Larkin scorned the excesses being committed at every side; instead, he worked assiduously, even though he often grew weary of it. He wrote a friend, "I would give 500 ounces of gold to chase out of my brain for a year or two every idea of trade." More and more he spoke of the day he would retire and return to Massachusetts. His relatives wrote assuring him they were anxious to "welcome you to happy New England."

At last, in 1850, he was ready to go; the fortune he had come to seek was made. He had gotten in on the ground floor of the Gold Rush inflationary spiral and it had made him a millionaire — California's first. After sending his family on ahead, he disposed of the house where he had seen his ambitions fulfilled far beyond his hopes. Placing his remaining interests in charge of an agent, he departed, taking the quickest route via the Isthmus of Panama. It must have been truly an exultant moment, to set foot upon the Atlantic Seaboard rich and famous only two decades after departing it a debtor.

Details are lacking of his luxurious, free-spending tour of New England, New York and Washington, D.C., but it is evident that it all somehow paled beside the dream. The rosy young cousins he had so yearned to impress had grown up into lackluster middle-agers. In Washington a new political regime seemed to have forgotten his patriotic feats, and in New York City, where he had decided to live in a fine Broadway mansion, he found the corridors of finance and power preempted by sophisticates in top hats and Prince Albert coats who looked upon him as a rustic outsider. This rankled, for he had discovered that, far from desiring to forget every idea of business, he yearned to return to it. His New York activity was largely confined to Brooklyn real estate deals. In less than three years he confessed he was homesick for California and ready to return. With his family he departed on one of the new steamers, joyfully anticipating a permanent return to the place he once had journeyed to with dread.

Back in San Francisco, Larkin found that the recurrent San Francisco fires provided ample scope for new development. Deciding to make San Francisco his residence as well as his business headquarters, he built a stately mansion on Stockton Street, just a few blocks from his namesake Larkin Street. There the Larkins, *au courant* in all the latest New York fashions, lent tone to San Francisco's rather uncertain social set. He made large investments in Sacramento real estate and joined in schemes for short railroads and shipping lines while developing his land holdings in the interior. He made a continual circuit of his scattered enterprises.

He was on a business trip to Colusa in October 1858 when he contracted typhoid fever. He returned to San Francisco for treatment, and there two weeks later he died; he was only 56. His burial place was a San Francisco cemetery overlooking the Pacific.

But Monterey is where Larkin wrote his name in history, and there is maintained, as a state historic monument, the storied house in which he set California moving toward its appointment with destiny. Luckily it has always been an object of respect and care. In 1922 it returned to the family when it was acquired by Larkin's granddaughter, Mrs. Alice Larkin Toulmin. Making it her home, she conducted a wide search for Larkin family relics and for furnishings appropriate to the dignified rooms with their wide-planked floors and simple woodwork. In 1957 she presented it to the state as an historical monument. Today a steady stream of tourists wander through its portals, later

Sheraton side table and oval looking glass in stair hall.

to muse in the silent enclosed courtyard, where between timeless adobe walls and under a timeless sun the busy merchant might have walked through just that morning.

LARKIN HOUSE is located at the corner of Jefferson Street and Calle Principal in Monterey. The house is shown by guided tours of 35-minute duration, conducted daily except Tuesday 9:15 a.m. to 4 p.m. The garden is open from 10 a.m. to 5 p.m. The 25-cent admission charge is good for other historic buildings.

Hearst's Dream Castle

SAN SIMEON

WHEN GEORGE BERNARD SHAW arrived in 1933 on his much-publicized visit to America, like any other tourist he brought a lively curiosity about this country's most famous and spectacular personality, William Randolph Hearst. Hearst, as the owner of dozens of newspapers, magazines and radio stations, was the most powerful publisher in the world. Moreover, his name had been placed before several presidential conventions; he operated a Hollywood production unit; owned vast real estate, mining and cattle empires; and was the largest art collector in the world.

Unlike the ordinary tourist, the Irish wit and playwright had bestirred the curiosity of Mr. Hearst, and he was invited for a visit. Shaw accepted — the only private invitation he *did* accept — and Hearst flew to get him in his silver-domed airplane and fly him to his favorite retreat, San Simeon, a magnificent dwelling complex situated on a mountainous California tract that flanked the Pacific Ocean for fifty miles and was half the size of Rhode Island.

There in golden sunlight the Irish bard conversed with the lordly American in his 84-foot Assembly Room, dined under a 16th-century Italian ceiling, rode in an elevator made from an ancient confessional, and met Marion Davies, the beautiful blonde actress friend of Mr. Hearst. Shaw took it all in while the world waited to hear what England's most legendary figure would say of his visit with America's most legendary

figure. Never one to disappoint an audience, Shaw made these observations:

Of Mr. Hearst, that he had "enjoyed Mr. Hearst as a social phenomenon and liked him as a man."

Of Miss Davies, "Marion is by far the most attractive of the stars who are not really eighteen."

Of San Simeon, "This is probably the way God would have done it if He had had the money."

Undeniably, money *had* been a factor in creating San Simeon's uncommon beauty and majesty. Hearst, the country's most lavish spender, had channeled some $30,000,000 into what he affectionately called his "Enchanted Hill." Indeed, he had paid out more for housing and decoration than any man in history, king or commoner, and was then bidding on art and antiques to the tune of an average million dollars a year, the cream of them earmarked for San Simeon.

But far more than money had gone into his unique achievement. To Shaw's comment on San Simeon might be added, ". . . and if He had had Mr. Hearst's experience with castles." Hearst had been studying and building castles all his life in preparation. A shimmering castle rising from that sun-kissed hill had been the most persistent dream of his childhood. Growing up for ordinary children means relinquishing childhood dreams, but for Hearst, a most unordinary child, growing up meant gaining the freedom and wealth to make his dream reality. The pursuit of it obsessed him;

Detail from Refectory ceiling. (*—All photographs: North Collection*)
At left, tiered facade of La Casa Grande.

» 83 «

despite the enormous pressures of his rushing, multifaceted career, he was ever slipping back to further his dream, and he directed toward it the full force of his intellect, his energy, his wealth and his indomitable will.

Born in 1863 in San Francisco, Hearst had an exceptional upbringing. His big, bluff father, George Hearst, was a multimillionaire gold miner but almost illiterate, although he served a term as a United States senator. He once complained that a political opponent had accused him of spelling "bird" b-u-r-d and asked, "If b-u-r-d doesn't spell bird, what in hell does it spell?" But Hearst's tiny, delicate Dresden doll of a mother lived and breathed culture. With her husband away at the mines, she haunted the local art galleries, leading her adored only child as soon as he could toddle. His precocity by age three delighted her; she wrote a relative that not only could he "tell all about Cocky Locky and Henny Penny" but he was learning to speak French. His father called him Billy Buster, but his mother called him Willie.

When Willie was ten, she took him on a months-long trip to Europe that ignited lasting passions. Medieval Edinburgh enchanted him, and he wanted to enter all the ancient buildings. Mrs. Hearst kept a diary of her son's comments, noting that upon viewing Windsor Castle he observed, "I would like to live there." In Paris, he suggested that she buy the Louvre. He became fascinated with the relics of the Frankish king Charlemagne, who helped preserve civilization during the Dark Ages; the young Hearst visited his tomb and sat in his chair. While his mother bought sculpture, he made his own acquisitions. He returned with a collection of porcelain figurines, beer steins, papal medallions and books on Charlemagne.

Back in San Francisco, the Hearsts acquired a mansion with an art gallery to accommodate Mrs. Hearst's sculpture collection and Willie's figurines and beer steins. Now a sophisticated blond youth with courtly manners, he could hold his own in the afternoon salon his mother hosted for artistic types and society matrons. Evenings, mother and son pored over art albums and planned their next pilgrimage to the European art capitals, all to the mystification of the culture-blind George.

But father and son shared one enthusiasm; they both loved the sprawling family rancho acquired when Willie was a baby, a wilderness tract in the craggy Santa Lucia Mountains, 200 miles south of San Francisco. They went down partly by train, partly by horseback and roughed it. There Willie was Billy Buster, galloping his pony and imitating the ranch hands. Later, George built a comfortable two-story house at the foot of the rocky escarpment that so fascinated Willie. He liked to climb it on his pony; he'd take a picnic lunch and sit long on the mountain crest staring out to sea, dreaming of the castle he'd build there. Such grandiose thoughts were hardly discouraged by the unbridled wealth and privilege that surrounded and isolated him. He was the only child in San Francisco with his own Punch and Judy show, and when he asked his father for money for ice cream he was likely to be flipped a twenty-dollar gold piece.

Hearst's childhood enthusiasm strongly influenced his adult life. His publishing career, although it absorbed prodigiously of his energies, never really claimed his heart. He had never given journalism a thought until his last year at Harvard, when he worked a stint on the *Harvard Lampoon* to help a friend pull the magazine out of debt. Hearst boosted circulation and advertising with some unorthodox promotion schemes, and as a result became curious about his father's recent publishing venture — also accidental. George Hearst had loaned money to the ailing *San Francisco Examiner*, and when the newspaper couldn't repay, he bought it to try to recoup his loss. Upon leaving Harvard, Hearst asked his father to give him the *Examiner*. The request dismayed both parents; his mother wished him to become a diplomat. While his father hesitated, Hearst went to work as a reporter on the *New York World*. Later that year George Hearst was elected to the Senate, and he relented and signed the *Examiner* over to his son.

The fledgling publisher, a handsome six-footer with piercing blue eyes and a walrus mustache, plunged into building up the *Examiner*. He campaigned spiritedly for reforms and spiced up the news columns, pointing his journal, like the *New York World*, toward the masses. Journalism quickly led him into political stances, and he seems to have early conceived the idea of building political power through newspapers and thereby making himself president (the *Examiner* had helped lift George into the Senate).

Hearst soon began to make other publishing acquisitions, which in time would expand into a chain of thirty newspapers, giving him the influence he coveted. His interest was never in the money; he often bought losing propositions and held on to them against all advice. His formula of supplying more entertainment than news (he introduced comics and features to newspapers), his splashy headlines and photographs, and his colorful reportage were for boosting circulation and, thereby, political power.

And he *did* gain political power, enormous power. In New York, his publishing headquarters, he was nominated again and again for state and city office; and in the presidential arena his name was either touted or placed in nomination every election year for two decades; for a decade more he was a force behind other nominees. But he was always more the art connoisseur than the politician, lacking not only the common touch but a talent for speech-making. The highest office the electorate ever presented him was that of U. S. congressman.

All the while, he was mindful of his dream castle. Early he knew where he wanted it — on his old picnicking spot overlooking the Pacific. After he married Millicent Willson, a dancer, he often took his young family camping there — camping elegantly in striped tents with floors and bathrooms, with servants and tutors in tow. Already he was making acquisitions for the castle: paintings, tapestries, della Robbia reliefs, ancient beds. And not just furnishings for the castle but *parts* of it. He purchased complete rooms of castles and monasteries — walls, ceilings, windows, all — and had them disassembled and stored. Sometimes he bought whole structures.

Meanwhile, he helped his mother plan two sumptuous family seats in Northern California, one on the McCloud River, the other a handsome Spanish-Moorish palace at Pleasanton. In the architect of the latter, he knew at once he had found the person to build his castle. She was young Julia Morgan, a diminutive Oakland-born woman with an iron determination concealed in her fragile frame. She had crashed barriers on two continents to win her credentials. First, she braved ostracism to study engineering at the University of California; then, she became the first woman to win an architecture degree at the École des Beaux-Arts. As early as 1905 Hearst discussed with her his plan to build a house on a mountaintop at San Simeon. Her training fitted exactly into his monumental building scheme. Further, he sensed she would not shy at challenge. But, lacking funds, he could not build yet. George Hearst had died and, concerned at his son's cavalier attitude toward money, had left his entire fortune to his wife.

In 1919 Phoebe Hearst died of influenza, willing $11,000,000, the bulk of her fortune, to her only child. A few months later, Hearst handed Julia Morgan a commission that would span three decades. Although by then a highly successful architect with dozens of churches, schools, and hospitals to her credit, she must have been astonished by the details of this assignment.

She learned of the accumulation of elaborate rooms, mammoth staircases, choir stalls, towering columns, balustrades and ancient mosaic floors waiting in far-flung warehouses to be incorporated into her design. Without road or port, how were they to reach the 200-foot-high building site? Not to speak of the problem of unifying it all into a scheme that involved scores of rooms on an untold variety of levels. Not only was there to be a castle, but an orbit of sizable guesthouses. Although the building site was mostly solid rock and nearly barren of soil, Hearst specified spacious, terraced gardens and groves of trees. At the very peak, where he wished his castle to rise, stood four huge oak trees to which he was fondly attached and wished to have moved to other locations on the grounds.

It was a challenge such as no architect had ever faced. Mixing architectural parts that spanned a thousand years! Never had Miss Morgan's Beaux-Arts grounding in the classic traditions been so useful. Her engineering training served handily too. Soon a road was climbing the mountainside and a wharf being constructed for bringing in the heaviest shipments by sea. The four obstructing trees, one weighing 600 tons, were extracted by encasing their roots in huge concrete tubs and hoisting them to other spots. To make gardens possible, water was piped from mountain springs five miles away and tons of earth carted up from lower meadows. Hearst didn't bat an eye at the staggering costs; he was used to such outlays. Once after purchasing and disassembling a 10th-century cloister in Segovia, Spain, he was obliged to construct a sawmill to supply wood for the 10,700 crates in which the stones would be packed and then build 21 miles of railroad to connect with the nearest line.

Hearst wanted three guesthouses to be erected first. Like the castle, they were to incorporate the art and architectural treasures he had been acquiring. Architect and client pored endlessly over the complex plans, working and reworking the details, she sketching, he oversketching. Miss Morgan was later to credit Hearst with possessing marked architectural talent: "If he had chosen that career he would have been a great architect."

The architectural wonder of the age began to take shape. To prevent the guesthouses from obscuring the castle, Miss Morgan built their top floors to open at the castle level, with three or four lower floors reaching down the mountainside to lower terraces. Of 10 to 18 rooms each, the houses were white-walled and tile-roofed, variously designed in the Moorish, Italian and Spanish Renaissance styles. Each had its grand sitting room and entrance hall and such splendors as red and gold Renaissance furnishings, Grecian urns and carved gold-leaf columns, an ancient loggia ceiling from Spain, and a magnificent carven bed that once rested the head of Cardinal Richelieu. The name of each house was suggested by its view: La Casa del Mar facing the sea, La Casa del Monte the mountains, La Casa del Sol the sun.

Slowly reaching skyward was the great shining castle, La Casa Grande. The basic construction — poured, reinforced concrete faced with Utah limestone — was as durable as a cathedral, which the tiered façade with its Gothic ornament and Renaissance grillwork rather resembled. But conferring individuality and a hint of the exotic was a wide, teakwood gable. The vestibule was floored with a Pompeian mosaic featuring a mermaid and sharks, which for centuries lay buried under volcanic ash.

Changes in massing and detail were made again and again; sections were built and rebuilt. Hearst seemed reluctant to arrive at the final form. During the slow emergence, he was experimenting with other castles. The McCloud River house had burned, and he replaced it with a Bavarian village composed of a castle and three subcastles; he purchased two ready-made castles, St. Donat's Castle in Wales and a moated and drawbridged pile on Long Island. But they were mere whims compared to his passion for San Simeon. He was ever slipping back to inspect progress.

The contents of the much-traveled packing crates were studiously blended into the expanding design. The size and shape of the august Assembly Hall were dictated by the dimensions of its ceiling, removed from an Italian *palazzo*. Brussels tapestries woven in 1550 adorned its walls between a marble doorway sculptured for Pope Julius II and a 16th-century French Renaissance fireplace. The Refectory, later to become Mr. Hearst's favorite room, united an Italian ceiling, Flemish tapestries and 500-year-old choir stalls from Catalonia, Spain; while the Gothic Study, where he would work and preside over meetings of his executives, brought together the artistic expression of five centuries and more than a dozen countries.

The decision to build the distinguishing twin towers did not come until three stories had been constructed and Hearst and Miss Morgan mounted the roof to inspect it. Admiring the view, Hearst decided he would like his living quarters on that level. "Build another story," he directed; "We'll call it the Celestial Suite." To fit this order into her design, Miss Morgan devised the magnificent baroque towers, each accommodating an octagon-shaped bedroom, connected by an oblong sitting room. Over each bedroom she set a bell tower equipped with bronze carillon bells from Brussels. In the end, Hearst decided to occupy the third-floor Gothic Suite instead, reserving the Celestial Suite, the loveliest in the castle, for distinguished visitors.

Late in 1925, La Casa Grande was ready for occupancy, and Hearst and his wife and five sons spent Christmas there. He couldn't look at it enough, and he was anxious to have it viewed by other deserving eyes. He returned often to play

The Refectory, Hearst's favorite room, combined priceless Renaissance art works from Italy, Spain and Belgium.

The magnificent Roman Pool is paved with hundreds of thousands
of pieces of blue and gold mosaic tile by artisans from Italy.

host, and there began that file of dazzling guests who made San Simeon the most exciting court of the 20th century. George Bernard Shaw was but one of many world figures who found a Hearst invitation too irresistible to turn down. Across the Pompeian mermaid strode President and Mrs. Calvin Coolidge, the Shah of Iran, Winston Churchill, Charles and Anne Lindbergh, Mayor Jimmy Walker, and every Hollywood name who *was* a name: Irving Thalberg, Charlie Chaplin, Delores del Rio, Darryl Zanuck, Clark Gable, Greta Garbo, Bette Davis, Beatrice Lillie, columnist Louella Parsons, and a youthful new producer named Howard Hughes.

Hearst happily surrounded himself with the accomplished, the witty and the beautiful. Although naturally shy, he liked having crowds of them at once. He worked hard at being the genial host, and sometimes to please his guests would yodel or do the Charleston, but he always seemed

a little formal and remote. He was ever thinking up new delights: throwing a costume party and putting at his guests' disposal the Metro-Goldwyn-Mayer wardrobe collection and make-up artists; chartering a plane to fly to New Orleans for fresh shrimp; showing the latest prerelease films in his luxurious gold and Turkey-red upstairs theater; staging overnight camping trips by horseback with a retinue of cooks and servants bearing champagne and caviar.

During daytime hours when Hearst was making decisions in the Gothic Study, guests amused themselves by inspecting each other or the creatures in the zoo — everything from tigers and elephants to Tibetan yak and Australian emu, altogether more than a hundred species comprising the largest private zoo in the world. The tennis courts often were enlivened by the likes of Bill Tilden or Helen Wills and, sometimes, by the host himself, who played an astonishing game standing regally in one spot, or almost, effortlessly commanding the ball with his long reach and placing it with remarkable precision. Or one might swim, either indoors in the $1,000,000 Roman Pool made of small gold and blue Murano tiles laid by artisans brought from Italy, or outdoors in the 102-foot-long white marble Neptune Pool with its Roman Temple for a cabaña. The grounds were virtually a sculpture museum of classic marble nudes, a surprise to those familiar with the Hearst newspaper policy of painting gym suits on photographs of scantily-clad athletes. Another garden pastime was spotting the telephones; they were concealed under trees, under stone seats and behind shrubs, so that wherever the master strolled he was but a tinkle away from the key people of his newspaper empire.

In turn, Mr. Hearst required certain things of his guests. Abhorring intoxication, he expected visitors to make do with the one cocktail served per day. And there was the unwritten law never to mention death; he even hated to see a dead leaf or flower in his garden, and groundsmen spent predawn hours removing them by flashlight and once painted a desiccated palm tree green until it could be replaced. He wished strict observance of his estate road signs "ANIMALS HAVE RIGHT OF WAY"; Winston Churchill was obliged to sit more than an hour waiting for a couchant giraffe to bestir itself. Guests likewise were to ignore the mice scampering down the paneled halls; Hearst, a zealous antivivisectionist, wouldn't hear of killing them. He expected everyone to attend the nightly movie (one of his favorite actresses was Shirley Temple), and to get into his party costume, whether the gladiator suit was flattering or not. And it pleased him if his guests fitted at least a few pieces in the outsized jigsaw puzzles always laid out in the Morning Room.

San Simeon was Hearst's greatest pride, the one project that never palled for him, and he never lost zest for perfecting it. In the late 1920s he added a recreation wing to the castle, and in the mid-1940s, when he lived there permanently, he completed another large wing. This brought the number of rooms, including guesthouses, to 146. Not enough, in his opinion — he had plans drawn for still another guesthouse.

But in the late 1940s Hearst suffered a heart attack, and his physician decreed he must no longer live at the remote spot. He wept as he made his last trip down his Enchanted Hill; he knew he would not return. San Simeon was close in his thoughts until his death in 1951, at the age of 88, in Beverly Hills. Only two days before, he asked a friend to go check on things there. Politics and film making had disappointed him, and his interest in publishing had waned, but he knew that in San Simeon he had created something of first rank. Moreover, he believed that, like his childhood hero Charlemagne, by collecting and restoring the best art of the ages he too had preserved an aspect of civilization for posterity.

In his will, Hearst directed that the buildings at San Simeon and their art works go to the University of California as a memorial to his mother, but the university regents found it unfeasible to incorporate the isolated property into its educational system. Hearst's sons remembered their father had talked also of presenting San Simeon to the state to be used in some way to advance

Opening into the castle court is the splendid door of La Casa del Sol, one of the three guesthouses.

At left is an aerial view of the Enchanted Hill, showing the access roads and the many service buildings involved in the estate. Opulent twin towers, at right, contain octagon-shaped bedrooms reserved for distinguished guests. Overhead pealed bronze carillon bells.

the art and culture of the public at large. They invited Governor and Mrs. Goodwin Knight to the castle for a week end and expressed their willingness to give the property to the state as a memorial to both their father and their grandmother, Phoebe Hearst. Knight, impressed, directed the Division of Parks and Recreation to investigate whether it might be incorporated into their jurisdiction.

In 1957 the state formally accepted. The gift included the buildings, their art works, the 123 acres surrounding them, and a small tract at the base of the hill, once Hearst's private airstrip, for use as an entranceway and visitor parking lot. The legislature appropriated $256,000 to cover the expense of preparing buildings, grounds and approaches.

In 1958 the property was opened to the public as the Hearst San Simeon State Historical Monument. Tours of the guesthouses, castle and grounds were offered the visitor, who purchased his ticket at the lower base and rode a bus up the hill to be taken on a tour by an informed guide. Fears in some quarters that the monument might be a tax burden were groundless; the operation has proven nicely self-supporting.

But Hearst, who cared little for fiscal reports, would be most pleased to know that yearly some 600,000 men, women and children come to gaze upon his cherished architectural gems and art treasures.

HEARST SAN SIMEON STATE HISTORICAL MONUMENT is located on State Highway 1, 94 miles south of Monterey and 42 miles north of San Luis Obispo. Three separate tours of about two hours each are conducted 9 a.m. to 5 p.m. daily except Thanksgiving, Christmas and New Year's Day. Admission is from $3.35 to $4.35 for adults, slightly over half price for children (those under six admitted free if they don't occupy a separate bus seat). Tickets may be purchased at the entrance to the monument, at a Computicket outlet, or by writing Department of Parks and Recreation, P. O. Box 2390, Sacramento 95811.

Sharing adjoining Santa Barbara sites are the homes
of Horatio Trussell (above) and Charles Fernald.

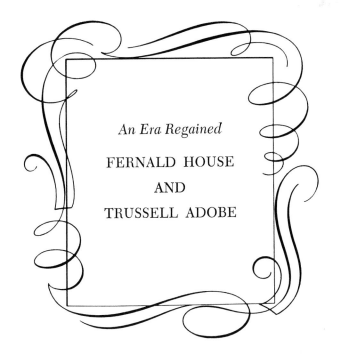

An Era Regained

FERNALD HOUSE
AND
TRUSSELL ADOBE

WHEN CHARLES FERNALD and Horatio Trussell were schoolboys back in Maine and heard of British royalty and read about the men who mutinied on the *Bounty,* they never dreamed they'd meet connections of those fabled casts. Still less would they have believed the meetings would take place in the obscure Mexican town of Santa Barbara.

California's sudden Americanization and the subsequent gold discovery swept in flush, frenetic times that beckoned to the most astonishing variety of human beings ever assembled. The two Maine youths rode in on the first wave, from their separate villages, and after sampling the offerings of the golden shores, they settled down in the warm valley town between the Santa Ynez mountains and the sea. It was there they met, became friends, and stepped into active, vital roles during the decade after the Mexican flag was lowered.

It seems appropriate that the Fernald and Trussell homes should stand but a few yards apart in a tree-shaded district of Santa Barbara. On Sunday afternoons, when the houses are open to the public, visitors stream back and forth between and mingle on the connecting lawn, or admire the old fashioned flowers in the garden where a bronze plaque is erected to describe the houses' pasts.

The two houses now stand together, but actually the two transplanted down-Easters never ex-perienced such close proximity. The juxtaposition of the Trussell Adobe and the Fernald House was accomplished in recent times by the Santa Barbara Historical Society, by the device of moving one house onto a site beside the other — for purposes of history.

The society acted to rectify a loss. Santa Barbara had lost a chapter of its past, or so it seemed. Its early American period, the half century following the inauguration of American rule in which Charles Fernald and Horatio Trussell figured, had largely been forgotten because of a preoccupation with the era that preceded it. So vividly remembered were the bygone Spanish days of the glittering fiestas and swaggering dons that they tended to obscure what followed after.

One Spanish figure in particular cast a formidable shadow over Santa Barbara history — the short, stout figure of Don José Antonio Julián de la Guerra y Noriega. That "y Noriega" he kept because his mother was even more noble than his father; indeed, the cool, imperious Don José was the nearest thing to a feudal lord California had ever seen. Spanish-born, he had come to Santa Barbara in 1806 as a military officer and in a few years was *comandante* of the Presidio. But with the advent of Mexican rule, his birth was held against him and he was denied higher office. But they couldn't hold him down. He wheedled land grants until he owned a third of a million acres, while lining his coffers by importing cargoes from a merchant uncle, and he shrewdly accumulated power until he dominated the very offices he was barred from, as well as the clergy. So awed were ordinary folk, they doffed their hats and crossed themselves when passing his casa, exactly as when passing the church. At home his grown sons, even married ones, nightly kissed his hand as they marched from the dining room straight to bed; for pocket money they would tar the end of a stick and fish through a crack in his counting room. But the man who held Santa Barbara in his pockets conferred benefits. Barred from the Mexican hierarchy, Don José ignored its revolutions; thus while turbulence wracked the province elsewhere, the pueblo was a haven where one might peacefully pursue his bent. In festive Santa Barbara, at the slightest excuse everybody dropped everything and held a fiesta.

Everybody loves a fiesta and its lore. A movement grew in Santa Barbara early in this century to revive Don José's smiling era. Variously this was accomplished with the annual "Old Spanish Days" fiesta, by the restoration and publicity given Mission Santa Barbara ("queen of the missions"), and by the resurrection of the original pueblo through restorations creating the El Pueblo Viejo historic district. Later the colorful El Paseo complex of shops and restaurants were honeycombed into the restored de la Guerra adobe in the heart of downtown Santa Barbara. So dominant were these Spanish exhibits that Santa Barbara gave the impression of having leaped agilely from the mid-19th century into the modern age, and the average Santa Barbaran knew almost nothing of how the Spanish pueblo was transformed into an American town.

Certain history-minded citizens deplored this neglect of the early American period and set out to correct it. But reviving that era in Santa Barbara presented more of a problem than in towns where some one big happening had seized the popular imagination. San Francisco had its Gold Rush legend, Sacramento its transcontinental railroad lore, Los Angeles its storied land boom. While Santa Barbara had no event of this caliber, its changeover years had been exciting and sig-

nificant nonetheless, and the historians set out to regain them and fit them into place. One means of doing this was to preserve worthy American-era landmarks as reminders to passers-by that the dons did not have the 19th century all to themselves.

Americans were prominently on the scene in Santa Barbara even before annexation. The *Yanquis* began arriving early. A seaman on shore leave, exhilarated by a fiesta, would bid for the hand of one of the local señoritas; then marriage bonds tied him to shore. The first was Daniel Call, who made himself useful as a carpenter. Alfred Robinson married one of Don José's daughters and became the leading trader. During the 1840s, Americans increased, all adopting the local customs, including the authority of Don José, who welcomed them as a buffer against the Mexicans.

After annexation, Americans poured in swiftly and Don José as swiftly changed his mind about them, as he saw his power collapsing like a pricked balloon. The cocky newcomers didn't bother to check in with him. One was Charles Fernald. He had wound his way from Maine to San Francisco in 1849, put in a stint panning gold, apprenticed briefly in a San Francisco law office and was on his way home again in 1851 when he stopped off in Santa Barbara to say good-bye to friends. He found the town trembling in terror. A gang of die-hard Mexicans had turned desperadoes, overrun the town and bullied the county law-enforcement officers into resigning. Because Fernald knew some law and had a purposeful cast to his chin, he was persuaded to take the job as sheriff.

He intended to earn some money and be on his way; instead, he was to stay the rest of his life. With a combination of zeal, luck and a law requiring citizens to hang lanterns on their properties (violators were fined fifty cents to a dollar), he routed the bandits and restored order. After turning in his guns, he noticed the town was short on lawyers, so he hung out a shingle. Now an established professional man, he returned to his Maine home town and claimed Hannah Hobbs as his bride. After their return to Santa Barbara, he was made district attorney.

For Captain Horatio Gates Trussell becoming a Santa Barbaran was an affair of the heart. For years he had plied clipper ships and steamers

Views of Fernald House stair hall and dining room show skilled wood-work of pioneer cabinetmaker Rosewell Forbush. Ornate chandelier was equipped to burn candles, the only lighting used by the fire-wary judge.

along the California coast before making Santa Barbara his home base, after marrying one of its belles. His bride was not Spanish, but a beautiful Tahitian, Ramona Burke, believed to have illegally swum ashore from a vessel anchored in the channel. Ramona was the great-granddaughter of George Stuart, one of the British crew of the *Bounty* who in 1789 mutinied and settled in the South Seas. George Stuart's bride had been the proud daughter of a Tahitian chieftain.

Captain Trussell and his bride from the sea appropriately ensconced themselves in a semi-nautical house. As he was preparing to build a modest dwelling and deploring the dearth of lumber, the steamship *Winfield Scott* was wrecked off the coast and supplied most of his needs. Timbers salvaged from the wreckage made possible construction, in 1854, of a house in a semi-American style. The captain, who first went to sea as a ship's carpenter, constructed the central section of the plentiful adobe, then concealed it with a frame cover, frame wings and a shingle roof, one of the first in Santa Barbara. Further, he cleverly made use of salvaged brass thresholds for interior doors.

The house expressed not only the captain's practicality but his background. It had New England formality in its symmetrically spaced, shuttered windows and in its rectangular porch with simple, square columns, and he gave it the familiar high-pitched gable roof. Later, the captain's plan did prove impractical in one respect: it did not lend itself to expansion. In the 1860s, he was obliged to sell it and build another house that would accommodate his ten children.

The captain and the young lawyer attained prominence in decades of giddy prosperity. Cattle boomed in the 1850s and early 1860s; every hillside around the town teemed with munching herds, raised not for their hides, but for beef on the hoof. Picturesque, shouting drovers whipped the big-horned cattle north to the San Francisco market, where they fetched handfuls of six-sided slugs of gold worth fifty dollars each. Never had Santa Barbarans possessed such spending money, and spend they did for all the luxuries cargo ships could unload. Commerce blossomed, culture budded. Meanwhile, Fernald became the leading attorney in the vibrant town.

Chaste New England window treatment of the captain's adobe.

When drought ruined the cattle business, a land boom replaced it. Newcomers began arriving in droves that nearly matched those of the departed herds for size and clatter, lured by reports of a heavenly climate and agricultural wonders. The depleted ranchos broke up into small farms for growing grain and fruit, and Santa Barbara quickly changed from an adobe town to one of brick and wood with gaslights and telegraph service. It got a college too, but so strong was the custom of easy-going gaiety, it soon closed its doors. Captain Trussell, now retired from seagoing, built a wharf to serve the port's multiplying cargoes.

By then Fernald had become a county judge and was ready to build a house. Like the captain, when choosing a style he remembered New England. In 1860 he constructed a simple, two-story square house of brick with a hip roof. But because his builder was Rosewell Forbush he got an interior far from austere. Forbush was an American cabinetmaker who had arrived in pueblo days and turned contractor during the land boom. Woodwork remained his love and he delighted in the new Victorian motifs. His devotedly detailed doors, panels, wainscoting and the curving mahogany staircase lend a most un-

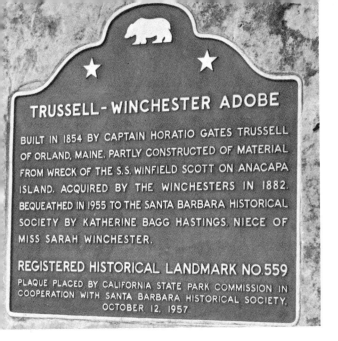

TRUSSELL-WINCHESTER ADOBE

BUILT IN 1854 BY CAPTAIN HORATIO GATES TRUSSELL OF ORLAND, MAINE, PARTLY CONSTRUCTED OF MATERIAL FROM WRECK OF THE S.S. WINFIELD SCOTT ON ANACAPA ISLAND. ACQUIRED BY THE WINCHESTERS IN 1882. BEQUEATHED IN 1955 TO THE SANTA BARBARA HISTORICAL SOCIETY BY KATHERINE BAGG HASTINGS, NIECE OF MISS SARAH WINCHESTER.

REGISTERED HISTORICAL LANDMARK NO. 559
PLAQUE PLACED BY CALIFORNIA STATE PARK COMMISSION IN COOPERATION WITH SANTA BARBARA HISTORICAL SOCIETY, OCTOBER 12, 1957

Puritan elegance. He was thwarted, however, in installing modern lighting fixtures; the judge, twice burned out in Gold Rush fires, would have no truck with either gas or kerosene — only candle-light would do. Chandeliers were equipped with candleholders, and later a table in the stair hall held candlesticks for carrying up to bed. House guests delighted in the romantic aura created by candle glow on polished woodwork.

The judge, now a true Santa Barbaran, reveled in lavish entertainments, and festive parties were in his plans. Accordingly, lower floors were arranged so that folding doors connected the front and back parlors; the whole could be thrown *en suite* to accommodate a ball or a grand reception. Against Forbush's handsome backdrop, the judge's fêtes blossomed, along with his career. Twice re-elected judge, Fernald then became Santa Barbara's mayor.

As the city's official host, he was inspired to remodel his modest house into something more fashionable. He engaged the architect Peter Barber, who was then designing most of the elegant new mansions and hotels. Barber transformed the unpretentious salt box into an imposing residence in the combined Stick and Queen Anne styles. Plastering the brick exterior to make it resemble stone, he emphasized the vertical line by flanking the windows and doors with slender strips. The low-hipped roof was remodeled into a cluster of steeply pitched gables lined with scroll-cut; pointing skyward were iron finials and decorative Queen Anne chimneys. The reaching parts

had a lofty look, considered appropriate for the abode of a judge, even a fun-loving one like Judge Fernald.

Now he was ready to receive the best, and the famous and the fashionable were increasingly enlivening the Santa Barbara scene. At the judge's candlelit eight-course dinners, served by a large retinue of Chinese servants, winter visitors mingled with the town's *beau monde*, among them Captain Trussell. A popular afterdinner diversion was a high-toned game of charades, for which the dining room would be cleared as a stage and its double doors flung back with guests seated in the library. One scintillating evening the acting out of the word "adjudicate" included scenes from *The Merchant of Venice, The Taming of the Shrew* and an aria from *Il Trovatore*. Bishop Kip, first Episcopal bishop of California, was a frequent guest, as was a certain Captain George Dewey, a cousin of Mrs. Fernald, later to become Admiral Dewey of Spanish-American War fame.

But all that paled beside the judge's crowning social triumph late in 1882, when to him fell the delicious pleasure of hosting Queen Victoria's daughter, the Princess Louise, and her new husband, the Marquis of Lorne, then governor-general of Canada. The pair already had paid respects to Governor Stanford and San Francisco, with a blare of press reportage about the emancipated princess who "smokes, plays billiards, flirts, travels or visits country houses alone." There was also a buzz of gossip that the royal marriage had been hastily arranged because of the princess' inappropriate interest in a certain Anglican canon. Santa Barbara was in a frenzy of anticipation, and at Judge Fernald's glittering formal dinner in their honor the royal retinue did not let the locals down. The princess and her ladies-in-waiting swept in wearing daring, low-cut evening gowns, while the marquis, not to be outshone, threw convention to the winds by carrying his gloves in his hat instead of wearing them, causing Santa Barbara males to peel in imitation. The princess was delighted with Santa Barbara and ordered a palette and paints to record her impressions. She charmed everyone, including the monks at Mission Santa Barbara, who admitted her to their private walled garden, where she sat down and painted a picture.

Decorative mahogany newel post of Fernald House staircase.

After that, the judge seems to have felt he had reached the apex and had nowhere else to go. He declined further public office and quietly dabbled in business enterprise. Commerce had taken a spurt with the arrival in 1887 of a railroad, a branch of the Southern Pacific's valley route, and that event inspired the judge to introduce streetcars into Santa Barbara. Afterwards, he founded the local chamber of commerce. Santa Barbara had come a long way from the fiesta-loving, bandit-fearing pueblo he had found in 1852. In fact, visitors sometimes exclaimed in surprise that "Santa Barbara seems typically American."

That was the era the Santa Barbara Historical Society set out to recall in the form of some visual reminders. Across the country Victorian Era architecture was long disparaged, until a re-evaluation returned it to favor. In Santa Barbara this ostracism was especially strong because interest in the Spanish restorations encouraged construction and remodeling in kind. Structures from the early American period were winnowed out like ragweed from a garden, regardless of quality or historic import.

Among those distressed by this trend was Mrs. Katharine Bagg Hastings, the owner and occupant of the Trussell Adobe and a connection of the Winchester family, which acquired it in the 1880s. After inheriting the house, she restored it, removing accretions of millwork, painting it white again and providing needed maintenance. Her snug, old-fashioned dwelling with its furnishings of a bygone era delighted her; moreover, she realized its historic worth and determined it must not go the way of the other Victorians. The Santa Barbara Historical Society, of which she was a member, entered into an agreement whereby she willed the society her house, along with its furnishings and sizable grounds on provision the society would preserve it as an historic exhibit.

In 1957 the society, having fallen heir to the Trussell Adobe, opened it to the public without charge. The landmark was in a firm position, endowed with a $30,000 living trust, the gift of Mrs. Edwin Gledhill, an historical society member then curator of the society's museum. The house also had a new roof and new paint, donated by another member. In addition to furnishings willed by Mrs. Hastings, it contained some of the original furnishings donated by descendants of Captain Trussell. A massive bedroom set of hand-carved maple had come around the Horn from Detroit as a wedding gift. A marine painting was the work of Frank Thompson, a nephew of Captain Frank Thompson, whom Dana depicted in *Two Years Before the Mast*. A mahogany square-back chair, of the sort often paired together to form a bed, originally served in the historic Dobbs Ferry Tavern; since George Washington frequented the tavern, he doubtless sat, perhaps even slept, in it. Soon after the opening, the State Park Commission's Historical Landmarks Division registered the house as an historical landmark and sent a representative to mark it with a plaque.

Two years later the society was distressed to learn that the Fernald House, which had been owned and meticulously maintained by the judge's family through the years, was threatened. The telephone company was negotiating purchase from the descendants for a building site.

A determination was made that the Trussell lot would accommodate another structure, and the

Trussell Adobe contains captain's practical original furnishings. View shows simple living room fireplace.

sections, and each was moved separately. Moving the begabled sections through the street necessitated cutting numerous telephone wires, which alone cost $6000. After being reassembled on its new site behind the Trussell Adobe, the house got new chimneys and fireplaces and an exterior coat of plaster to restore its former appearance. A circular driveway provided access to the street. Many of the furnishings dating from the judge's occupancy were donated by his descendants and installed in original positions. Half of the rooms were furnished as period rooms for public viewing, the rest being reserved as office space for the historical society and other civic organizations.

Juxtaposed, the two houses, each in a different style, constitute a museum of period architecture and décor. The Trussell Adobe represents how adobe construction was blended with New England tradition, while the Fernald House exemplifies the Victorian style most used in Santa Barbara. Although the society's plot can not accommodate further refugees, it still offers sanctuary of a kind. The respectful treatment of these two Victorian Era structures has conferred status on others and has slowed the rampant destruction. Owners who used to see in their vintage houses only the salable land beneath are now seeing charm and history — and some are deeming these worth keeping.

society obtained the family's permission to move the doomed house to a site that had been the Trussell orchard. The telephone company then donated toward the moving cost the $1200 it had planned to pay for demolition.

The transfer proved complicated. Prior to moving, the plaster-coated brick walls had to be replaced with wood; chimneys and fireplaces were also removed. Next the house was sliced into three

The TRUSSELL ADOBE and the FERNALD HOUSE are located at 412 W. Montecito Street in Santa Barbara. Both houses are shown on Sunday afternoons from 2 to 4 p.m., except on Christmas and New Year's Day. No admission charge.

Old *carreta* stands before south wing of "T" plan adobe, above, built by Ygnacio Palomares. Wide *corredor* of casa's central wing, below, suggests the leisure of California's "golden years."

Pomona Pastoral

ADOBE
DE PALOMARES

THE GLORIOUS PANORAMA often painted of the roseate "days of the Dons" rather suggests the Spanish nobility deserted their castles on the plains of Spain for the slopes of the Pacific, there to rule from country seats of surpassing elegance over domains of infinite riches. A soupçon of truth in a caldron of fiction. Early California, in reality, was far more earthy and humble.

But Ygnacio Palomares, on whose domain later rose the city of Pomona, would have believed the roseate version. He saw himself a don surrounded by loyal subjects. Encircling his casa like a feudal village were the casas of his offspring and those of relatives and friends who had come to live on his land; beyond them camped the obedient rancho Indians. His greatest pleasure was to stand in his doorway of a morning and survey his domain. Once he boasted: "Every smoke plume you see rising is from the home of one of my children or one of my friends to whom I have given land." His life was all he could ask for. Certainly, he was a don and his sons would be dons after him.

In fact, Ygnacio Palomares was not of noble birth, but the son of a footsoldier, and his abode was an unpretentious adobe. He never had much money, and his pleasures were the simplest. Yet, he was a representative figure of the "golden years." His rancho, of roughly 7500 acres, was an average-sized Mexican-era grant and typical in

its operation, as he was a typical ranchero in his background, habits and attitudes.

He acquired his rancho in a typical way. During Spanish rule few ranchos were granted and these mostly to military retirees, but in the Mexican era, when Palomares gained his rancho, land was quite freely given. It was required, however, that the land applied for not be in use by another citizen, and that usually meant outlying land, and outlying land nearly always meant Indians. Locally, the troublesome San Gorgonio tribe had put a damper on land applications, and some grantees after settling had come scurrying back to the pueblo.

In the spring of 1837, Palomares, a young family man in the Pueblo of Los Angeles, found himself with a problem that made him ready to brave Indian territory. His problem was the Widow Valdez. He and his friend Ricardo Vejar had been pasturing their herds in a hilly district (now Beverly Hills) that was also the favorite grazing place of the widow's cattle. She had curtly invited them to take their cows elsewhere.

Ygnacio and his friend scouted the surrounding territory on horseback and decided on a tract well removed from the widow's sharp tongue. It lay about 25 miles west, part of a grassy valley nestled in an arm of the San Gabriel Mountains. Cattle from the San Gabriel Mission had grazed there before secularization, and some abandoned

Tooled leather chair in the sala. (—All photographs: Alfonso Fages)

mission Indians still inhabited the district. In fact, the young rancheros were counting on the *man-sared* (gentled) Indians both for rancho work and to act as a buffer against the obstreperous San Gorgonios. Ygnacio composed a letter to the governor in Monterey. He described the tract, declared it to be unoccupied (Indians didn't count) and asked to be granted two square leagues (roughly 15,000 acres) "for myself and for Ricardo Vejar who does not know how to write."

The two friends differed in other ways. Ygnacio was a serious, somewhat pompous young man with the visage to go with it — a brooding face with heavy brows over close-set, sunken eyes and a tight mouth. Ricardo, the son of a wood carver who had come up from Mexico to work on the missions, was round-faced and jolly.

The grant was given, and one August morning the Palomares and Vejar families loaded their possessions onto oxcarts and pack animals. Driving their cattle before them, they set out over hard, dry earth, following roughly the route of the present San Bernardino Freeway. The retinue on horseback included the pueblo priest, who went along to bless the rancho.

Their stopping place was by chance. Government officials had measured the grant in the usual desultory way, employing a leather line that stretched in the dew and shrank in the sun, and using such property markers as a hacked tree here, a pile of bones there. The families had planned to settle in the center of their rancho, but unable to ascertain the boundaries, nobody could tell where the center was. So they had to guess.

The party drew rein in an oak grove beside a spring. There they gathered under a giant oak, where the priest said mass and pronounced a blessing on the land. Afterwards, the Vejars proceeded several miles due south. The rancho was to be held as undivided property, the Palomareses occupying the northern half, the Vejars the southern.

The first item of construction was a corral, not for the cattle but for the Palomareses. Stout poles barred stock and wild animals from the site where the family cooked, ate and by night slept under hides stretched over stakes. But soon adobe bricks were drying in the sun, fashioned by the civilized Indians, who had been induced to camp near-by

and make themselves useful. The rancho's first casa began to take shape, square room by square room. Other Indians tended the herds, while their squaws undertook household tasks under the critical eye of Don Ygnacio's wife, Doña China.

In that simple way did the rancho begin, and as simply did it proceed. The cattle freely roamed the valley and foothills, requiring neither feeding nor fencing. At rodeo time they were rounded up with much shouting and whooping; calves were branded and the herd's increase slaughtered for hides and tallow. Hides were processed by soaking in salt water and stretching on poles, tallow by rendering fat in iron pots and pouring into leather bags. These, the rancho's only marketable products, periodically were transported by oxcart to the port of San Pedro and bartered to ship captains for a few luxuries.

Don Ygnacio considered himself rich, but he had precious little money. Why would he need it? All necessities came from the rancho. Bean patches supplied the staple *frijoles*, cornfields the *tortillas*, gardens the vegetables for the daily soups and stews (always of beef — *Californios* spurned pork, mutton, fish, bear and venison). Medicines too were home-grown: rosemary for weakness, thyme for coughs, rue for earache and asthma, mint for cholic, swallowwort for sore eyes, sage to mix with soot and salt for fever and ague. Baby powder was made by pulverizing dried rose petals. A little fruit was grown for eating and canning, grapes for wine and brandy-making. Sheep's wool was made into cloth, tallow into soap and candles, hides into bridles, saddles and shoes. What use were the gold pieces displayed in the *sala?* For an occasional christening and for tossing at the feet of señoritas when they danced the *sol.*

Pleasures too were of the rancho. Males diverted themselves with bear and cockfights and, mounting horses, vied with each other to seize a coin from the ground at full gallop or grab a rooster buried up to its neck in sand. Scarcely less vigorous were the popular *bailes*, held in the sala bedecked with scarlet paper flowers. Sometimes an imbued *caballero* would ride his horse right into the room. The dances had a childlike air. In the *fandango* somebody would shout "*Bomba!*" (Listen!), upon which all would join hands and

In his old age Don Ygnacio slept
in this canopied four-poster bed.

sing: "Now I see a rat, now I see many; some have big ears, some haven't any." Everybody danced — Don Ygnacio solemnly with a married daughter, a grandmother with a grandson, small sisters with small sisters. The *bailes* were marvelously gay, but a far cry from Spanish court life.

But in one way Don Ygnacio *was* princely. He did not have to toil. He had servants, the Indians, to do his every bidding. He might stand in his doorway all morning if he liked, and always he took an afternoon siesta. In exchange for their labor, the Indians were permitted to live on the rancho, raise their own food and partake of gifts of beef at slaughtering time. As hoped, the rancho Indians were a deterrent to the San Gorgonios; the fierce tribesmen, after a show of defiance by burning the Palomares beanfield, retreated to the mountains, except for an occasional foray on the rancho horse corral.

Mission-trained Indians were the mainstay of most ranchos, and their subservience may have sparked the notion among rancheros that they were one with the Spanish nobles, for even the

grandees did not possess such obliging retinues. After prospering, Don Ygnacio, like some other rancheros, took pains to find a coat of arms to lay claim to. His was composed of a castle with seven towers with a dove perched on each. His claim to noble ancestry was a trial to his daughters, for he branded all the local young men, including the Vejars, ineligible suiters, even though there was no other choice at hand. For all his storms and sulks, the daughters eventually took local husbands, his favorite daughter Teresa marrying a Vejar.

Identifying with old Spain, Ygnacio disdained the new styles for men, the short hair and long trousers, that came up from Mexico. He insisted on wearing knee breeches with leggings and continued to braid his hair, or rather have Doña China braid it, into a queue which hung below his wide-brimmed, flat-crowned hat with chin strap, also outmoded. His solemn airs and appearance may have prompted his appointment as justice of the peace after the district became more populous. He disconcerted the citizenry by attempting to enforce religion and morals as well as law. He was especially hard on profaners; the luckless offender was tied to a poplar tree before the Palomares casa with a lump of rock salt in his mouth.

Equally conservative in politics, he longed for a return to Spanish rule and looked down on the "upstart" Mexicans who had usurped power. Yet, when a faction led by Governor Alvarado sought to revolt from Mexico and institute local rule, he called *them* upstarts and clung to Mexico. Joining Pío Pico in an attempt to overthrow Alvarado, he was captured and jailed for a time. His experience made him look with favor upon *Americanos* as preferable to the revolutionaries, a conversion that proved fortunate for a group of Americans trapped in a house in Chino during the fighting that ended the Mexican War. Some vengeance-minded *Californios* wanted to shoot the gringos, but Don Ygnacio was among those who insisted they be spared.

Americanization caused scarcely a ripple on the placid pool of Don Ygnacio's existence. The only change was the Gold Rush-sparked demand for beef in Northern California. Don Ygnacio sent his vaqueros north with cattle, which fetched

Heavy early pianoforte dominates west end of the large sala.

higher prices than he'd ever heard of. His new riches seemed providential and inexhaustible, and they brought him to a decision: his old casa no longer befitted his position. Something finer was needed.

This was in the early 1850s, and architectural choice had widened. The two-story Monterey style, combining Spanish and New England design, had been popularized by the house Thomas Larkin had built in 1834 in Monterey; also many *Californios* were building in the pointed Gothic and towered Italian Villa styles introduced by the Americans. Don Ygnacio didn't even consider them; unhesitatingly he clung to tradition. A short distance from his old casa, at the crossroads of the highway to San Bernardino, he constructed a 13-room, narrow, strung-out adobe in one of the familiar plans, the "T." Each narrow wing was flanked by the familiar covered *corredor*.

In nearly every detail he employed the tried and trusted. Although lumber was plentifully available from a mill operated by one of the new Mormon settlers, and support framing would have permitted a thin shell of brick, he retained the ultra-thick walls with their deep interior recesses for doors and windows. The upper reaches of the house were finished in the old-fashioned way of stretching cloth overhead in lieu of a ceiling. Generations of children, trapped in the sala with grownups, had diverted themselves by following the course of spiders and other insects that pre-empted the space. Anticipating bigger than ever *bailes* and assuming the priest from San Gabriel Mission would continue to come and say mass at his casa, he constructed a palatial 20x30-foot sala. His casa was coated inside and out with a mixture of fermented cactus juice and lime. His one daring concession to the 19th century was a wooden shake roof.

With his fine new casa and with cash rolling in from the beef market, Don Ygnacio felt the rancho's best years were ahead. He could foresee no alteration in the pleasant, leisurely rhythm of his days. Some rancheros were turning part of their acres to orchards, vineyards and crops. He saw no sense in that. Why go to the trouble of clearing land and irrigating? Cattle was the thing. A man's stature would always rest on the size of his herd and the quality of his horses. Settlers were multiplying and the gringos coming by and looking for a bit of farmland puzzled him. Passengers whizzing by in the fast Concord stages bound for St. Louis and Salt Lake City puzzled him. "Why," he asked Doña China, "would anybody want to go to such places?"

Even the great drought did not wither his faith. In the early 1860s three rainless years parched the grass, dried water holes and brought death to thousands of cattle. Bleached skeletons mounted in heaps. Money ran out, and supplies dipped low. Only fleas seemed to thrive. Into that gloom came the terrible smallpox epidemic. Whole families fell sick; most of the Indians died, the rest fled. Don Ygnacio's youngest daughter died. Doña China was inconsolable and made her sons chase away the mourning doves that made her sadder. Through it all, Don Ygnacio's calm was a mainstay. "Have patience," he soothed, "these bad times will end."

His old friend Vejar lacked patience. His cattle were dead—and he had owned more than Ygnacio—and his son Chico had gambled away the family gold. By then the rancho had been legally divided, and Ricardo talked of mortgaging his half. Ygnacio recoiled at the idea of risking land for mere money. The drought would end, he argued; then they would rebuild their herds. The Indians would return, prosperity would return. Unheeding, Ricardo made his mark on a gringo's paper.

At last the drought was over, and the smallpox epidemic was broken with a miraculous new vaccine. Confidently, Don Ygnacio prepared to start anew. Then he himself fell ill of a mortal disease. It was time, he said, for his sons to take his place; adjuring them to return the rancho to its former glory and to honor the name of Palomares, he made his last confession and peacefully died.

He died the don, and Doña China saw to it that he was buried the don. Extravagantly, she ordered Los Angeles' new plumed and glass-paned hearse; it took two days to coax it over the rutted roads. Friends and relatives came from every rancho between the ocean and the mountains and solemnly marched behind the magnificent plumed hearse to the plot Don Ygnacio himself had chosen.

Death had spared him knowledge that the drought had ended the cattle era of Southern California, that a new agricultural economy had replaced it. And it spared him witnessing the sad fate of his friend Ricardo. When time came to pay his debt, he lacked the money, and most of his rancho was taken from him, like many another ruined ranchero. The languid culture had simply collapsed beneath the weight of Yankee economics. The golden years had vanished. In the 1860s and 1870s almost every rancho in California passed from *Californios* to Americans, either by foreclosure or sale.

The Palomares rancho went the latter route. The year after Don Ygnacio died, his heirs sold part of the land to an American. Doña China kept the casa and brought in a relative to live with her and run a small store that catered to stagecoach passengers and wagon trains. But the taxed land was a burden, and after a few years she went to live with her children, selling the remaining acres, except for plots the sons possessed. An American bought the land for a nursery to serve the emerging orchards Don Ygnacio had spurned.

Cattle was forgotten; now fruit growing was the thing. Windows of the old casa looked across the road at the largest orange grove in the world. A branch railroad line from Los Angeles sparked population growth, and in 1874 a town was incorporated, its name Pomona, after the goddess of fruit. The casa sheltered a succession of American families until they could build their own homes on one of the new subdivisions; later it became a

Palomares
cattle brand.

primitive dormitory for farm laborers. Finally, abandoned to weather and vandals, it became a ruin.

The ruin had all but disappeared — both arms of the T had moldered into the earth — when a chance event brought rescue. In 1934 the City of Pomona purchased a strip of land for watershed, and it happened the crumbling adobe occupied a corner of it. The discovery prompted historic reminiscence, and reminiscence sparked a movement to restore the home of Pomona's first settler as a historic monument.

The Historical Society of Pomona Valley launched a fund-raising campaign. Despite the Depression, which had dealt the valley its hardest blow since the great drought, pledges flowed in — from women's clubs, service clubs, the Pomona Chamber of Commerce, and from more than 300 individuals. The city council assigned the city engineer to assess the casa's needs. The assessment caused despair when it revealed a state of deterioration so acute as to require almost complete rebuilding, and to duplicate the old structure would cost an estimated $55,000.

Then help came from, of all things, the Depression. That is, the federal government agreed to complete the building fund and rebuild the casa as a W.P.A. project. Work began in April 1939. Every solid wall was saved, every sound brick and piece of wood. Thousands of new adobe bricks were molded on the site from ground that had absorbed the old ones, and walls were rebuilt exactly where the others had stood. A studied effort was made to recapture authentic detail: thresholds were rounded as though worn by count-

less feet, and old-time door locks, hinges and window latches were hand-wrought in replica.

Equal care was taken with furnishings and landscaping. Palomares descendants supplied many family heirlooms, including Ygnacio's saddles, bridles and spurs and Teresa Vejar's much-embroidered wedding dress. The eminent landscape architect Charles Gibbs Adams, descendant of one of Pomona's founders, re-created the patio and garden, guided by memories of the eldest living Palomares. Among his settings, many the gifts of Pomona residents, were California holly, sweet lime, Spanish broom, yucca and a thick-trunked rose tree, a gift of Estella Vejar, granddaughter of both Ygnacio Palomares and Ricardo Vejar, who was returning it, having transplanted it years before. The single plant remaining from Don Ygnacio's days, a giant wisteria vine, was given a new pergola.

The Historical Society of Pomona Valley accepted responsibility for maintaining and exhibiting the house, while Pomona's parks department assumed jurisdiction over the grounds. Hundreds of townspeople attended ceremonies opening the restored casa on April 5, 1941. Father Joseph of Los Angeles led a procession of Palomares and Vejar descendants singing the old Spanish house-christening song as he moved through the casa sprinkling holy water at each threshold in the time-honored way that Don Ygnacio would have approved.

———

ADOBE DE PALOMARES is located at 491 E. Cucamonga Avenue (Arrow Highway) in Pomona. Open Tuesday through Sunday, 2 p.m. to 5 p.m., except Thanksgiving and Christmas. Admission free.

The sala, which rocked with dancing at fiesta time, was more solemn when the San Gabriel Mission priest came to say mass.

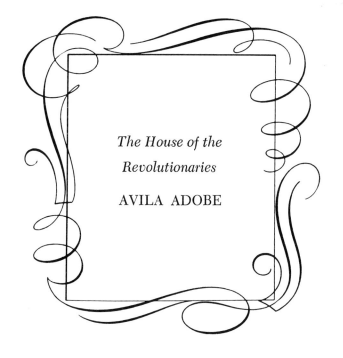

The House of the
Revolutionaries

AVILA ADOBE

IT IS OLVERA STREET, the eternal fiesta on the fringe of Los Angeles' downtown. In stalls alive with glass blowers and candlemakers you jostle shoulders with tourists fingering displays of hoop earrings, bangles, clay bulls, piñatas and tiny pots of cacti. From the open door of a crowded basement cafe rises the aroma of enchiladas and the strains of a guitar.

Suddenly, amidst this bustle, you come upon the homey, cracked facade of an old adobe. Its veranda sags out of plumb; the ancient roof is slightly askew. Mounting creaking plank steps, you lift the rusty, iron latch of a carved door and step into Los Angeles history of a century and a half ago.

This is the Avila Adobe, Los Angeles' oldest house, which in its prime gave hospitality to governors, generals, diplomats and priests. As the door closes, excluding the market's din from the cool, dark corridor, it is easy to imagine them there. They must have visited the family chapel that opens to the right, with its velvet hangings, its flickering candles, its burning-eyed portrait of the household's patron saint. They probably sat in Encarnacion Avila's spacious sala, still grand enough for any of them with its brocade, gilt-framed portraits and rosewood piano. Walking on, you wonder which of the casa's great bedrooms with their high, carved beds rested the head of General Kearny after his victory at La-

guna Rancho, the battle that ended the Mexican War.

Later, you investigate the history of the casa to discover that its true spirit is more akin to the lively market outside than to the cathedral calm within. In fact, the house was so notorious for the plots and counterplots hatched there by the hotheaded Avilas that it was dubbed "Casa de Los Revolucionarios." Revolution was a highly popular activity in Los Angeles' pueblo days, and it is quite appropriate that this house remains to symbolize the tumultuous early settlement.

Los Angeles was born in controversy. The Spanish military governor Philip de Neve founded it over strenuous objections by the Franciscan Order, which saw California as a series of religious flocks clustered about the missions. De Neve envisioned California dotted with farm towns. He had already defied the padres by starting a pueblo in San Jose, but it was languishing due to his error in settling it with ex-soldiers, who lacked enthusiasm for the soil. For Los Angeles he was determined to find some dirt farmers who weren't afraid of plows. In 1781 he rounded up eleven families of mixed Indian, Spanish and Negro stock from farm villages in Western Mexico. Marching them north, he settled them on a fertile-looking site on the trail from San Gabriel Mission to its port at San Pedro, at the point where the trail crossed the river.

Rustic wall shrine on corredor. *(—Uncredited photographs: El Pueblo de Los Angeles)*

Problems arose from the start. The settlers were pestered by Indians, whose village site had been appropriated. They were beset with droughts and epidemics of crows. And instead of finding comfort at the mission, they found themselves at odds with the pueblo-disapproving padres, who ignored their spiritual needs. The Angelenos felt they were entitled to an occasional mass and so demanded. But masses were not forthcoming, and in lieu of them the resourceful Angelenos adopted a custom that startled visitors to the pueblo. Upon waking each morning, the man of the house struck up a hymn and every person in the adobe sat up in bed and chimed in. From casa to casa the chorus spread, until the whole pueblo sang, accompanied by the vocalizing of awakened poultry, dogs and livestock. What the custom lacked in piety was made up in cheerfulness.

The settlers' troubles were further aggravated by the viceroy in Mexico City, who conceived that Los Angeles might double as a penal colony. When he began exiling criminals there as punishment, Angelenos were indignant. As a matter of fact, several of the original settlers had been convicts, but they had reformed and were no more receptive than the rest to the jailies-come-lately. On top of this, Mexico began to send shiploads of orphans, and the military to send its dischargees, such as had been the downfall of San Jose. The viceroy was advised that what Los Angeles could use was a shipload of "healthy young women," but this request went unheeded. Thus, plagued by Indians, church, military, home office, even Mother Nature, Angelenos not surprisingly began to feel persecuted.

They didn't take it meekly. Forgetting they were named for the angels, they riposted with rude complaint. All administrative officials were sent from Mexico, and Angelenos early perfected the art of bedeviling them, progressing until they had become adept at deposing the mightiest governors and military commanders. Revolution became their favorite pastime, and as bickering and criticism became a habit, they turned it upon each other with the result that even the humble town government became a hotbed of conspiracy.

Early ringleaders in this continuing mutiny were the Avilas. Cornelius Avila, the progenitor of the Avila family in California, arrived two years later than the original settlers, but by 1800 twelve adult male Avilas were throwing their weight around the pueblo. In 1810 Francisco Avila was listed as one of the pueblo *comisionados;* an 1812 document shows the Avilas to be one of several families owning rancho lands.

By 1818 Francisco was in a position to build the finest house in the pueblo, now grown to a settlement of 600 souls. Eighteen rooms were ranged around a court, each with 18-foot ceilings beamed with hand-hewn timbers cut from cottonwood trees along the river. The most impressive feature was French doors, first in the pueblo, but there were also imported hangings and furniture, probably acquired in contraband trade with foreign vessels. These grand touches must have contrasted startlingly with the dirt floors the casa at first had due to a scarcity of lumber. Architectural historians believe there was only one plank floor in the entire province when Spanish rule ended in 1822, that in the governor's house at Monterey. Billowing over dirt floors in nearly every casa were snowy, lace-edged bed and table linens.

For all its impressive length, the facade of Francisco's adobe was no more elegant than the rest. It followed the traditional squared-off, one-story, flat-roofed design, and the roof surface was tarred, not tiled. So boxy and bereft of foliage were these early adobes, one writer described them as looking "like so many brick kilns ready for the burning."

Francisco built the house for his bride and second wife, Encarnacion Sepulveda. Descriptions of Francisco are lacking, but a surviving portrait of Encarnacion shows she was handsome and statuesque. Francisco soon was granted another outlying rancho, and in the glow of his new acquisitions he donated a brace of bells for the newly completed Plaza church. To appease Angelenos the mission padres finally had donated seven bar-

Avila
cattle brand.

During the early 1920s the Avila Adobe was in this state of dismal neglect, but a demolition order aroused indignation that sparked a dramatic rescue.

rels of brandy to be sold by the drink to raise money for the building fund.

Francisco's new adobe became the gathering place for the multiplying Avila clan, whose acknowledged leader was the brother José. José Avila has been described as herculean, fiery-tempered and overbearing. Nonetheless, in 1825 he managed to get himself elected alcalde. This unique Spanish municipal position had singularly wide latitude, combining both administrative and judicial powers, but José is said to have stretched his prerogatives to include pre-emptorily jailing whoever gained his displeasure. Angry citizens finally threw him out of office.

The late 1820s were ceaselessly turbulent for the Avilas. They feuded with the spirited Carrillo family, which lived across the plaza, and disputed with succeeding alcaldes, especially José Sanchez, who had aligned himself with California's new governor, Manuel Victoria. To spite Sanchez, the Avilas made it up with the Carrillos and joined them and Pío Pico in plotting against the gov-

ernor. The governor got wind of this and had Sanchez lock up José Avila in the Los Angeles *calabozo*. When iron bars failed to quiet José, Sanchez humiliated him before the whole town by locking him to a chain with a log attached.

Anti-Victoria plotting continued apace, and in 1831 conspiracy leaders issued a pronouncement, declaring the governor's military power to be ended. In Monterey the governor flew into a rage. Summoning troops, he headed south to put the upstarts in their place.

Here a word on revolutions is in order. Revolutions in the California style were the subject of jest among foreigners. Not only did they involve but a handful of men, but they were bloodless. After issuing blustering, sword-rattling *pronunciamentos*, the opposing forces met, shouted insults and shot over each other's heads; then they chose representatives to work out a compromise, or to decide whether the official in question might remain in office. If not, and were he Mexican, he would be escorted to a ship and his departure

Fragile French furniture of sala contrasts with the plank floor and rafter ceiling. (*—Jack Sheedy*)

celebrated with a riotous fiesta. An occasional dead horse or mule was the only victim left behind on the "battlefield." These pacific climaxes to such belligerent dramas have been laid to the fact of close family ties: the province contained scarcely a hundred families, nearly all related by marriage; *Californios* called each other "cousin" as a matter of course. But whether cousinship was the cause, it is undeniable that *Californios* were notably unsanguine — or always had been before.

Alerted that the governor was roaring southward, the conspirators assembled a force. One of their first acts was to storm the jail and release José Avila, chaining Alcalde Sanchez to the log in his place. The army that rode north to meet the governor included a sizable contingent of Avilas, José among them.

The opposing forces met in San Fernando Valley and reined their horses to take each other's measure. The governor haughtily ordered the rebels to come over to his side. They as haughtily refused, upon which he ordered a volley fired over their heads. At this moment, the governor's aide, handsome Captain Romualdo Pacheco — having misunderstood an order, it is believed — rode for-

Renaissance-style bureau with ornate crest top, in bedroom.

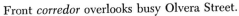

Front *corredor* overlooks busy Olvera Street.

ward into the space between the opponents. José Avila, armed with a lance made of a stake with a bayonet attached, believed the captain was challenging them to single combat. He impulsively galloped forward, lance leveled. As both sides gaped in disbelief, the men rushed at each other like knights on the Field of the Cloth of Gold. Pacheco swerved to avoid the lance thrust, and Avila, a man possessed, drew his pistol and shot Pacheco through the heart. Avila was charging Governor Victoria when a bullet knocked him from his horse. From the ground he seized the governor's foot, dragged him from the saddle and slashed at him with his sword. His young nephew, leaping into the fray, also stabbed at Victoria. At that point another bullet struck José, killing him.

That ended the battle — the first in California history to spill blood between men of Spanish ancestry. Victoria recovered but was persuaded to resign. He limped up the gangplank of a Mexico-bound ship, and Pío Pico was named provisional governor.

Not long after this melee, afterwards known as the Avila Insurrection, the Avila ranks were further depleted by the death of Francisco. He left Encarnacion with two daughters and a cache of gold, buried nobody knew where (and nobody ever discovered). That the Avila casa continued to serve family tradition is indicated by the fact that in 1836 the premises were searched by Governor Alvarado's troops, seeking evidence of a plot against him.

In 1846 came American annexation, and Commodore Stockton arrived to claim Los Angeles, which with a population of roughly 4000 now called itself a *ciudad*. Stockton set up a garrison force of fifty men, put a young Marine lieutenant in charge and departed, confident all was well in hand.

That was all he knew about Los Angeles. He was scarcely back in Monterey when the Angelenos rose up, captured their conquerors and declared themselves to constitute the government of California. American forces dashed south to nip the rebellion in the bud, but it took three months of fighting and maneuvering to regain Los Angeles. During this time the Americans suffered heavy losses and the *Californios* proved that when not tilting with cousins they could be most pugnacious warriors.

The rebels finally were defeated by the combined forces of Commodore Stockton and General Kearny at a battle on the San Gabriel River. On January 10 the Americans re-entered Los Angeles, the troops marching snappily down to the plaza behind a brass band to find the pueblo bolted and still. Expecting vengeance, families were huddled behind barred doors; some had fled to the countryside. Encarnacion, characteristically, had not remained neutral; she had supplied the rebels with horses from her rancho. Now she was in hiding at the home of a Frenchman, having left her casa in charge of an Indian boy.

If the Angelenos' first instinct was protest, their second was celebration. Stockton wisely stationed his band in the plaza playing a nonstop concert. Before long the puebleros and their children were peering around corners, then slipping

into the square. Soon they were cheering and stamping to the music. Among them was Encarnacion's young caretaker who, enraptured by the music, had deserted his post. Meanwhile, Stockton's aides were scouting for a suitable occupation headquarters, and finding Encarnacion's casa open and inviting, they set up command there. Thus by chance did the Casa de Los Revolucionarios provide the stage for the last act in the drama of California's conquest.

The Stars and Stripes was run up over the casa, and its corridors echoed the tramp of military boots as the officers Stockton, Kearny and Frémont and the scout Kit Carson conducted the affairs of occupation. General amnesty was declared; the defeated rebels were merely required to put away their weapons and help restore peace. Stockton sent an emissary among those in hiding, assuring them it was safe to emerge, while taking precautions that *this* peace would not be purloined by die-hard Angelenos. During the five days the Americans occupied it, the Avila casa to all intents and purposes was the capitol of California.

The families returned to their casas, reconciled. The soldiers returned, and so did a chastened Encarnacion. Offered compensation for the use of her casa, she would accept nothing.

The next American contingent to arrive in Los Angeles was the U.S. Land Commission, there to investigate land titles. It was given a warm welcome by the Avila clan, which threw a grand ball in its honor. In the subsequent hearings all of the Avilas' land titles were approved.

After Encarnacion died, in 1855, the house underwent a long decline. In 1857 an earthquake severely jolted the house, destroying the south wing that had flanked the plaza. The city began expanding in another direction, and the district gradually was deserted by the old families. Chinatown encroached and deterioration accelerated until Olvera Street had become a filthy, crime-ridden alley, a place of drunks and derelicts where wastepaper wafted and rats slithered among garbage cans. Encarnacion's once proud casa was a flophouse for destitute Mexicans.

Then, in 1926 it reached its nadir. The health department hung a condemned sign on the old adobe and scheduled its demolition. Fortunately, about that time Mrs. Christine Sterling wandered into the slum district behind the new city hall, and picking her way through Olvera Street, she came upon the condemned house. She made inquiries and learned it was the oldest house in the city. Mrs. Sterling, a history aficionado and member of a pioneer California family, was shocked that so historic a house was to be destroyed.

She carried her indignation to the late Harry Chandler, publisher of the *Los Angeles Times*, and he agreed the house should be preserved. The upshot was a spirited *Times* campaign to "Save Los Angeles' most historic house." At first the only response came from school children, who collected pennies to give the house a new roof. The newspaper persisted, and finally the public awakened. Contributions flowed in, some in cash, some in donations of restoration materials. Avila descendants still held title to the house, and they co-operated in its restoration by deeding it to the city. After an expert restoration, a search was made for appropriate furnishings. Then the house was opened to a public now educated as to its value.

The Avila Adobe then became the nucleus of an evolving project that would grow into one of the largest restorations in the West. When visitors showed reluctance to brave ruts and rubble to reach the house, a program was started to spruce up all of block-long Olvera Street. The Los Angeles City Council passed an ordinance to close it to traffic and to encourage repair of all its structures. Five citizens gave funds to pave the street with red tiles.

Across the street from the Avila house Mrs. Sterling found two other structures of historic interest, former residences of the prominent Sepulveda and Pelaconi families. These came in for extensive repairs, and the Pelaconi house became the popular Casa La Golondrina Cafe. In line with a plan to convert the street into a typical Mexican thoroughfare, shops were opened in repaired structures, while on the paved mall sales booths were set up under bright-hued canopies.

Olvera Street was given a grand opening on an April night in 1930. Thousands crowded there to enjoy mariachi bands and dancing to clicking castanets. At once the gay little street became the most popular tourist attraction in the city. From

then on success was the spur to keep going until all of the original pueblo had been restored.

But financing was to present some thorny problems. Restoring very old, deteriorated structures is more costly than demolishing and rebuilding anew. Mrs. Sterling and her rescue team had discovered around the plaza a number of historic buildings worth preserving. Only the plaza church, which had remained in continual use, had been maintained. The cost of restoring these buildings and reclaiming the dilapidated plaza would be formidable. In the 1940s a plan was advanced to restore the plaza district as part of an urban-renewal project, but investigation showed the area had lost most of its residential character and therefore wouldn't qualify.

The fortunes of the plaza brightened in 1952 when the state designated the forty-acre district a joint state and city park to be known as Pueblo de Los Angeles State Historical Monument. The legislature appropriated $750,000, which was matched by a city and county fund. Following purchase of the land parcels that make up the district, work was begun to restore those buildings of historic interest and to adapt the rest for appropriate use. In 1965 the city and state park administrations conferred power on an 11-member appointive commission to develop and govern the monument. Additional appropriations have been forthcoming from time to time, augmented by fund-raising activities of Los Amigos Del Pueblo, a supportive organization, and by private donations.

Restoration priorities had to be revised in 1971, due to the Los Angeles earthquake. One hundred and fourteen years after losing its south wing to an earth jolt, the Avila Adobe again suffered major damage. It was closed for more than a year during extensive restorative work financed by a federal earthquake-relief grant of $49,008, by a $100,000 donation from Los Amigos Del Pueblo and by public subscription.

More than $4,000,000 has been spent to date on the ever-evolving monument, which annually draws more than 2,000,000 persons. The master plan calls for reconstructing several lost structures, including the architecturally significant Lugo House, and for blocking off all streets leading to the plaza. Promised too is development of Pico

House into a de luxe, period-style hotel with authentic early California cuisine and décor.

Interestingly, the proposal that the plaza district be made a state park came from Park Commissioner Leo Carrillo, famed movie actor and kinsman of José Carillo, who once lived on the plaza and was often among the conspirators at the Casa de Los Revolucionarios. After a century and a half, the Carrillos and the Avilas were in league again to save the pueblo, this time not from Mexican despots, but from the persecution of time.

THE AVILA ADOBE is located at 14 Olvera Street in Los Angeles, three blocks north of City Hall. Open daily, including Sundays and holidays, from 9 a.m. to 5 p.m. Admission is 25 cents for adults, 10 cents for children.

Colorful Olvera Street, fragrant with the candlemakers' wares, offers a taste of Los Angeles' Mexican and Spanish heritage. (—*Los Angeles Area Chamber of Commerce*)

A Rebel's Refuge

PIO PICO

MANSION

FOREVER EMBROILED in some risky conspiracy or business deal, Pío Pico used his San Gabriel Valley rancho as a rural hideaway. One can imagine his dismay were he to come galloping home on his fine horse and silver-mounted saddle to find his haven as it exists today: flanked on one side by railroad tracks, on the other by a roaring freeway, and enveloped by the busy town of Whittier.

But the last Mexican governor of California — a homely, mediocre man who craved esteem but whose gaucheries and pugnacity denied it even when in exalted position — would be delighted to find his modest home accorded the distinction of a state historical monument. Here at last is something that can not be turned to jest, nor wrested from him. Ironically, his follies, which invited American annexation, by the same token made him last of a line, thereby giving him a front position in history.

Just as Pío Pico endured so many close shaves throughout his tumultuous political and business careers, so did his casa survive a hairbreadth escape. In the early 1900s, more than a decade after his death, when the abandoned rancho was held by Whittier as water-bearing land, a contractor constructing a bridge approach to the San Gabriel River decided the dilapidated buildings would provide excellent fill. He had hauled away the chapel, the mill and other auxiliary structures, and had begun on the casa when history buffs discov-

ered his depredation and indignantly halted it. They organized the Governor Pico Museum and Historical Society to preserve the home of Pío Pico, and they are to be forgiven if in their zeal to amend the vandalism they restored overgrandly. In 1917 they succeeded in having the property taken over by the state and it came under jurisdiction of the park department, which undertook re-restoration in the interests of authenticity. Numerous mistaken "improvements" were removed, including a pseudo-mission false front that had been tacked onto the end of the house.

The simple don would have been intimidated by the grander version, but he would feel at home today in the plain, U-shaped adobe house with its shady, brick-paved patio. The central portion has the second story he added in his later years. If he looked closely he could find patio bricks with nicks made by the iron-shod horses he liked to ride right up to the door. He would remember the round stone well; even the fig tree he doted on has been replaced. He could wander familiarly through the small, dark rooms with their few small windows — some glassed, others barred and shuttered — and over the wide-plank floors upon which he once cast coyote skins for throw rugs. He wouldn't recognize the furniture as his own, but he would certainly approve the style — French copies of the 1870s. One wonders what he would say of two other features. A square, rosewood

Old well in patio. (*—California Dept. of Parks & Recreation*)

Contemporary sketch of Pío Pico. (—*Bancroft Library*)

grand piano in the living room is there despite the recorded testimony of a former neighbor to "no piano in the sala — only a guitar." And a large upstairs room, romantically called the "grand ballroom," is scoffed at by realists who point to the low eaves which make standing impossible except in the room's very center.

Squat and sturdy, the casa rather suggests the shape of its master. Potato-nosed and thick-lipped (there was an African strain in his ancestry), he sought to distract from his unprepossessing aspect with flashy jewelry, brass buttons, medals, ribbons, a diamond stickpin, a gargantuan watch and chain, ornamental garters and a walking stick whose handle was an ivory lady's leg encased in a high gold shoe with diamond buttons. But his most charming features were his merry shoe-button eyes and irrepressible enthusiasm.

Unlike the silver-spooned Spanish statesmen of his era, Pico had been encumbered as well by early poverty. Both his parents had come as children with the ragtag second Anza expedition of settlers. After he became rich, Don Pío dramatized his rise with the boast, "My father did not leave me a vara of ground nor a mule!"

Pío de Jesus Pico was born in 1801 in a brush shack on the grounds of Mission San Gabriel,

where his father was a military guard. Only 19 when his father died, Pío moved the family to San Diego and supported them by setting up a dram shop at which he boosted profits by devising horn tumblers with false wooden bottoms that made customers think they were getting an extra tot. After expanding his operation into a general store, he built his mother an adobe casa with two salas. Ugly duckling though he was, his doting mother kept her go-getting son well secluded from designing señoritas. At 26 he was still complaining complacently that his mother wouldn't let him go abroad at night.

He found an early emotional outlet in politics, displaying a talent for intrigue that in an era when revolution was the national sport would make him something of a superstar. He probably inherited this bent from his father, who once was briefly imprisoned for fomenting a revolt at the mission. At 27, Pico was named one of the municipal electors to choose the *diputados* who formed an advisory legislative council to the governor at Monterey. The following year he was elected a *diputado* himself.

At his first session he passionately aligned himself with a Southern California faction against a Northern one and initiated what was to be his major political preoccupation: seeking to persuade the body to move its proceedings to Los Angeles. The governor that year evaluated each council member and of Pico noted: "of little capacity, not illustrious, some aptitude."

Two years later Pico, demonstrating where his aptitude lay, was ringleader of a rebellion against the succeeding governor, Manuel Victoria. In San Diego he and his co-conspirators signed a declaration proclaiming the governor's military powers dissolved. Reportedly, Victoria thereupon vowed to hang Pico if he could put his hands on him.

When Pico heard that the governor was roaring south with his army, he commandeered troops from the San Diego Presidio and dispatched them north. With Pico himself keeping out of the fray, the forces met northwest of Los Angeles. During a brief confrontation the governor's aide was killed and the governor wounded, after which Victoria was persuaded to resign and depart for Mexico.

Cattle brand
of Pío Pico.

After a tumultuous political career, Pico settled down at this San Gabriel Valley home. (*Governor Pío Pico Mansion Society*)

Pico's followers put him in the vacated governor's chair, but opposition forced him to step down after twenty days. In his first revolution, Pico had demonstrated his daring to enter the tiger's mouth and his instinct for avoiding the teeth — but, alas, a propensity also for losing the glory.

Don Pío remained single until he was in his mid-thirties, when he entered into matrimony (which would prove childless) with a Los Angeles spinster. He was a governor before he was a husband. He'd had one previous love, for a San Diego beauty who, after spurning him, enlisted his help in eloping with another. In politics he never gave in that way.

By this time he not only was cutting a political swath but was on his way to amassing a fortune. The missions were being secularized and parceled out to persons with pull. He acquired several leagues of land near San Diego and became an important ranchero during the era of the profitable hide and tallow trade. Between state duties he would don his red-sashed splendor, buckskin leggings and high-coned hat and gallop about his ranchos overseeing his vaqueros.

But it was in the political arena that he truly came alive. After long agitation, Mexico had given California a legislature, and Pico took a strident position in it. In 1838 he tried to overthrow the government of Governor Juan Alvarado of Monterey, thereby incurring the enmity of Alvarado's uncle, General Mariano Vallejo. The revolt failed; Pico was captured and charged with being a traitor, but he succeeded in bargaining his freedom.

He discovered a new adversary to rail against in the legislature: the "hordes of Yankee immigrants who have begun to flock into our country." He felt they were not keeping their place; everywhere he looked they were clearing farms, erecting mills, sawing lumber — generally seizing the country's economy. "Whatever this astonishing people will next undertake I cannot say, but on whatever enterprise they embark they will be sure to be successful." Tolerating this "astute enemy" was a mistake, in Pico's view. He preferred the British colonists, who were not so everlastingly aggressive and who understood the importance of leisure, as did the Mexicans. He accused the Northerners of letting Americans cross the Sierra illegally and of pampering them when they arrived.

Meanwhile, Don Pío kept his vision of having the capital shifted to what was, in his view, the only logical place: the City of the Angels. Unable to convince the legislature, he succeeded in having the shift decided in Mexico by executive decree. At last the capital moved to Los Angeles,

Entrance to Pío Pico Museum.
(—*California Dept. of Parks & Recreation*)

but in exasperatingly short order it was returned north by the next governor, who preferred Monterey. At this Pico completely lost his temper and got himself fined $200 for unseemly conduct.

After years of being at loggerheads with the Northern California politicians, Pico in 1845 suddenly found himself in accord with them. They both desired the overthrow of Governor Manuel Micheltorena and the twain met congenially on the barricades against the unwelcome appointee from Mexico. Pico now found a talented partner in revolution in his soldier brother Andrés, who soon would be promoted to general.

Micheltorena had anticipated conspiracy and had been aligning Americans on his side by issuing them land titles. Thus, when the sides squared off for a showdown, Micheltorena had behind him a sizable army of tall, well-armed allies. The governor's forces looked like the victor, but Pico saved the day by the remarkable feat of winning over the immigrants he had so maligned. He got word to them that the land titles they had been granted were worthless, but if they would back him, he would issue proper titles. The Americans succumbed to this lure and agreed to hold fire. Discovering his impotence, Micheltorena surrendered and returned to Mexico.

Again revolution rewarded Pico with the governorship. His second term was the stormiest in the history of the province. The alliance with the Northerners scarcely lasted out his investiture. He angered them not only by whisking the legislature to Los Angeles, but by seeking to move the treasury there as well. (It traditionally was operated in connection with port collections at Monterey.) When balked in that, Pico sought to install his own treasurer. His standing feud with Military Commander José Castro reached new heights of invective. He infuriated Americans by failing his promise to secure their land titles, as well as by making known he would welcome a British protectorate to help expel them. He inflamed the clergy by making wholesale disposal of mission land, delivering much of it to his family and close friends. Worse, he broke with long-time Southern California confederates, who thereupon allied themselves with the Northern faction. His harangues with subordinates came close to blows. An American observer in Los Angeles reported to American Consul Thomas Larkin in Monterey: "The present government of California cannot exist six months; it will explode by spontaneous combustion."

Meanwhile, the Northern faction, and especially Commander Castro, was alarmed by the arrival in California of an American expedition led

Sun-splashed patio has a timeless air. (—*California State Library*)

Corner of Governor Pico's
Victorian parlor.
(—Martin Cole)

by John Frémont. Castro feared invasion was imminent and demanded that Pico fortify the country. Unable to believe the situation had changed so swiftly, Pico told Castro he was making a mountain out of a molehill. Castro insisted the situation truly was critical and urged Pico to hasten to Monterey for a junta of military and political leaders. Pico couldn't see anything afoot except a scheme to seize and depose him should he be so simple as to enter the trap. He refused to attend the junta and forbade its meeting.

When Castro held the junta anyway, Pico was convinced that a coup was brewing. Well, he knew how to handle coups. Summoning his troops, he began a rapid march north along the coast, bent on taking Castro by surprise. He left behind orders in Los Angeles to defend the capital in case Castro sneaked south around the Tulares.

Pico had proceeded as far as Santa Barbara when the bomb of the Bear Flag Rebellion exploded. Galvanized into rationality, he issued a ringing proclamation: "Fly Mexicans, in all haste in pursuit of the treacherous foe . . . punish his audacity." Dashing back to Los Angeles, he hastily

assembled an army and dispatched it north to merge with Castro's forces.

But before Pico's army reached its destination, Commodore Sloat had sailed into Monterey and claimed California for the United States. Castro and his army fled southward. He joined Pico briefly and the two former enemies tearfully consoled each other before Castro crossed into Mexico.

Pico's final performance as governor on August 10, 1846, is somewhat cloudy in history. He later claimed in writing that he summoned the legislature and advised it that "in view of the fact that the Comandante General was failing us, it should authorize me to take command of the forces and go out to fight against Frémont. The deputies opposed it pre-emptorily, saying that they would agree in no way that the Governor should expose his person to the risk of being prisoner and . . . resolved I should leave the country." But the minutes of the legislature's last meeting report that it was Pico himself who suggested he escape to Mexico. There is no mention of an offer to ride into battle.

Gnarled pepper trees shade park at rear of mansion. (*—California Dept. of Parks & Recreation*)

Pico remained in Mexico for ten lonely, angry months. One wonders if in isolation he gained perspective to see the tragic flaw of his public life: that he did not direct his remarkable energy toward meaningful goals. Unfortunately for his country, this limited, short-sighted man had seen his destiny as that of leader and was able to convince his betters by sheer persuasion.

Mexican California had passed into history, and Pico's career had passed its prime. But his escapades were far from over; even his return to California was typically Picoesque. A Mexican newspaper report that the Americans were permitting California functionaries to resume their duties led him to suppose the edict applied to him. When he popped up in Monterey demanding the governor's chair, the astonished American governor clapped him behind bars. There were plans to incarcerate him in Oregon so that his absurd claim would not excite sedition, but again

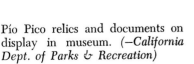

Pío Pico relics and documents on display in museum. (*—California Dept. of Parks & Recreation*)

his famous luck held. At that moment came news of the ratification of the Treaty of Guadalupe Hidalgo, and the pretender was freed with a stern warning.

Humiliated and titleless, Pico had at least the consolation of finding his fortune nearly intact. He still had his ranchos, some 190,000 acres near San Diego, and he felt optimistic enough to make another acquisition. It was at this time that he acquired his San Gabriel rancho, paying $4624 for the 8891 acres, then called Rancho Paso de Bartolo, not far from his birthplace. He built his comfortable casa and there with his wife settled down to a rancho life scarcely different from when the Mexican sun was shining.

Pico felt nothing was too good for the home he affectionately called "El Ranchito" because of its small acreage; he furnished it to accord with his notion of a proper country seat for the rightful governor. Of course, he selected his appointments with the same taste that he chose his garters and walking stick. An American woman, who visited there in the 1860s, years later recalled with undiminished wonder the assemblage of curlicued sofas, center tables, gaudy chandeliers, ancient weaponry and the porcelain cuspidors, imprinted with moss roses, that were liberally scattered about all the rooms. This treasure-trove of rococo was set against a writhing background of large-figured carpeting and wallpaper that was all spliced together of unmatched strips, a decorating touch omitted by the modern restorer.

Like other rancheros, Pico saw his hide and tallow trade dwindle in the late 1840s, but a more profitable demand soon replaced it. A handy man at Sutter's Mill found a shining pebble in a millrace and a hundred thousand gold hunters swarmed through the Golden Gate. To southern ranchos came the astonishing news that cattle which had been worth $2 a head for their hides were worth $50 to $200 a head for their beef. Soon shouting vaqueros were overseeing huge northward cattle drives, which returned so much cash the rancheros could scarcely find hiding places for it.

Doing well with his ranchos, Pico couldn't resist trying his hand at the commercial enterprises the "astute enemy" so excelled in. He invested in some of the fashionable new ventures, including oil, and in 1869 took a flyer in the hotel business. He and his brother Andrés built and equipped the Pico House hotel in Los Angeles at a cost of more than $100,000, lavishing on it such innovations as gaslights and bathrooms (two), as well as a sumptuous fountain court.

Don Pío became a well-known figure about town, where he resided part-time after his wife died suddenly of a mysterious seizure. He served briefly as a Los Angeles city councilman. A visitor described him as "one of the picturesque sights of Los Angeles . . . with his stocky figure, square head and bright eye, contrasting with his bronzed skin and close-cropped hair and beard, he has a certain resemblance to Victor Hugo."

Denied revolutionary outlet, more and more he indulged the satisfactions of his second love — gambling. Not only did he approach business with a gambler's exuberance, but he laid huge stakes on bullfights, cockfights and horse races; for a time he had his own string of race horses. He was forever lending, borrowing, wagering.

In 1883 he was in need of $62,000 to pay a debt, but with his affairs going downhill, he found it difficult to make a touch. Finally he located an American businessman willing to loan him the money, but on the stern condition that he sign a blanket mortgage on all his properties. Although his holdings were worth an estimated $200,000, he rashly signed. When the debt fell due, he was unable to meet it. He managed to stave off collection for years with vehement and costly litigation, but in the end he lost all — his hotel, his ranches and his San Gabriel home. His legendary luck had run out.

One day in 1892, at the age of ninety, he said good-bye to El Ranchito's adobe hacienda and, "with defeat in his eyes," drove with a few possessions to Los Angeles, there to live on the charity of a friend for his two remaining years. Not long before the end, California's once highest official suffered a crowning indignity: an officer of the law snatched his broad sombrero from his head to satisfy a creditor's claim.

PÍO PICO MANSION is located at 6003 Pioneer Boulevard, Whittier. Open from Wednesday through Sunday 10 a.m. to 5 p.m. Closed Mondays, Tuesdays, Thanksgiving, Christmas and New Year's Day. No admission charge.

This stately Los Angeles mansion was the scene of Civil War celebrations, railroad and harbor planning, and modern movie making.

House of Regales

GENERAL
PHINEAS BANNING
RESIDENCE

NOT FAR INLAND from Los Angeles' pungent, braying, clanging port of San Pedro, in a park of ancient, towering trees stands a three-story mansion that seems to have strayed from some Georgia plantation. A whiff of antebellum: tall, white columns, pedimented roof, broad verandas, fan-lit doorway. The house has similarly impressed movie-makers. Several period films have been shot there, including *Gone With the Wind* and *The Littlest Rebel,* one of whose high points was Shirley Temple's slide down the banister of the grand staircase. Was it built, one wonders, by some nostalgic, exiled gentleman of the Deep South?

On the contrary, its builder, Phineas Banning, was a bluff, back-slapping, self-made Delaware native of Dutch and Danish ancestry, who far from being nostalgic for anything was the most go-ahead man in the West. In a sense he was the first true Californian. He was obsessed with modernizing transport by developing the harbor and by availing Southern California of all the latest contrivances for getting about and communicating. A dogged force when it came to pushing through his schemes, he had more to do with shaping the growth of Southern California after Americanization than any other man.

How does one reconcile Phineas Banning with this elegant house? This big, hurrying, jut-jawed man, although his own thick hands were always

engaged with some tiller or throttle, yearned wistfully for culture. He built his white, classic mansion, the finest house south of San Francisco, as a lure so that culture and gentility would come to him. He especially planned it as a setting for musical entertainments, and his "regales," as he called them, became enormously prestigious — the Southern California equivalent of attending the opera. On these gala evenings, beautiful women in décolletage and crinoline animated the grand salon under glowing chandeliers. At other times he employed the sumptuous rooms, with their carved marble and gold leaf, his groaning dining table and free-flowing wines to win financial and political backers for his visions. There were also many happy gatherings of family and intimates to celebrate hard-won victories. It was a house that pulsed with excitement.

To realize how far Banning carried Los Angeles, visualize the city as he found it in 1851. While working on the Philadelphia docks, a runaway Delaware farm boy, he'd caught the California fever, and when at 21 he was offered the job of accompanying a shipment to San Pedro, he snapped it up. But what a letdown lay in store! His ship had to anchor several miles offshore and launch a small boat, and when being rowed in, it capsized on a sand bar, dumping passengers and cargo into the surf. Could this be the port — a weather-beaten warehouse, a few oxcarts and dry-

Early letter press in Banning's study.
(—*Uncredited photographs: Los Angeles Recreation and Parks Department*)

» 123 «

ing racks of stinking cattle hides? Transportation to Los Angeles was a bone-jarring seven-mile ride in a wagon with crosswise planks for seats. In the dusty town he wandered into a general store and was waited on by a clerk with two guns strapped to his waist. Later, looking out the window of his hotel room, he saw a man shot dead before his very eyes. He asked about mail service and learned that an occasional mail pouch was tossed on the beach by a passing ship, and if it didn't get carried away by tide, the finder brought it into town. Banning's initiation to Los Angeles would have a lasting effect on him.

Optimism triumphed over disappointment; he stayed and found a niche for himself. Robust and ready, he quickly progressed from warehouse laborer to clerk, and after coaxing his employer to replace the jolting wagon with a stagecoach, he drove the stage.

Acquiring, on credit, partnership in a wagon service to points north, he plunged into modernizing it. He ordered better wagons, added fancy stages with upholstered seats, extended routes as far north as Salt Lake City and whittled travel time. An employer once had commended Banning's "accustomed promptness," and he now took the phrase as his advertising slogan, even signing his letters "With accustomed promptness." But improvements multiplied more swiftly than profits, and Banning's slogan did not always apply to paying debts. His creditor slapped a writ of attachment on his receipts.

He fretted over the harbor. It exasperated him that not only were ships unable to dock, but even when anchored offshore were obliged to flee for open sea with the slightest squall. The local view was that the shallow, exposed shore lacked sufficient natural assets to warrant developing it. But the alternative to not developing it, Banning insisted, was to let Los Angeles die on the vine. He only got shrugs.

Nobody could understand Banning's sudden interest in a backwater slough formed by river floods. He built a scow and spent his free time poling about in it, taking depths and providing laughs. "Banning's paddlin' in his hog wallow." In 1854 he married Rachel Sanford, the sister of an associate, and soon afterward he, his in-laws

and friends purchased 2400 shore acres including the slough. The slough was now his prime interest. Around this time a newly arrived German immigrant had Banning pointed out to him as an important figure and was most astonished to behold him "coatless and vestless, without necktie or collar, and wearing pantaloons at least six inches too short, a pair of brogans and socks with large holes." Banning had no time to read the fashion pages.

But by 1858 he could pause for a celebration. Having bought out his partner, he was on his own, dispatching stages and wagons up the dusty roads. Further, he now held personal title to 640 acres at the head of the slough, which he called "the estuary." There he had built a wharf, warehouse, stables, a carriage factory and, for his family, a modest home. And there he had laid out a town, called Wilmington after the city of his native state. Glowing with expectations, he invited out the population of Los Angeles, loaded them on barges and cruised them up "the estuary" to his landing, gay with trappings and flowing with refreshments.

If Banning had expected ballyhoo to prime the pump for harbor developments, he was disappointed. He proposed that port interests share the cost of dredging the channel. Then ships of fairly large draught could dock, he argued; the port might even be made to rank second to San Francisco's great natural harbor. Too expensive, he was told. Nor did he get anywhere seeking harbor appropriations in the state legislature or in Washington.

Disgusted but determined, he put into play a little scheme of his own. Each day when the tide was going out, he cruised the channel dragging long ropes behind him, churning up silt for the tide to wash out. He lost some silt, but gained a lot of raillery; wags dubbed him "Port Admiral." However, a rapid reassessment of Banning's channel-raking occurred one day in 1859, when a medium-sized brigantine made its way through the deepened channel and into the estuary — the first ship to discharge its cargo at the dock.

Banning nurtured another dream. So buoyantly did he view the future, he already visualized his great columned mansion and had chosen a site, about a mile north of his landing. He began planting trees and shrubs, and he had ships' captains bring him seeds and cuttings — Jacaranda trees from the Amazon, eucalyptus from Australia, cypress from Italy. But construction would wait until he could afford the best.

While never slackening efforts to get a harbor, Banning dabbled in other projects. His telegraph company opened service to San Francisco and Yuma, Arizona. He also ordered with much fanfare from Leeds a wood-burning "steam wagon" touted to pull 38 tons at a speed of five miles per hour. Unfortunately, his English import provided only titillation. A welcome crowd gathered in Los Angeles, where a newspaper extra proclaimed: ". . . our citizens are anxiously, hourly expecting to see Major Banning heave in sight at the foot of Main Street." Meanwhile, back in Wilmington, Banning was seated at the controls, sputtering with frustration while under him the vehicle's wheels spun around and round in the sandy soil, immobilized. Abandoned, the contraption long stood there rusting in the salt air, a grotesque object lesson. (His title of major was won in the local vigilante organization; a later general's rank was earned in the state militia.)

Next he conceived a scheme to build a railroad between Wilmington and Los Angeles and succeeded in getting it franchised by the state legislature, only to have local opposition cry it down. Soon the Civil War absorbed his energies; the Union Army established Camp Drum in Wilmington, as a precaution against Southern California going Confederate, and gave Banning contracts to supply troops throughout the West. An ardent Union man, he used his influence to combat Confederate sentiment in Los Angeles. For that and for keeping supplies moving he was commended by President Abraham Lincoln.

Next to the harbor, the vision that most excited him was his great, shining house. By 1864, flush from war contracts, he was ready to build it. Ships' captains were advised that he planned a real show place and was in the market for first-rate materials and fixtures. Into the harbor came fine hardwood for paneling and cabinetwork, stained glass from Belgium and great marble fireplaces in a variety of colors. Also he bargained

Impromptu recital recalls Banning's stylish "regales."

with captains to lend him their ships' carpenters in exchange for tar. There were three generous floors with thirty grandly sized rooms, plus a square cupola for scanning the harbor. Next came furnishings: Oriental rugs, mirrors, French sofas, brocade hangings, rococo chandeliers. For the latter he acquired fittings to utilize the latest in lighting fixtures, lamps that burned camphine, a refined oil made from turpentine.

For a housewarming he threw his first regale. He and his stylishly gowned wife stood in the wide entrance hall welcoming guests as they alighted from carriages that rumbled up the great winding driveway — the Abel Stearnses, the Juan Temples, former Governor Downey and, arriving by horseback, officers from Camp Drum, resplendent in their gold-trimmed dress uniforms. All agreed the music was grand, but the hit of the evening was the new camphine lamps.

High four-poster bed arrived by ship from New Orleans. Banning's son Hancock was room's occupant.

Far from being a paved road to success, Banning's career was full of ups and downs. A ferry he operated blew up with disastrous results; an oil venture failed; a sector of the business community boycotted his freight service; and time and again his harbor bills met defeat. Most distressing of all, his wife died in childbirth, leaving him with four young sons.

Hard work brought peace and sometimes victory. In the late 1860s the County of Los Angeles at last was persuaded to issue bonds for a railroad from Wilmington to Los Angeles. Banning acquired a controlling interest and won the contract to build it. About the same time he opened a shipyard to build small steamers, and in 1869 launched the first steamer built in Southern California. Later that year the railroad opened with a jolly free excursion. Flushed with satisfaction, he was married again, on Valentine's Day, 1870, to Mary Hollister of a prominent San Luis Obispo

family. Once more the camphine lamps were turned up for gala dinners and regales.

The Angelenos' attitude toward Banning as somebody who was slightly demented on the subject of transportation changed, thanks to the railroad. That short line they so reluctantly accepted proved to make the difference between Los Angeles' remaining just another cow-country trading center and its becoming the hub of Southern California. It happened that the Southern Pacific Railroad was then building its line south from Oakland, and the plan was to run it on to Arizona, by-passing Los Angeles. Banning saw that this would be disastrous for his harbor plan; he began dangling lures to bring the Southern Pacific to Los Angeles, and a prime inducement was the opportunity to connect with his port railroad. Banning transferred his line to the Southern Pacific and it rerouted to Los Angeles.

In turn, Southern Pacific's sudden interest in the neglected port was exactly what was needed to spur government action. Early in 1871, Banning went to Washington to plead for a harbor bill and this time found Congress receptive to voting funds for a mile-long breakwater. More harbor funds were voted in 1872 and 1873. The following year the Southern Pacific completed its line from Oakland to Los Angeles, thereby making Wilmington the terminus of a branch of the transcontinental railroad. The harbor was on its way.

By ushering in the railroad Banning had killed his stage and freight business, but he happily shifted his energies to the harbor project. Perhaps because he had suffered so much ridicule for it, he came to identify himself with that untamed shore. He hovered affectionately over every step of the breakwater; when federal funds ran low, he hurried back to Washington to pump up a new appropriation. With some apprehension he realized he had vastly underestimated how much harbor work was needed to meet the depth and safety demands of major shipping. A second really sizable breakwater was needed, and the cost would run to millions!

Banning had enlisted others in his campaign for a second breakwater when an unexpected hitch developed. Two rival groups undertook to get federal funds to develop ports at Santa Monica and

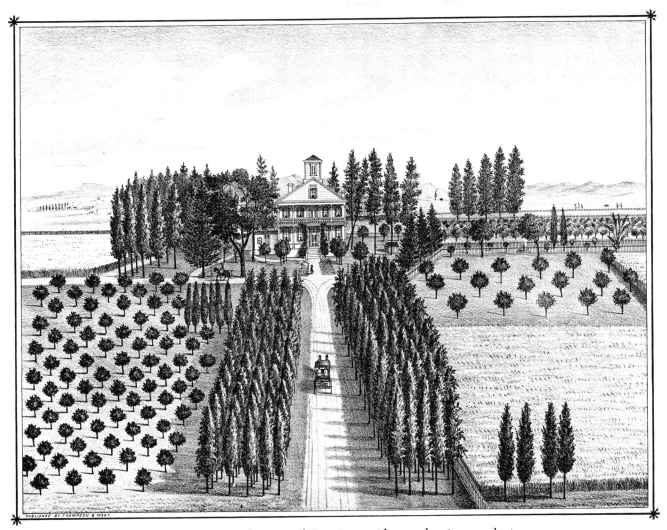

Late 19th-century pen drawing of Banning residence, showing eucalyptus grove planted by Banning, appeared in Thompson & West's *History of Los Angeles County*.

at Redondo Beach. Congress, confounded by demands for three harbors, called a halt to harbor appropriations until the Californians could thrash it out among themselves.

As the controversy reached its zenith, Banning was knocked out of the battle. Ironically, the man who had devoted his life to transportation was felled by a transportation accident. When on a business trip to San Francisco, rushing as always, he swung himself off a streetcar and into the path of a heavy express wagon. One wheel passed over his chest — a serious injury.

He was returned to the quiet of his big white house and ordered to rest completely. For once he did; his great 200-pound frame was weighted down by an unaccustomed weakness. Devotedly attending him were his wife and three pretty daughters, one of whom was soon to reign as the first Rose Pageant queen. He reclined on his wide

veranda and took his ease in his summer house, watching the progress of his latest horticultural pride, a wisteria vine planted with seeds brought from China by his Chinese cook. In February 1885 the added strain of flu brought death at age 56.

But thanks to his diligent groundwork, the fight for San Pedro would be won — although not until 1896, when Congress at last committed itself to funding a deep harbor at a site to be chosen by a board of engineers. That body, after intensive study, selected San Pedro. In 1899 President McKinley pressed a button to start the breakwater work that eventually would cost $75 million and rank the harbor — not second to San Francisco's, as Banning had dared hope — but second only to New York's.

The realization that they were getting a great world port that would catapult them into worldwide prominence so elated Angelenos that they wished to thank some living man for so dazzling a gift. Hastily, they conferred the title of "Father of the Harbor" upon the politician who had picked up the banner from the fallen leader. But with time citizens realized their error and accordingly shifted that designation to Phineas Banning, the man who looked at a slough and dreamed he saw a harbor and never rested in pursuit of his dream. It was Banning who had a Liberty Ship named in his honor, had a high school dedicated to him and has a Southern California town for a namesake.

Banning has also been honored through his house, which has been publicly owned since 1927 and, more recently, has been designated a landmark by both the state and the City of Los Angeles. In the mid-1920s the house stood vacant and neglected. History-minded organizations were always saying the house ought to be made a historical monument, while parents frequently remarked what a fine park and playground the estate would make. City organizations, especially women's clubs, began to pool their ideas concerning Banning House. Out of co-ordinated thinking came the goal of acquiring the house and the twenty remaining acres of the estate for a combined public park and historic house. Since acquisition would be expensive, it was decided to seek financing through a public bond issue. A spirited campaign during the optimistic year of 1927 resulted in passage of a district bond issue for acquiring the estate. Following purchase, for $278,000, the property was deeded to the Los Angeles City Recreation and Parks Department (Wilmington had become part of Los Angeles through annexation).

After the house had received paint and other renovations, furnishing thirty large rooms presented a formidable task. The decorators were fortunate in receiving from Banning's descendants many of the original furnishings, as well as help in placing them correctly. In Banning's upstairs study, adjoining the master bedroom, is displayed his cherry roll-top desk; beside it on a stand is an odd metal contraption, a letter press innovative to that early day. A bookcase that came around the Horn contains his books — law volumes and novels, one by Thomas Mann. Near it is a huge, overstuffed horsehair chair that once supported his massive frame.

In downstairs halls and salons hang the Victorian paintings of the Romantic School that Banning ordered for his new house, interspersed with oil paintings of the Banning family. A large front bedroom, luxurious with ornately carved Italian furniture, was the room of Lucy Banning, that first Rose Pageant queen, whose colorful life included five marriages, the last to a Japanese wrestler.

Banning's stables and a vast coach house are also part of the exhibit. On display are several horse-drawn vehicles including a surrey with "fringe on top" and a fine phaeton coach.

Converting the grounds, with their rare and beautiful trees and shrubs, into a park required little work. The eucalyptus trees planted from seedlings brought from Australia now soar overhead. One standing west of the main driveway is believed to be the first of that species ever planted in California. The Banning flower gardens to the rear and south of the mansion are maintained as a horticultural attraction. The center of interest is the huge wisteria vine that spreads along the U-shaped pergola that supports it. The vine, which is in full bloom during March and April, was the inspiration for the community's most important annual event, the Wilmington Wisteria Festival, held each April on the grounds of Banning Park to inaugurate the yearly opening of the house. Crowds gather to enjoy the fragrant white and purple blossoms and a program that includes the presentation of Wisteria Princesses, a musical concert and a play about the Banning family. The festival, continuous since 1950, is co-sponsored by the Wilmington Chamber of Commerce and the Los Angeles Recreation and Parks Department. The Native Daughters of the Golden West, wearing costumes of early California, act as festival hostesses.

The near-century-old vine with its tree-sized trunk and awesome 200-foot spread has become a botanical wonder — an appropriate symbol of its former owner, who though a man of vigor and aggressiveness was also a lover of beauty, as his stately house remains to tell.

The GENERAL PHINEAS BANNING RESIDENCE is located in Banning Park at 401 East M Street, Wilmington. Banning Park is open year-round, while the residence is open on Sunday afternoons from April to mid-October. Tours from 1 p.m. to 4:30 p.m. Admission is 25 cents for adults and 10 cents for children.

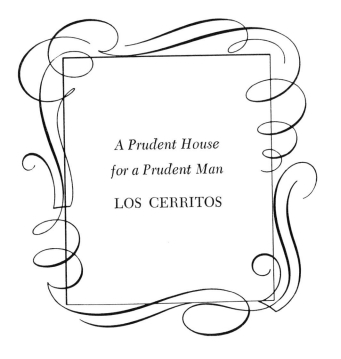

A Prudent House
for a Prudent Man

LOS CERRITOS

THEY SAID OF DON JUAN TEMPLE that he got what he wanted by prudence. And prudently is how, in 1844, he went about building a house on the 27,000-acre rancho he had acquired as a side line to his prosperous Los Angeles general store. Its location was the rolling coastal district that comprises most of present-day Long Beach.

Construction waited until a ship could sail around the Horn for New England brick for a firm foundation. Meanwhile, lumbermen were felling virgin redwood near Monterey for stout support beams. With equal caution Temple settled on two traditional features: the walls would be of adobe, so suited to the dry climate; the roof of serviceable *brea* (asphalt), free for the taking from the La Brea tar pits in Los Angeles. His careful architectural plan wedded the familiar U-plan with walled-in patio to the convenient two-story-with-galleries arrangement recently introduced by Thomas Larkin at Monterey. The closed patio was retained as a security against *bandidos* or marauding Indians; other defense measures included barred and shuttered windows and a row of rifle apertures under the roof. As befitted the house of one of California's most affluent citizens, workmanship was first-rate throughout.

Thanks to this sound planning, Temple's Casa de Rancho Los Cerritos remains substantially with us today, presenting the paradox that the finest and best-preserved adobe residence in Southern

California was built, not by a native, but by an adopted son.

Born plain John Temple in Reading, Massachusetts, he was one of about a score of Americans who settled in California before 1830, mostly New Englanders and all sea arrivals. Yankee commerce with California was an extension of the China trade. Contraband commerce it was, of course; Spain forbade the Californians to trade with foreign vessels, wishing to keep all the trade for herself. But early in the 19th century Spain became preoccupied with rebellious colonies and raiding privateers, and one day in 1805 the Yankee ship *Lelia Byrd* speculatively put into San Pedro harbor near Los Angeles. Instead of firing on her, the lonely, luxury-starved Californians welcomed her and eagerly swapped meat and otter skins for silk and jewelry, cutlery and tin pans. Thus began a long-lived exchange between Yankee traders and the coastal towns from San Diego to San Francisco, although Spanish officials occasionally cracked down and bartering had to take place by night in secluded coves.

The illegality of these calls discouraged seamen from jumping ship. The sole American colonist in Los Angeles during Spanish rule was a Bostonian named John Chapman, and he wasn't there by choice. He had shipped on a French privateer, which had turned to pillaging California coastal towns, and as the pirates were making

Rear *corredor* at Los Cerritos. (*—Historic American Buildings Survey*)

off after one raid, a vaquero managed to lasso him. What emerged dripping from the surf was a mild-looking pirate indeed: a tow-headed youth with a shy smile. He was permitted to do penance by building a gristmill and roofing the plaza church. Afterward, he had his choice of a bride among the local señoritas, all enamoured of his blue eyes. Pirate Chapman ended up a ranchero.

But after Mexico broke with Spain in 1822 trade became legal, and soon sombreroed and booted Yankees were to be seen strolling about the Los Angeles Plaza. Several were shipwreck survivors, but usually the defection could be traced to the spell cast by a coquettish señorita. Many are said to have announced they would marry none but a man with *ojos azules*. Parents were highly approving of these marriages, although not so taken with eye pigment as with Yankee business acumen.

What with the language barrier, many couples consummated their marriages before they ever conversed. In Santa Barbara, a seaman diligently memorized the Spanish words for "I love you" (*Yo te quiero*), but when he announced them to a young lady at a tender moment, she surprised him by hopping up and putting the kettle on. In his excitement, he had reversed the words to "*Yo quiero té*," which means, "I want a cup of tea." But before the evening ended he managed to straighten it out, and they somehow pledged their troth.

John Temple's case was different. He visited Los Angeles as a seaman, fancied the climate and sniffed business opportunity. Los Angeles lacked a store; its citizens were obliged to travel the nine miles to San Gabriel Mission to buy from the padres. After accumulating a stake, Temple returned to Los Angeles in 1827 and prudently went about building his future.

First, he took Catholic instruction and got himself baptized, taking the name Juan. Next, although he hadn't selected a bride, he asked the church to investigate him for marriage. Whenever a Yankee ship docked he searched for friends to testify on his behalf. Meanwhile, he studied Spanish, applied for citizenship and scouted for a suitable wife. He courted in turn the belles of Los Angeles and San Diego and was looking over

what Santa Barbara had to offer when, in 1830, his marriage approval came through. He proposed at once to Rafaela Cota of Santa Barbara, and what with his clean-cut features and strong jaw, even without *ojos azules*, he had no difficulty gaining her hand. After the wedding, he carried her off to Los Angeles.

There, as a bona fide Mexican, Spanish-speaking Catholic married into an established California family, he opened a general store and prospered at once.

Soon he branched into real estate speculation and acquired a handsome town house, a say in community affairs, and the courtesy title of don. An indication of his status is that when the pueblo organized its first vigilante committee in 1836 to quell a spreading family feud, the meeting was held in Don Juan's store. Temple then acquired something he hadn't counted on, but which became a pleasant addition to his life: he gained a business rival in Abel Stearns, who opened Los Angeles' second general store after a sojourn in Mexico. Stearns was also a Massachusetts native, coming from Salem. The men became close friends and later co-operated in numerous business ventures.

All that lacked in Don Juan's life was a rancho, and this need was filled in 1843, when he purchased for $3000 (half coin, half merchandise) 27,000 acres that had formerly been part of the sprawling Nieto estate. He paid $25 more for the rancho branding iron and the rights to use it, for he intended his rancho, named Los Cerritos for its small hills, to be a working ranch, specializing in hides and tallow. About the same time, Abel Stearns purchased an adjoining rancho.

As the site for his house, Don Juan chose the crest of one of the small hills overlooking the Los Angeles River. The house was grandly sized with a 100-foot, two-story, main section to which attached two 90-foot wings. Adobe bricks, made down by the river and tamped by Indian feet, were laid three feet thick at lower wall levels. Temple laid out a large, luxuriant garden, planting it with exotics, Italian cypress, pomegranates, rubber and pepper trees, oranges and figs, all kinds of palms and ferns. This lush Eden was watered by a cistern into which river water was pumped

by means of a hydraulic ram. Some of his plants are still thriving.

The Yankee ranchero applied himself earnestly to the task of directing an operation that included 15,000 cattle, several hundred horses and large crews of Indian vaqueros, tanners, harness-makers, blacksmiths, carpenters and domestic servants. There were roundups in the spring, *matanzas* in the fall, and always hides and tallow being readied for market. In the 1840s San Pedro shipped more raw leather than any other port on the coast, Los Cerritos being one of its big suppliers. From there the smelly cargoes sailed around the Horn to New England factories, then back again to San Pedro as fancy lace-up shoes and shiny pumps to be sold in Don Juan's Los Angeles store — probably the most traveled shoes in the world.

Don Abel's Rancho Los Alamitos was equally busy, but the two households ever found time to join in gay entertainments. And what did these two Latinized Yankees do for fun? Why, hold fiestas, of course. At such times the courtyard at Los Cerritos fluttered with gay festival trappings, while near-by barbecues sizzled in open pits. Bullfights were held in a bullring just north of the courtyard; horse races matched the equine best from the two ranchos. Nighttime brought dancing to strumming guitars and clicking castanets, the favorite dance being the *jota,* in which couples

Juan Temple's building plan mingled the Monterey Style, introduced by Thomas Larkin, with Spanish adobe tradition. Below, early ironware and crockery in Los Cerritos kitchen. (—*Long Beach Public Library*)

faced each other while hopping briskly from one foot to the other.

Presiding over the unbridled merriment were the merchants' bejeweled doñas. Likenesses are lacking of Doña Rafaela as a young woman, but Temple's brother Pliny, who came out to look over California and his new sister-in-law, wrote home that "Brother John" had taken to wife "a short, thick-set woman." A portrait at middle-age shows a firm-mouthed, double-chinned woman with a no-nonsense, satisfied expression. But Don Abel, although himself so homely with his long, bony face that he was called *cara de caballo* (horse face), is known to have captured a stunner. Having waited until forty to marry, he won a flower-faced beauty of 14, Arcadia, daughter of the prominent San Diegan Juan Bandini. This unlikely union caused it to be sung behind his back: "Two little doves sang in a laurel, How lovely Doña Arcadia! How ugly Don Abel!" But Doña Arcadia seems to have reveled in all the pampering Don Abel lavished on her, including a town house so grand it was called El Palacio, and carried her sunny disposition into marriage. One wonders if Don Juan and Don Abel, sporting their red sashes and dancing the *jota* with their high-combed wives, ever reflected on the amazing gulf between their life styles and that of their boyhood chums back in Massachusetts.

These two Yankees seemed to have crossed the border without a hitch, but complication was brewing. By the 1840s resentment was growing against gringos, especially those arriving overland, who had never gotten the welcome the seafarers had. With their rifles and buckskins and brusque ways they were considered a wild set of men, and doñas kept their daughters well hidden. The swelling ranks of Americans were considered a threat. However, this feeling had not yet penetrated the realm of the two popular merchants, and they never suspected it would.

Then in July 1846 came the shocking Bear Flag Rebellion, followed in dizzying succession by American annexation and the flight of Governor Pío Pico. Commodore Robert Stockton and his troops debarked at San Pedro, marched north past Los Cerritos and occupied Los Angeles. Less reconciled than the Northern Californians, Angelenos burned with anger and expected naturalized Californians to share it. But emotions were by no means so simple among those who had relinquished their nationality, only to have it follow and confront them. Resisting the passionate partisanship of his wife, Juan Temple endeavored to stay neutral.

Then Stockton departed, leaving behind a garrison force of fifty soldiers and appointing a reluctant Juan Temple as alcalde. The officer left in command was a tactless, high-handed man who arrested leading citizens for trivial cause. Temple was caught in the middle, between his wife, in-laws and friends, who besought him to overrule the bullying officer, and the commander, who demanded unquestioning support. Feeling mounted and Temple saw revolt coming. He decided to resign as alcalde and seclude his family at his rancho. He and his wife and daughter departed Los Angeles in a *carreta* in which, it is said, Doña Rafaela, unknown to her husband, carried 200 pounds of gunpowder concealed in her personal valises for delivery to the rebels.

Several days later the Angelenos rose up and overpowered their conquerors; they forced part of the occupation troops to depart and imprisoned the rest. To Don Juan's distress, Los Cerritos was requisitioned as command headquarters for the *Californios* and as prison for American captives. Among the prisoners was Benjamin D. Wilson, uncle of the World War II general, George S. Patton, Jr. Wilson had arrived overland and married a Spanish wife but had chosen to fight with the Americans. He fared little worse than the master of Los Cerritos, who had sought to remain neutral. Temple not only had his rancho seized but was imprisoned for a time as well. He wrote home to Massachusetts: "I and Brother Pliny have passed many anxious days and nights during the insurrection, our persons and families exposed to insult and imprisonment (having both of us been prisoners) and our lives and property at the mercy of a lawless set of men."

At Los Cerritos, rebel leaders prepared for a retaliatory attack by the expelled troops. When the Americans returned, the rebels met them with eight-foot lances and a four-pound cannon mounted on the front of an immigrant wagon. Their ferocious defense again routed the Americans. This was known as the Battle of the Old Woman's Gun, because the cannon had been hidden from the Americans by an elderly Mexican woman. It is unknown whether to the battle's name should be added "And Doña Rafaela's Gunpowder," but throughout the insurrection, despite the imprisonment of her husband, Temple's wife remained steadfastly Californian.

Los Cerritos played one more part in the Mexican War. In Don Juan's perfumed garden was planned the wily military deception which prevented Stockton from advancing on Los Angeles after landing in San Pedro Bay on October 23.

The nearly weaponless *Californios* gathered a vast herd of wild horses from the rancho and assembled them behind a gap in the hills about three miles from the landing. Mounted troops were scattered among the barebacked horses, and while Stockton watched from shipboard, the troops and horses were kept passing and repassing the gap. They stirred up such clouds of dust Stockton couldn't see that most of the horses were riderless. Believing he was facing a vast army of cavalry, he weighed anchor and sailed for San Diego.

Of course, Stockton didn't stay thwarted. Soon he was joined by General Stephen Kearny, dispatched from Santa Fe to help bring the *Californios* to heel. Kearny lost one battle, but his and Stockton's forces merged and confronted the enemy in an action on the San Gabriel River, where they soundly defeated them. On January 10, 1847, the Americans marched on Los Angeles and reclaimed it without bloodshed. And that marked the end of resistance.

Don Juan's painful neutral stance turned out to have been prudent after all. He not only regained the friendship of his fellow Angelenos, but the U. S. Land Commission confirmed all of his land claims. His greatest business success followed the annexation: the Gold Rush boom lent opportunity for lucrative loan-making, and with the profits he contracted for public and commercial buildings. He erected Los Angeles' first courthouse, its first theater, and in partnership with his brother put up the Temple Block buildings.

Expanding his enterprise into Mexico, he invested in land on the West Coast and in a fleet of ships that plied between Acapulco and San Francisco. His most spectacular feat was obtaining operating rights to the Mexico Mint in 1856, when Mexico was depleted by revolution; he became known as the richest man in Mexico. He managed to retain the mint throughout Maximilian's reign, and his heirs held it until 1893, when it reverted to the Mexican government. In his flamboyant business career he was a forerunner of those 20th-century global financiers who wield their legendary fortunes, franchises and fleets oblivious to war and politics.

But always Don Juan liked to get back into his saddle at Los Cerritos. The rancho had made

Dining room with mannequins in period costume appears as when
in use by the Jotham Bixby family. (—*Long Beach Public Library*)

a profitable transition from hide and tallow into beef, which came into demand with the Gold Rush. Then, in the winter of 1863-64, the great drought descended on Southern California. Los Cerritos cattle died by the thousands; carcasses were thick along the dried-out water courses. Don Juan, then seventy, decided not to restock and sold his rancho to Flint, Bixby and Company for a fraction of its value. Don Abel, whose Rancho Los Alamitos lost 50,000 head of cattle, let his rancho go to its mortgagee. He too had made a fortune in business while also pursuing an active political career after annexation.

In a few months Don Juan was dead, leaving a large estate to his wife and only daughter. Inheriting her father's cosmopolitan bent, his daughter had married a Frenchman and gone to live in Paris, where the widowed Doña Rafaela joined them to live out her days.

Flint, Bixby and Company stocked the ranch for sheep raising. Some 30,000 sheep, led by imported Merino rams, ranged the slopes in small flocks watched over by crook-wielding shepherds and their dogs. In spring and fall, crews of skilled Mexican shearers would descend on the rancho for a noisy month of shearing and bailing that yielded an annual wool clip of 200,000 pounds. Later, Jotham Bixby acquired a controlling interest in the ranch and turned much of it to cultivation. He also made a significant alteration in the house, replacing the flat *brea* roof with a New England-style roof, high-peaked, gable-ended and shingled.

In the 1880s the rancho was caught up in an ambitious land scheme. An Englishman named William Willmore envisioned a city on the undulating slopes and contracted to buy the rancho from Bixby, who vacated and moved to Los Angeles. But Willmore's dream proved premature, and the land reverted to Bixby. He later sold it off, parcel by parcel, as settlers began arriving in a spill-over from the Los Angeles land boom. Eventually the moldering casa was sold too, along with its tangled gardens, to Bixby's nephew, Llewellyn Bixby. He rehabilitated the house and watched the subdivisions multiply until Los Cerritos was enveloped by a city. Long Beach had shot past the 55,000 mark when, in 1921, the hills for which the rancho was named were showered by an oil gusher. The strike opened a fabulously rich oil field that was named after the highest of the *cerritos,* Signal Hill.

Over the years Llewellyn Bixby lovingly restored the old house and gardens, retaining as many original features as possible, such as the hand-wrought woodwork and the original brickwork in the patio. His most salient changes were in replacing his uncle's New England roof with a slanting tile one, and removing part of the second floor to fashion a two-story-high living room with interior balcony. In 1937 the Historic American Buildings Survey designated Los Cerritos as "most worthy of careful preservation for the benefit of future generations."

After Llewellyn Bixby died in 1942, his widow continued to live in the historic house. When she indicated her willingness to sell it, numerous groups urged that the city take steps to ensure its preservation. In 1954 the city council voted to lease the building and grounds, with the option of purchasing the property. The following year the city, which had ample coffers thanks to Signal Hill, exercised its option and paid out $80,000 for the big house and its grounds for use as a combined historic house and historical library-museum. The Long Beach Public Library system took over its direction and opened it to the public.

The Yankee trader in John Temple would be pleased to know that the oil that lay hidden beneath his rancho, and which in his day would not have been worth the drilling, would emerge when needed and provide the financing to perpetuate his memory.

LOS CERRITOS is located at 4600 Virginia Road, Long Beach. House and gardens are open Wednesday through Sunday from 1 p.m. to 5 p.m. Closed on Mondays, Tuesdays, Thanksgiving, Christmas Eve, Christmas, and New Year's Day. No admission charge.

The gate to Los Cerritos opens into the former private garden of Juan Temple. Casa entrance then was through the courtyard on the west. (*—L. T. Kean*)

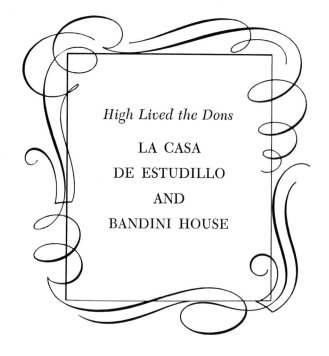

High Lived the Dons

LA CASA
DE ESTUDILLO
AND
BANDINI HOUSE

SAN DIEGO IS WHERE California began, with the arrival in 1769 of a small, hungry band of Spaniards led by a diminutive, limping priest, and today the city cherishes its Old Town as a reminder of those intrepid beginnings. Actually, Old Town's oldest structures, La Casa de Estudillo and Bandini House, are much too grand to represent that humble prelude when Father Serra hobbled amongst the rocks and cacti of the sun-scorched camp assuring everybody that things would get better, that California was a place worth staying in.

What these big, imposing adobe houses really symbolize is an element absent in that first arrival and quite rare in California history — the Spanish aristocracy. Mainly, California was settled by men poor enough to covet a land barren of nearly everything but beasts and Indians. But always Spartan pioneering draws a quota of the high-born, lured from boredom into romantic uncertainty, and that is how California came to attract an Estudillo and a Bandini, the former a proud Castilian who came as a military officer for his king, the other a genteel Andalusian, connection of a noble Italian family, who arrived as a ship's lieutenant. They stayed, married and raised families, counseling their scions to keep the family honor burnished bright, even among the primitives.

It was their proud, energetic sons, José Antonio Estudillo and Juan Bandini, who in the 1820s

built the handsome houses of our story, filled them with the best furnishings the clipper ships could bring, and established a standard of high living and hospitality that was the talk of the Pacific Coast.

Handsome, stocky Estudillo and small, elegant Bandini were good friends and former sporting companions. Both recently had buckled into married life, Estudillo marrying the daughter of a sergeant in his father's command and Bandini marrying Estudillo's sister. San Diego was experiencing an atypical era of excitement. After being founded with the erection of a mission and presidio — the first in a chain of north-winding Spanish settlements designed to halt the south-winding Russian migration from Alaska — San Diego had lagged behind the rest. It could boast only of being first: not only was it California's first town, but its bay had been the first discovered by the Spanish explorers; Cabrillo had touched there in 1542. But once settled, it had languished in doldrums so tranquil that even the pirate Bouchard, who had ravaged towns up and down the coast, ignored San Diego.

But now San Diego, the cactus patch, was blossoming thanks to, of all things, the new Mexican governor's case of rheumatism. Preferring to keep his aching knees in a balmy climate, in 1825 he had moved the capital down from Monterey. Now *politicos* and *hidalgos* from all over Cali-

Cupola, La Casa de Estudillo. (*—Uncredited photographs: Donald Nicol*)

fornia were wending their way toward the once forgotten port, and whaling and trading ships were casting anchor in the bay. San Diego looked promising, and so the two ambitious young aristocrats decided to establish there.

Estudillo was the first to build a family seat, in 1827, breaking ground on the south side of the plaza for a house even finer than the governor's. Before the year was out, Bandini began building right alongside, planning to make his abode equally as impressive. Building a fine house in early California didn't mean building ostentatiously, but rather solidly and on a generous scale. The prevailing taste was for blocked-off rectangular exteriors bare of any ornament. The building material was adobe, hard, smooth bricks made of sun-dried clay and straw and locally utilizing cactus juice. The builders were Indians who had learned construction crafts under the tutelage of mission padres.

The plan of their houses followed the shape of a "U," the inner part forming a patio closed by an adobe wall with a great double gate for admitting *carretas*. The tile roof sloped in a shallow cant to the outside wall, leaving a high wall on the patio side, against which leaned the roofs of the flanking *corredores*, or covered verandas, onto which opened numerous rooms. Supports for the roofs were timbers bound in place with rawhide thongs. The massive walls were five feet thick at the base, diminishing upward, with deep-set windows which in the sleeping rooms were barred and shuttered. Each bedroom had its niche for a shrine. Floors were of wide redwood planks, hand-hewn. The Estudillo house had one eye-catching, incongruous feature that Bandini omitted to give his: an octagon-shaped cupola centered atop the roof.

Carefree years followed for the privileged young families in their splendid new casas. San Diego pulsed with excitement, and the Bandinis and Estudillos were at the thrilling center of it all. They were ever entertaining the governor's set with gay *bailes* and fiestas. Bandini was a marvelously agile dancer, and at the balls he always led the loveliest señorita onto the floor. He introduced the Spanish waltz, which he'd learned in Peru, and it quickly spread the length of Califor-

nia. For his contribution he got himself excommunicated by a disapproving padre, but when halting the craze proved impossible, the ban was quietly lifted. There was lots of gambling and frequent bullfights in the plaza, during which the Estudillo cupola bulged with feminine charmers cheering their favorite matador.

The peppery local politics offered another engaging pastime for the young aristocrats, although in this they sometimes were outshone by the future governor, Pío Pico, then operating a general store and grog shop in San Diego while entrenching himself as a political kingpin. In 1828 Bandini was elected to serve as revenue collector, with Estudillo as his assistant. Pico soon went to Monterey as a *diputado*. Thanks to its population growth and its able politicians, San Diego succeeded in obtaining a charter of incorporation, even before Los Angeles received one.

Alas, San Diego's boom was only an interlude. The Northern California political faction succeeded in wresting the capital back to Monterey, and with it went all the trade and excitement. San Diego began to drowse again. In the decade of the 1830s, California politics rose to a feverish pitch, with much intrigue and baiting of the Mexican officials, but sleepy San Diego went quietly along doing nothing. Its population shrank until the town lost its corporate status and its alcalde and had to be governed as a department of burgeoning Los Angeles. As if that weren't humiliating enough, the Presidio dwindled to a skeleton force of barefoot sentries who planted potatoes on the ramparts.

With commercial and social life at a nadir, Bandini and Estudillo turned their attention to their outlying ranchos, which Governor Echeandía had granted them in appreciation of their hospitality. Estudillo adjusted to the quieter life better than did the high-strung Bandini, who craved excitement. Since Mexico's break with Spain he had resented the new government and tried to take a lead in censuring it, but being confined to political backwaters he found that role difficult. His threats and pronouncements made scarcely a ripple.

In 1831, however, Bandini was able to join forces with Pío Pico in a revolt against Governor

View of La Casa de Estudillo from Old Town's historic plaza.
Windows and doors recess deeply into five-foot-thick adobe walls.

Victoria. The dissenters succeeded in getting the governor overthrown, but his successor was not to the don's taste either. In 1836 he again joined Pico, this time opposing Governor Alvarado, and persuaded the Presidio force to march on the capital with them. But the Pico-Bandini-Presidio band was easily defeated by the Alvarado forces. Afterward, the Presidio contingent failed to return from the action and the Presidio was closed. San Diego was deader than ever and Bandini more bored.

San Diego could no longer hold him. The missions were being secularized, and he took a job administering San Gabriel Mission, south of Los Angeles, and wangled grants to two ranchos north of San Diego. Moving between his scattered enterprises exhilarated him, and everywhere he cut a social swath with his dancing, wit and gallantry. Richard Henry Dana wrote of Bandini's "most graceful dancing" at a Santa Barbara wedding, attired in "white pantaloons, neatly made, a short jacket of dark silk gaily figured, white stockings and thin morocco slippers upon his small feet."

After his beautiful daughter Arcadia married a rich Los Angeles merchant, the American Abel Stearns, Bandini entered into a mercantile venture in Los Angeles with his son-in-law. He also obtained a concession to mill lumber in the San Bernardino Mountains. Still restless, he went prospecting in Mexico and set up gold and copper mining operations there. Unfortunately, in business Bandini displayed more daring than acumen and often was obliged to cover losses with high-interest loans. His concerned son-in-law tried to offer advice, but he was too proud to take it.

Meanwhile, José Estudillo had matured into a solid family man and dedicated town father. He

The Bandini House was headquarters for American officers
in 1846 when United States forces occupied San Diego.

improved his estates and took a leading part in civic affairs, serving earnestly, in succession, as tax collector, treasurer, mayor and judge. La Casa de Estudillo became less a place of gay entertainment than of more vital activities. The patio rang with the voices of children, not only with his own large brood but with nieces and nephews he had adopted after his wife's sister died. The Estudillos also donated one room of the casa for use as a public school, and on Sundays the family chapel was opened to the townspeople when the mission priest came to say mass. Doña Victoria had become known for her many charities; a steady stream of sick and needy wound its way to her open door. Estudillo's public service included helping other settlements expand their agriculture; the first pineapples introduced into Hawaii were stored in his house en route from Mexico.

Their good works came back to them in the form of more and larger land grants. Also, Estudillo was placed in charge of the secularized Mission San Diego as well as outlying Mission San Luis Rey. To the flamboyant Juan Bandini on his important comings and goings, Estudillo, now grown quiet and portly, must have seemed a solid burgher indeed. While the town was proud of Bandini, marveling, "Why, he seems to belong to the world!" it was reliable Don José Estudillo on whom they depended.

The friends had divided in another way. They held opposing views on the increasing presence and power of Americans in California. Bandini, who by now had soured completely on the Mexican regime, was saying, "We'd be better off under the *Yanquis* — they'd bring peace and prosperity." The Estudillos were staunchly loyal to Mexico.

Flowers bloom year 'round in the vast courtyard of La Casa de Estudillo. (*—California Dept. of Parks & Recreation*)

Then on July 7, 1846, in an extension of the Mexican War, Commodore John Sloat claimed California. On July 29 San Diego awoke to the sound of martial music and found a throng of 150 tall Americans raising the Stars and Stripes in the plaza. Among them were Captain John Frémont and the famed scout, Kit Carson.

Bandini, who was near-by at one of his ranchos, rushed into town to welcome the Americans and assure them, "La casa es suya." The American officers were pleased to establish their headquarters at the Bandini casa. The Bandini daughters sewed up an American flag in honor of the occasion, and one of them, while standing on a ledge admiring the dragoon officers, fell into the arms of the handsomest, the West Pointer, Cave Couts, who would soon become her husband.

Juan Bandini called on all San Diegans to follow his lead and co-operate with the prosperity-bearing *Yanquis*. Few did; most burned with resentment and showed it. The Estudillos decided

on a neutral course: Don José removed himself to one of his ranchos, while Doña Victoria opened their casa as a refuge for frightened women and children. Town males continued to smolder, and as soon as Frémont sailed out of the harbor, a group of *Californios* made a dash on the Americans, who were obliged to scramble onto an anchored American vessel. But with an assist from Bandini, who managed to hide the town cannon, the Americans readvanced and once more raised their colors in the plaza. Bandini's confederate, Pío Pico, by then in the governor's chair, was still urging all Californians to eject "the treacherous foe." But in a few days he too would bow to the inevitable and flee to Mexico, where he denounced Bandini for having "traitorously embraced the enemy's cause."

Bandini was now giddy with optimism. The energetic Americans were at the helm, and he had two American sons-in-law to lend prestige. He confidently expanded his numerous enterprises and looked around for new investment opportunities. When the Gold Rush began he observed that a heavy traffic of prospectors was crossing from Mexico through San Diego, demanding lodging and provisions. Without perceiving that this demand might be ephemeral, he plunged heavily, with borrowed funds at usurious rates, into the construction of a store and a large hotel. He was nonplused when "all of a sudden trade left entirely," leaving him with two white elephants and insistent creditors. His newest son-in-law lacked the means to help, and Stearns now demanded mortgages in exchange for his financial bailings-out. One historian recorded that the sons-in-law also objected to the "gambling proclivities of the don's young sons and the expenditures of Doña Refugia Bandini in preparing one elegant fiesta after another even while feeling 'awfully downcast' about money matters."

Money worries and family troubles mounted. They may have been the basis of the discontent that caused Bandini to turn on the *Yanquis*. He announced his disenchantment with their rule, averring California to be "in a much worse state than before." He threatened to move across the border and resume his Mexican citizenship, and finally did, in the mid-1850s, only to find that regime not to his liking either. "It is impossible to expect any good from a country governed in

Tufted velvet French armchair, La Casa de Estudillo.

Child's room, La Casa de Estudillo.

Estudillo dining room.

Brazier in center held preheated coals.

such a manner," he wrote in 1858 to Abel Stearns, announcing his intention to return to California. With characteristic optimism, he said he planned to "start to work anew to found ranches."

It was too late. His health was gone, and soon after his return he had to go to Los Angeles for treatment of a serious illness. There, in the Stearns' town house, he died in 1859, not yet sixty. By then he was penniless, all his properties having been signed over to mortgagees, including his San Diego casa, which went to Abel Stearns. His sole legacy to his widow was $171 worth of personal possessions.

By then his old friend Estudillo had also died; he too was still in his fifties. But his departure had been in much different circumstances, since he was at a pinnacle of esteem and success. Even though he had not welcomed them, the Americans had accorded him great respect and entrusted him with official responsibilities. In the first election following annexation he was chosen county assessor. He took a leading part in civic affairs of the Americanized town and was making ambitious plans to move the business district nearer the bay so as to stimulate port activity, but he

died before they could be effected. He left a large fortune and many mourners.

Ironically, the San Diego prosperity that Bandini had despaired of seeing and Estudillo had faithfully sought arrived in the decade following their deaths. In the late 1860s San Diego saw boom years. The port began to thrive and numerous hotels sprang up around the plaza; one of them operated in the Bandini casa. A. L. Seeley bought the house and remodeled it into the Cosmopolitan Hotel, adding an upper story and surrounding it with covered double verandas with fancy balustrades. Seeley was an operator of stagecoach lines, and his hotel was a bustling transfer point to Los Angeles and the East.

Moreover, the laurels of success which had eluded Bandini were to be bestowed on several of his progeny. His daughter Arcadia, during her second widowhood (her second husband was Colonel Robert Baker, builder of Baker Block), was known as one of the richest women in the country. His son Arturo became a scholar and author of books on California; his son Juan was manager of the *Los Angeles Herald*. Jack Carrillo, his grandson, became a world-renowned engineer, the

Juan Bandini's cattle brand.

» 142 «

Corner of sala,
La Casa de Estudillo.

builder of New York's Idlewild Airport, while Jack's actor brother, Leo, rocketed to stardom in the role of "The Cisco Kid" and was long a top name in films and television.

The two good friends' casas still stand side by side on the plaza. Although they have had many owners and undergone many vicissitudes, somehow they still suggest the men who built them a century and a half ago. La Casa de Estudillo, solid, proper, dignified, soberly unadorned, wears the distinction of being at once a landmark of city, state and nation. It was transferred to state ownership in 1968, the gift of San Diego businessman Legler Benbough. On May 12, 1971, it was dedicated a National Historical Landmark with a representative of the president on hand to present a plaque and declare it "of exceptional significance to the history of the United States." In the audience that day was Robert Estudillo of Tijuana, a great-grandson of José Estudillo.

The casa's present-day furnishings — great carven chests and armoires, four-poster beds that soar 11 feet toward the ceiling, mahogany tables and chairs, a rosewood pianoforte — were painstakingly assembled by the Colonial Dames of America. They studied actual ships' manifests for the period 1820-1845 to determine exactly what items of furniture the Estudillos ordered from Europe and the Orient.

Bandini House stands there with its showy additions, romantically befringed with banana palms and creeping vines, but with shutters closed, presenting something of a problem. Its function has yet to be resolved. In recent years, it has been tried unsuccessfully as a complex for shops and as an art gallery; presently it is closed. But always plans hover over it for some grand restoration that will confer glittering status, the accolade it has so long awaited with a mien that combines at once both hauteur and humiliation. Of the two casas on the plaza, somehow it is Bandini House which most irresistibly commands the eye and bestirs the imagination.

LA CASA DE ESTUDILLO AND GARDEN is located in Old Town San Diego State Historic Park across from the plaza between San Diego Avenue and Calhoun Street. Open daily including Sunday from 10 a.m. to 6 p.m. in summer, from 10 a.m. to 5 p.m. in winter. Closed on Thanksgiving, Christmas and New Year's Day. Admission 25 cents for persons 18 years of age and older, free to all others. BANDINI HOUSE stands next door.

Villa Montezuma stands as a monument to the architecture, life and times of San Diego's most exciting period — the boom years of the 1880s. At right is the elegantly detailed staircase leading from the main entry hall.

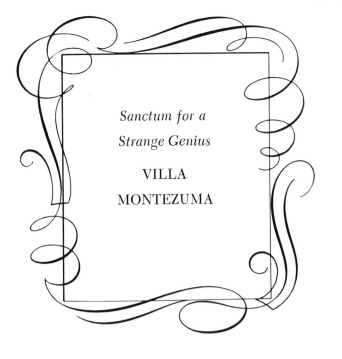

Sanctum for a
Strange Genius
VILLA
MONTEZUMA

WHEN THE *San Diego Sun* ANNOUNCED early in 1887 that "Jesse Shepard, formerly of Paris, France," would build a residence at the corner of 19th and K streets, it created a sensation, as it was meant to. People took it as a sign that San Diego had truly arrived if a man of Shepard's eminence had decided to call it home.

Shepard was probably the most impressive personage yet seen in San Diego. Reed-tall and handsome with a detached air of *savoir-faire*, dressed in elegant Continental clothes, wearing jewelry given to him by royalty — he took everybody's breath away. And it wasn't just his aspect. A bachelor then approaching forty, he was one of the best-known concert artists in the world. Both a pianist and a vocal virtuoso, he had played and sung in command performances for crowned and titled heads all over Europe, including Czar Alexander II of Russia.

After performing in Northern California, Shepard paid a professional visit to San Diego, which recently had gained a rail connection to the East and was in the throes of its great land boom. There he met the leading citizens, nearly all speculating in real estate, and certain of them thought what a catch it would be if this fascinating man might be induced to stay. With Shepard as a local asset along with the splendid climate, how could San Diego fail?

Shepard had grown up in rural Illinois but had spent all his adult life on the move. Recently he had conceived a plan compatible with settling down. Thus, when his admirers offered to present him a building site and part of the cost of constructing a house for himself, to their surprise and delight he accepted.

Shepard's plan was to become a writer. In the Paris artistic salons he had mingled with the literati and made friends with Alexander Dumas. Lately he had grown dissatisfied with his musical career, realizing it wasn't quite the genuine article. He wasn't the usual sort of concert pianist; virtually untrained, he was known as an improviser. His parents, impecunious English immigrants, had been unable to provide more than a few music lessons. But he had early discovered that his great natural talent — the ability to span an octave and a half with his long fingers — his striking appearance and a gift for improvising moody compositions combined to electrify audiences. The caliber of his audiences escalated so swiftly that by his early twenties he was in Europe delighting royalty.

In time, he did not depend on piano playing alone in his concerts but used his equally wide-ranged voice and added notes from a variety of musical instruments to enhance his compositions. What's more, his detractors claimed he enhanced his aspect with rouge, mascara and a studiously

Lyrical ceiling fretwork of polished redwood. (—*All photographs: Historic American Buildings Survey*)   » 145 «

disheveled wig. Doubtless he regretted how deeply he was involved with theatrical effect and looked up to writers, whose efforts had to be laid unadorned upon the printed page. He was challenged to emulate them.

For writing he wanted a house exactly suited to his temperament, for he believed that writing, like his music, was something that flowed forth if the psyche were properly nurtured. He set about to prime the muse, as all of San Diego watched to see what this extraordinary man would come up with.

He didn't disappoint them. His architectural style was vaguely Queen Anne, an English style that had ridden in on the craze for quaintness and was then rare in Southern California. Shepard engaged the architectural firm of Comstock and Trotsche, but his claim that the house was his own design is validated by the fact that it is quite unlike anything the firm did before or after.

Queen Anne, something of a catch-all style, was the epitome of variety, but Shepard's house was especially so. Only the striking excellence of its parts prevented it from degenerating into clutter. The astonishing roof bristles with no less than five towers and six gables. Exterior walls were sheathed alternately with shingles of several cuts, half-timbering, molded plaster panels, carved wood panels, pebble-encrusted panels and lathecut strips. Windows were cut in every size and shape: rectangular, round, square, fan-shaped, wide-arched, narrow-arched, needle-shaped.

Transcending all was the exquisite handling of the various units: the frothy, airy square tower; the lyrical, decorative panel with cornice; the stately entrance; the imaginative window groupings. In treating each almost as a separate architectural subject, he foreshadowed his preference for the essay, just as his painstaking attention to detail prophesied that he would be a polisher of sentences and a master of aphorism. In line with his planned seclusion, he omitted the style's usual veranda and balconies while sheathing his windows with dark stained glass and giving the rambling house only two exterior doors. The third floor of the large square tower, approached by a narrow staircase, was designed for his writing room.

The interior throughout was one of utter grandeur. Its effect, too, was achieved with brilliant little architectural essays in which artistic genius triumphed over rather modest expenditure. Shepard was far from rich. Always insouciant about money, playing only when he wished, he now found himself obliged to mortgage the house before he could finish it.

But in his hands moderate-cost materials could assume near-royal splendor. Planing mills recently had begun turning out fancy-cut boarding and detailing ranging from beveled strips to rosette newel posts; one could select from hundreds of designs in illustrated catalogs. Shepard tapped this modest source, choosing pieces in walnut and redwood and assembling them in wood mosaics that are a sheer delight. He used them fancifully as treatment for fireplaces, doors, windows and staircases and, more loosely, as wall panels and ceilings. His ceilings incorporated another utilitarian product, Lincrusta-Walton, a plastic material simulating tooled leather. He attained lyrical heights by overlaying it with a lacy fretwork of polished redwood. His stained-glass windows weren't imported, but made in San Francisco from his own designs, some portraits of musical and literary greats.

Also, there were personal touches expressing a side of Shepard then unknown to San Diegans. Four color windows in the music room depict flowers that symbolize the four seasons, reflecting Shepard's conviction that nature exerted a strong guiding force on his psyche. On the opposite wall a pair of colored windows represent the Occident and the Orient, with Occident symbolized by a rigid knight in armor before a battlemented castle, while Orient is shown as a serene-faced man strolling in flowing robes, with a graceful minaret in the distance. The latter figure wears the face of Shepard, who thus expressed his preference for the ways and philosophy of the East. Always something of a mystic, in Russia he had joyfully discovered spiritualism, and while there he had taken instruction in conducting séances. Thereafter, along with his musical career, although quietly, he had practiced spiritualism wherever he went. However, by the time he reached San Diego he had grown disillusioned with the phenomenal

Magnificent art-glass window in Music Room depicts Sappho attended by cupids; on either side are panels representing Milton's "Il Penseroso" and "L'Allegro." The room once vibrated with Jesse Shepard's famous piano concerts.

side of spiritualism, although he still believed in spiritualism as a means of courting artistic inspiration. Also revealing his eastern affinities was the Byzantine dome which capped the square tower immediately over his writing room. Shepard's house was thus singularly biographical.

Christening his house Villa Montezuma, Shepard moved into it in September 1887 accompanied by his secretary-companion Waldemor Tonner, a former Chicago tailor. Soon crates of paintings, *objets d'art*, Persian rugs and a huge polar bear skin began arriving. A reporter from the *San Diego Union* was permitted an inspection, and he couldn't have been more impressed. "Art, pure and simple, is found in everything," he rhapsodized.

As soon as he was settled, Shepard began spending long hours in his writing studio, which

he called his "Sanctum Sanctorium." Already he had launched his literary career. In June one of his essays had appeared in *The Golden Era*, a West Coast journal which recently had moved from San Francisco to San Diego. His publishing debut elated him. He wrote an uncle, "I shall let music take a second place in the future, as I wish to do a great deal of magazine and book work."

Writing was not his only San Diego occupation, however. He seems to have made an agreement with his sponsors to act as an unofficial civic host. Throughout the fall and winter he opened Villa Montezuma to receptions for prominent San Diegans and visitors to the city; he regaled them with his playing and singing and, no less, with his fabulous house. On these occasions the lower rooms blossomed with great bouquets of flowers, a different variety for each room. Always he concluded his performance with a composition of his own, the "Grand Egyptian March," which simulated the sounds of marching armies, trumpets, drums, tambourines, battle clashes and cannon booms. The finale invariably created a sensation.

Faithful to his regimen in the Sanctum Sanctorium, Shepard quickly established himself as a regular contributor to *The Golden Era*. Most of his writings dealt with persons and places that had impressed him in his travels and were laced with strong convictions on a variety of topics. He was opposed to materialism, militarism, literary realism, political liberalism and the worship of machines, while admiring literary romanticism, nature, mysticism and religious faith.

Medieval-style fireplace of Music Room is a medley of lathe-cut panels, black walnut shingles, and decorative glazed tile.

That writing was his true vocation he now had no doubt. Around mid-year 1888 he conceived the idea of going to Paris to seek a publisher for a collection of his essays, but he was running short of funds. He had splurged on furnishings and was having to make heavy mortgage payments (the prevailing interest rate was 24 per cent), while his publications brought but modest stipends. Only by borrowing was he able to finance the trip for himself and Tonner.

By fall Shepard was in Paris, calling on publishers. His book was accepted, and the following spring a volume titled *Essays and Pen-Pictures*, most culled from *The Golden Era*, was published in both English and French. For authorship he took another name, one that combined his middle name with that of his mother's family: Francis Grierson. He explained that he did not want his "serious work" to be associated with a "mere musician." No doubt he also wished to jettison his spiritualist reputation.

Returned to San Diego, Shepard happily read his favorable reviews and letters of congratulation. But despite its critical success, his book brought but negligible financial returns. By now he was badly strapped for cash. Efforts to extend his borrowing locally were fruitless, as was an appeal to a relative, even though Tonner wrote a follow-up letter saying Shepard's financial predicament had put him "in such a state of mind that he could neither write nor do anything else." Mortgage payments fell in arrears and foreclosure was threatened.

About this time rumors flew that Shepard was conducting séances for pay at Villa Montezuma. His sponsors indignantly denied this in the newspaper, but apparently he did resort to this means of replenishing his coffers. A later memoir by a prominent San Diego woman stated that her mother "went to a séance he [Jesse Shepard] gave, and she said he played continuously all through the demonstration."

All this forced Shepard to reassess his San Diego situation: clearly, it wasn't working out as planned. If he were to continue writing — and this was his deep desire — he would have to give up Villa Montezuma; its expenses were too burdensome. Moreover, he yearned for the artistic stimulation of Paris, for which receptions for bankers and realtors were not a satisfactory substitute. He sold Villa Montezuma and its furnishings for considerably below their cost, as the real estate boom had waned. He returned the building money his sponsors had advanced and folded away the rest for situating himself in Paris, where he hadn't a doubt that dazzling literary success awaited him.

In December 1889, slightly more than two years after opening his remarkable house, Shepard closed its doors behind him forever. He departed San Diego in high style. His farewell to a city loath to let him go was a fashionable benefit concert at the Unitarian Church. His many admirers crowded there to hear him play and sing for the last time and to enjoy one of his prose poems recited by a local matron. He closed with a ringing rendition of the "Grand Egyptian March."

San Diego never forgot him. Although the town had held the remarkable man less than three years, such was his impact upon it and so strongly had he imprinted his personality upon his house that a part of him seemed to remain. His name sparked conversation; Villa Montezuma was pointed out to visitors. Reports of his writing career came back from time to time, and several books followed in regular succession. Maeterlinck hailed Grierson "the supreme essayist of the age." But his works were too cerebral to be either popular or financial successes.

Shepard seems to have craved a wider readership. Departing Paris, he secluded himself in England to write an ambitious memoir of his Illinois boyhood. He labored at it for eight years, living frugally above shops. When published under the title *The Valley of the Shadows*, his book drew high praise for its brilliant insights and lyric prose style. But again, his appeal was for the cultivated few; he had not reached the masses.

He never did. His writings never returned more than a modest living; often he had to supplement his earnings with musical performances. A return to America on the eve of World War I interrupted his literary flow. Lean times followed. He died suddenly in Los Angeles in 1927 at the age of 79; he had just completed playing a concert, for which the faithful Tonner was passing a collection plate.

Dining Room's Renaissance-style fireplace incorporating fleur-de-lis and Greek pediment is set against polished redwood wall paneling.

It was part of Shepard's mystic belief that his disembodied spirit would remain after his breath had flown; perhaps, then, he is enjoying the revival of interest in his writings. His books, forgotten at the time of his death, have found new appreciation. Such eminent modern critics as Bernard de Voto, van Wyck Brooks, and Edmund Wilson point to him as a key figure in the intellectual climate of his times. New editions have been printed, along with volumes discussing his works; there has been a recent biography of him and another is in progress.

Shepard would likewise be pleased at the appreciation given his San Diego house, which opened to the public in the fall of 1972 with a ceremony rivaling that of his San Diego departure.

Preservation efforts had been under way since early in 1970. Fortunately Shepard's house, unlike his books, had never been eclipsed. San Diegans had always prized it, and each owner in turn had given it loving care. Even when it served for a time as a boardinghouse, the interior was meticulously cared for and left unaltered except for the addition of another entrance. In recent decades, however, owners had found maintaining so large and multidetailed a house burdensome, especially the exterior, where some weathering had set in. The foundation, too, had weakened, and the large gables needed shoring. Thus its future looked uncertain; there were rumors it might be purchased for a mortuary or remodeled for offices.

When it became known that Villa Montezuma could no longer survive as a residence, there wasn't any question among San Diegans whether the house deserved preservation. The only question was *how*. The San Diego Historical Society took the lead in seeking an answer. Its board of directors and its Women's Committee inspected the house and discussed possibilities, then deployed across the city to confer with other civic groups.

Rather quickly came the suggestion that financing be sought from the historic preservation grants-in-aid program of the federal Department of Housing and Urban Development, which was empowered to assist worthy preservations for public use. Next, the society and other groups co-operated in working out plans to purchase the house and operate it as a combined architectural monument and neighborhood center. The proposal was then considered and approved by the San Diego Model Cities program and a H.U.D. grant applied for. Meanwhile, the interested organizations together put up $30,000 to buy the house and hold it pending federal action.

Since H.U.D. grants-in-aid must be matched dollar for dollar, a campaign was launched to raise matching money. An appeal for public donations was made through the local press and in society publications. Interest was fanned by opening the house to the public for daytime viewing during a week in early December with the house be-

decked with Victorian Era Christmas decorations. During evening hours benefit dinners, cocktail parties and receptions were separately hosted by the San Diego Historical Society's Women's Committee, by the Contemporary Arts Committee of the Fine Arts Society and by the Native Daughters of the Golden West. All proceeds went to the Shepard House Preservation Fund.

In mid-1971 a H.U.D. grant of $41,469 was awarded the city to apply toward Villa Montezuma's restoration. By then the preservation fund not only was ample to match the grant but showed promise of meeting the projected $101,484 for the combined purchase and restoration. A major donation came from the San Diego Junior League. The house title was then transferred to the city and the work of restoration begun. While carpenters labored to strengthen the underpinnings, skilled craftsmen made studied replicas of missing shingles, lathecut, tiles and glass panes. As its contribution to the project, the San Diego Gas and Electric Company removed an unsightly pole and tangle of crisscross wiring from the corner before the house and laid utility lines underground.

The house that opened to an expectant public in October 1972 is a near miracle of preservation. Eighty-five years seem to have breathed as gently as a zephyr upon its jewel-toned, polished interior. With its authentic period pieces, studiously selected to complement the setting, the house constitutes a museum representing the height of Victorian taste in architecture and decoration. And it is more. Shepard, who as a yearning youth discovered the world of culture by climbing into a neighbor's window and venturing onto a piano stool, would certainly approve the other aspect of the house: a neighborhood cultural and educational center for the working-class neighborhood that has replaced the former luxury residential district. There in a glorious setting all ages may enjoy art exhibits, drama, lectures, musical entertainments — even music lessons.

VILLA MONTEZUMA is located at 1925 K Street in San Diego. It is open 10 a.m. to 5 p.m. Tuesday through Sunday. No admission charge.

A Gallery

OF HISTORIC HOUSES

As the foregoing historic houses and their stories give us the bones and sinews of California history — that is, its main points: governmental, social, and architectural — these ninety additional houses fill in its flesh and blood. They round out the picture, for each house played its particular role in the eras past and has something significant to tell us about our heritage. Each in its way is a landmark in the rich and exciting history of California.

A word of caution: schedules and entrance fees may change, so advance inquiry might avoid disappointment.

ANAHEIM

MOTHER COLONY HOUSE (1857)

414 N. West St.; Wed. 3-5, Sat. 10-12,
closed major holidays; free.

Anaheim's first frame house was one of the first buildings of the Mother Colony of German settlers. The redwood dwelling served as residence and office of George Hansen while he supervised the colony's development; it was later occupied by a branch of the old Spanish Carrillo family. Now city-owned and in the care of the public library, the house contains exhibits of furnishings and relics of early Anaheim. (*—Mother Colony History Room, Anaheim Public Library*)

ARCADIA

HUGO REID ADOBE (About 1839)

Los Angeles State and County Arboretum,
301 N. Baldwin Ave.; 8-6:30 except Christmas; free.

"I have built a new house . . . flat roof'd and corridor'd," wrote Hugo Reid in 1840 of this reed-thatched adobe in his successful petition to the Mexican governor for the grant of Rancho Santa Anita. Reid, a Scottish sea captain, settled in California in 1834 and championed the Indians after marrying an Indian princess. Restored by the state, the adobe is furnished in the style of early California. (*—L.A. State and County Arboretum*)

QUEEN ANNE COTTAGE (1880-81)

Los Angeles State and County Arboretum,
301 N. Baldwin Ave.; 8-6:30 except Christmas; free.

After amassing a fortune speculating in stock of the Comstock Lode, E. J. "Lucky" Baldwin set out to rival the "Bonanza Kings" with his own racing stables, private race track and this charming residence with stained-glass picture windows, marble fireplaces and walnut woodwork. Baldwin built it for the third of his five wives, but he misnamed it — the style is more Carpenter Gothic. (*—L.A. State and County Arboretum*)

BAKERSFIELD

PIONEER VILLAGE

3801 Chester Ave.; weekdays 8-3:30, Sat., Sun.,
holidays 12-3:30 (May-Oct. until 5:30); 50 cents.

This Queen Anne house, built by Bakersfield pioneer William A. Howell in 1891, is one of 33 structures brought from Kern County sites and arranged as a representative Central California community vintage 1870-1910. *Bakersfield Californian* donated Howell House. Other residences are Weill House, Weller Ranch House, Barnes Log Cabin and Sheepherder's Cabin. Kern County Museum is operator. (*—Jennifer Ellis*)

GUILD HOUSE (1905)

1905 18th St.

This late Victorian residence with Queen Anne detail was built by Bakersfield businessman Charles Barlow. Acquired in the 1960s by the Child Guidance Guild, it was restored under the direction of the Kern County Museum and contains period furniture, *art nouveau* lamps of Tiffany glass and a hand-carved English fireplace that came from Gumps in San Francisco. Proceeds of a lunch-hour restaurant downstairs (except in summer) benefit Guild projects. (*—Jennifer Ellis*)

BELMONT

WILLIAM C. RALSTON HOME (1866-68)

College of Notre Dame campus; Tues. 9-11, Thurs. 9-10 and 3-4, Sat. 10-11, except national holidays; 25 cents.

The former showplace of Comstock millionaire and banker William C. Ralston, this handsome villa (expanded from an 1854 structure) could accommodate 120 guests. Now serving the College of Notre Dame, the magnificent rooms include the mirrored ballroom, the grand banquet hall and the foyer, which is a replica of that in Ralston's first Palace Hotel. (*—College of Notre Dame*)

BENICIA

BENICIA CAPITOL (1852)

First and G Sts.; daily 10-5.

This brick building has the rare distinction of having been designed to resemble a Greek temple for use as a city hall, which instead served as the third capitol of California (from Feb. 1853 to Feb. 1854), afterwards being used as a county courthouse. It has also accommodated a school, library, theater, church and police station, and today is exhibited as an authentically restored and furnished State Historical Monument. (*—Bancroft Library*)

FISCHER-HANLON HOUSE (1856)

135 East G St.; garden and carriage house open daily 1-5; free.

When a fire ravaged Benicia's California Hotel, Joseph Fischer, Swiss-born merchant and cattleman, bought it, moved it and converted it into this residence. In 1969 three of his descendants, Marie and Catherine Fischer and Marie Hanlon, donated it to the state. The interior is not yet on exhibit, but the surrounding gardens and a carriage house with vintage vehicles and other displays are open to the public. (*—Historic American Buildings Survey*)

MASONIC TEMPLE (1850)

*110 West J St.; open for special events
and by appointment.*

Built of lumber and hardware shipped around the Horn at a cost of $18,000, this, the first Masonic Temple in California, was donated by the pioneer physician Robert Semple, a charter member of Benicia Lodge No. 5 F.&A.M. The lower floor was used for a time as the county court. Still in use, the building is one of three Masonic halls in the state where any Masonic lodge may confer degrees. (—*Historic American Buildings Survey*)

BERKELEY

CLAREMONT HOTEL (1914)

Ashby Ave. and Domingo Ave.

Architect Frank Lloyd Wright called this hotel which perches near the crest of the Berkeley hills "one of the few hotels in the world with warmth, character and charm." Klondike millionaire Erick Lindblom built it to be a fitting resort for visiting millionaires from the East and from Europe. The hotel enjoyed its greatest success during the 1920s and 1930s when it was a fashionable social center and offered ballroom dancing to big name bands. (—*Berkeley Chamber of Commerce*)

SOUTH HALL (1873)

University of California campus.

This distinguished red brick and gray stone building in the French Mansard style was the first building to be constructed on the University of California campus after its transfer from Oakland. Carpenters and masons were still at work on South Hall at the time of the first Berkeley commencement in July 1873. Since completion, it has continuously served classes. It was recently restored by architect Kenneth Cardwell. (—*Bancroft Library*)

BRENTWOOD VICINITY

JOHN MARSH HOUSE (Mid-1850s)

Marsh Creek Rd., 6 mi. W. of Brentwood.

This Gothic house of seven gables was built by Dr. John Marsh, a Harvard graduate who came west in 1837 and practiced medicine after acquiring a large land grant. Constructed of stone quarried near-by, the house was built for Marsh's bride, Abbe Tuck, who like Marsh was a Massachusetts native. She died before the house was completed; he was murdered soon after occupying it. Preservation is in process by the John Marsh Memorial Association. (—*Historic American Buildings Survey*)

BRIDGEPORT VICINITY

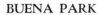

BODIE HISTORIC DISTRICT (1860s, 1870s)

Bodie State Historic Park, Bodie Rd., access from U.S. 395 about 6 mi. S. of Bridgeport; daily 9-6, May 30 to Labor Day; free.

These bleak reminders of the once bustling mining town of Bodie, which produced $100 million in gold, are among 168 deserted structures maintained by the parks department in a state of "arrested distintegration." Named after Waterman Body, who discovered gold there in 1859, Bodie was one of the toughest mining camps in the West. Park contains museum. (—*California Dept. of Parks & Recreation*)

BUENA PARK

KNOTT'S BERRY FARM GHOST TOWN

8039 Beach Blvd.; daily except Christmas; $1.50.

Adjoining the Ghost Town Fire Department is the Gold Trails Hotel, built in Prescott, Ariz., in 1868. The hotel was the first of dozens of vintage structures that Walter Knott moved to Buena Vista from all over the West to create a typical prospecting village of the 1800s. Other points of call are the blacksmith shop, saddlery, Wells Fargo Office, general store, livery stable, saloon, a hand-hewn log cabin and covered-wagon camp. (—*Knott's Berry Farm*)

CHINO VICINITY

YORBA-SLAUGHTER ADOBE (1850-53)

17127 Pomona-Rincon Rd.; open by appointment

The famous Butterfield stages stopped here to obtain fresh relay teams from the Yorba stables. This fine example of the hacienda-type adobe was built by Raimundo Yorba with Indian labor; in 1868 he sold it to Fenton M. Slaughter. His daughter, Julia Slaughter Fuqua, rescued the house from ruin in the 1920s, restored and furnished it with many family heirlooms. The adobe is now being readied for regular exhibit to the public. (—*San Bernardino County Museum*)

COLUMBIA

COLUMBIA HISTORIC DISTRICT (1850s, 1860s)

Columbia State Historic Park; daily; free.

The pictured Hildebrand Building, containing the town post office, is one of 40 period structures restored and governed by the state parks department in this famous Gold Rush town. The post office, operated continuously since 1852, has quaint boxes installed in 1861. The 12-block district contains such buildings as jailhouse, church, school, courthouse, fandango hall and stage drivers' retreat, also many functioning businesses and services. (—*California Dept. of Parks & Recreation*)

DEATH VALLEY

SCOTTY'S CASTLE (1924-1931)

Near northern end of Death Valley National Monument; daily 9-6; $1.

Centered in Grapevine Canyon is this $3,000,000 castle in the Spanish Provincial style. It was built by Chicago financier Albert M. Johnson and his mysterious friend Walter Scott. Highlighted by Austrian woodwork and German metalwork, the castle contains the original ornate furnishings and art objects. This National Parks Service property is shown by forty-minute guided tours. (—*Colourpicture Publishers, Inc.*)

ENCINO

LOS ENCINOS STATE HISTORICAL MONUMENT

16756 Moorpark St.; daily 9-5; 25 cents.

Once part of Los Encinos Rancho, this park contains three historic buildings: Osa Adobe (pictured), built by Vicente de la Osa in 1849; Reyes Hut, built in the late 1870s by Francisco Reyes, later a Los Angeles mayor; and Garnier House, a French Provincial house built of limestone in the late 1860s by Eugene Garnier. The park, operated by the Encino Historical Society, contains warm springs where Portolá camped and a 1000-year-old oak. (—*California Dept. of Parks & Recreation*)

EUREKA

CARSON MANSION [INGOMAR CLUB] (1884-85)

Second and M Sts.; open by appointment.

Embracing elements of nearly every Victorian architectural style except Romanesque, this house wears probably the most elaborate exterior of any house in the country. It was designed by the Newsome brothers' architectural firm for lumber baron William Carson. Interior paneling is of South American mahogany, Oriental teak and other rare woods. Numerous motion pictures have been filmed in it. Today it is occupied by a businessmen's club. (—*Historic American Buildings Survey*)

CARSON HOUSE (1889)

202 M St.

Across the street from the Ingomar Club is another house built by William Carson, this one as a wedding gift for his eldest son, J. Milton Carson. A fine example of the Queen Anne style, it has fish-scale shingles and a plethora of fancy lathecut. After being cut up into apartments, the house was a candidate for demolition when Robert Madsen purchased and restored it in 1964, making it into a handsome complex of shops and offices. (—*Trinity Color Techniques*)

FREMONT

A. A. COHEN HOTEL (1869)

Stanford Ave. beyond Weibel Winery.

Standing on the site of Warm Springs, a popular bathing resort since Indian times, is this old hotel built by transportation magnate A. A. Cohen. The beautifully detailed structure in the French Renaissance style was included in the Historic American Buildings Survey. After Governor Leland Stanford bought the estate for a vineyard, the hotel was used as a residence by his brother Josiah; later it was a convent. It has been returned to resort use. (*—Historic American Buildings Survey*)

GLEN ELLEN VICINITY

JACK LONDON STATE HISTORIC PARK

One mile west of Glen Ellen off State Highway 12; daily 10-5 except Thanksgiving, Christmas, New Year's; 25 cents.

Jack London's widow built the "House of Happy Walls" in 1919 as a memorial to the spectacular literary figure; it is now a museum of London possessions and manuscripts. The park, once London's ranch, also contains the author's grave and the ruins of Wolf House, the dream mansion which fire destroyed before he could move into it. (*—California Dept. of Parks & Recreation*)

GLENDALE

CASA ADOBE DE SAN RAFAEL (1860s)

1330 Dorothy Dr.; weekdays by appointment.

This adobe hacienda with 18-inch-thick walls was built on land once part of an early Spanish crown grant made to José Maria Verdugo in 1784. Tomas Sanchez, first sheriff of Los Angeles, built it after acquiring through marriage 100 Verdugo acres. When the crumbling house was threatened by a subdivision scheme in the 1930s, a citizens' group persuaded the City of Glendale to buy it. Restored with W.P.A. funds, it is run by the parks department. (*—Glendale Div. of Parks & Recreation*)

GRASS VALLEY

LOLA MONTEZ HOUSE (1850s)

Mill and Walsh Sts.; daily 9-5; 50 cents.

Secluded behind foliage, this house wears an air of mystery appropriate to its former owner. Lola Montez, the beautiful Irish-born dancer, came to California in 1852 at the end of her affair with the king of Bavaria. When her act was panned in San Francisco she retired to Grass Valley for two years. There she held an artistic salon and discovered the talent of Lotta Crabtree. Her house, later given a second story, is now privately owned. (*—Historic American Buildings Survey*)

JACKSON

A. C. BROWN HOUSE (1859)

*225 Church St.; daily except Tues. and
most holidays; free.*

Missouri-born Armstead C. Brown came to California in
1851 and after moderate success at mining returned for
his family and homesteaded. Later he built this Classical
Revival house with Italianate touches and there raised 11
children. He practiced law and became a county judge.
Now county-owned, the house is a history museum. The
ornate wrought-iron fence also encloses a carriage house.
(*—Historic American Buildings Survey*)

JENNER VICINITY

FORT ROSS COMMANDER'S HOUSE (1812)

*Fort Ross State Historic Park; Highway 1, 11 mi. N.
of Jenner; 9-5 (hour longer in summer); 25 cents.*

This high-roofed log house, built for the commander of
the Russian base, is believed to be the second oldest wood
structure west of the Rockies. Most of the original wood
was retained when the house was restored in 1950. It is
part of a cluster of buildings that served the Russian community that lasted until 1841. The quaint Russian Ortho-
dox Chapel, which burned in 1970, is being reconstructed.
(*—California Dept. of Parks & Recreation*)

LA PUENTE

JOHN A. ROWLAND HOME (1855)

*16021 E. Gale Ave.; Wed. 1-4 and first
Sun. of month 1-4; 50 cents.*

One of the oldest brick dwellings in the state, this 12-room
mansion was the home of John Rowland, coleader of the
Rowland-Workman Party, first American wagon train to
reach Southern California. Rowland, a prosperous fruit
rancher, built it for his second wife, 26-year-old Charlotte
Gray, whom he wed when 61. La Puente Valley Historical
Society restored it with some original furniture. (*—La Puente
Valley Historical Society*)

LAKE TAHOE VICINITY

VIKINGSHOLM (1929)

*Emerald Bay State Park;
daily July 1 to Labor Day; free*

Designed by a Swedish architect to represent an 8th-cen-
tury Norse fortress, this 38-room castle is considered one
of the finest examples of Scandinavian architecture in the
Western Hemisphere. It was built as the summer home of
Mrs. Lora Knight of Chicago and is now a state parks
property. The methods and materials used in its construction are those used in ancient Scandinavia. (*—California
Dept. of Parks & Recreation*)

EHRMAN MANSION (1903)

*Sugar Pine Point State Park;
daily, summer months; free.*

Long considered the finest summer home on Lake Tahoe, this stone mansion was designed by architect Walter Danforth Bliss for San Francisco businessman Isaias W. Hellman. It passed through marriage to the Ehrman family, which sold it to the state in 1965. Some of its rooms retain their original appearance; others serve as an interpretive center and museum of the area's history. (—*California Dept. Parks & Recreation*)

LONG BEACH

LOS ALAMITOS (1806)

6511 E. 7th St.; Wed.-Sun. 1-5 except holidays; free.

The oldest house in this book and one of the West's oldest is this ranch house whose central adobe portion was built by Juan Nieto on land granted to his father, Manuel Nieto, in 1784. In 1842 the Yankee trader Abel Stearns acquired it but later lost it to foreclosure. In 1881 it was bought by the Bixby ranching family and in 1906 Fred Bixby restored it and constructed additions. The Bixbys presented the house to the City of Long Beach in 1969. (—*Camp Wells Russell photograph*)

LOS ANGELES

CHARLES LUMMIS HOME, "EL ALISAL" (1894)

*200 E Ave. 43; daily except Sat. 1-4;
closed Thanksgiving, Christmas, New Year's; free.*

This stone and concrete house was largely constructed by its owner, Charles Lummis, author-editor-archaeologist who founded Southwest Museum. L-shaped, it has three-foot walls, handcrafted doors and hand-hewn ceiling beams. Now under jurisdiction of the Los Angeles parks department, it serves as a museum of Indian artifacts and headquarters for the Historical Society of Southern California. (—*Historic American Buildings Survey*)

ANDRES PICO ADOBE (1840s)

*10940 Sepulveda Blvd. (Mission Hills);
Tues.-Sun. 1-4 except Easter, July 4, Thanksgiving,
Christmas, New Year's; free.*

Indians built the original section of this adobe, believed to have served San Fernando Mission. It became the home of ranchero Eulogio de Celis; later Andres Pico, brother of Pío Pico, bought and expanded it. In the 1960s the San Fernando Valley Historical Society rescued the building from demolition and the City of Los Angeles acquired it. (—*San Fernando Valley Historical Society, Inc.*)

LEONIS ADOBE (1840s)

23537 Calabasas Rd., Calabasas community;
Wed., Sat., Sun. 1-4 and by appointment; free.

Standing on former San Fernando Mission land, this adobe ranch house is one of the best examples of its type in Southern California. In the 1870s the original adobe was remodeled into a Monterey-style dwelling by Miguel Leonis, who owned a vast cattle empire and was a Los Angeles political power. In 1965 the Leonis Adobe Association purchased the house and skillfully restored it. (*—Historic American Buildings Survey*)

DRUM BARRACKS (1862)

1053 and 1055 Cary Ave., Wilmington community.

This wood-framed building of colonial design and roofed with split-cypress shingles is one of few landmarks of the Civil War in California. It served as officers' quarters for the garrison that was set up to keep secessionist elements in check and was named after General Richard Coulter Drum, the commanding officer and head of the Department of the West. The Los Angeles parks department now owns it and is preparing it for exhibit to the public. (*—Historic American Buildings Survey*)

HALE HOUSE (About 1898)

3800 N. Homer St., Highland Park community.

This exuberantly ornamented, late Victorian mansion was the home of the James Hale family when it stood in the then fashionable Mount Washington district. In the late 1960s it was acquired by the Cultural Heritage Foundation and moved to Heritage Square. Decoration on the picturesque frame exterior includes molded plaster and metal, hand-carved wood, lathecut and wrought iron. Irregular tours are conducted while the house is being restored. (*—Julius Shulman photo, courtesy of Cultural Heritage Board*)

HOLLYHOCK HOUSE (1918-1920)

4800 Hollywood Blvd.; open on request after
restoration is completed in Aug. 1973.

An A.I.A. plaque marks this Frank Lloyd Wright house, noted for displaying his genius for fitting a building to its site and for its striking Mayan elements. Built for Aileen Barnsdall, it and the adjoining Barnsdall Arts and Crafts Center were Wright's first commissions in the Los Angeles area. The design incorporates an abstract hollyhock, a flower that once grew abundantly on the property. (*—Los Angeles City Recreation & Park Dept.*)

LOPEZ ADOBE (1878)

Pico St. and Maclay Ave., San Fernando community.
This charming adobe with an outside stairway was the second home of Geronimo Lopez, an early resident of Rancho San Fernando who operated the first post office in the valley. When the town of San Fernando began booming in the 1870s, he moved to town and resided in this house his son Valentino built for him. The Lopez Adobe Preservation Committee, backed by several civic groups, is presently preparing the adobe for regular exhibit to the public. (*—Historical American Buildings Survey*)

MARYSVILLE

MARY AARON MUSEUM (1850s)

Seventh and D Sts.; Tues.-Sat. 1:30-4:30; free.
The 1856 *Marysville City Directory* listed among the "new brick houses" this castellated Gothic residence built by Warren P. Miller, an architect who had recently come west from New York State. Today it serves as a history museum, having been presented to the city by Frank Aaron as a memorial to his mother, a former occupant. The museum specializes in 19th-century relics. In the patio is a fountain that graced a square in early Marysville. (*—Hometown Prints*)

MONTEREY

THE CASAS GUTIERREZ (1840s)

Calle Principal near Madison; business use.
A combination of adobe and wood construction, this house was typical of Monterey dwellings of the Mexican and early American periods. It was one of two adjoining adobes with a connecting wall built by the Gutierrez family on land granted to Joaquin Gutierrez by the municipality. One of his 15 children lived in the second adobe. Gutierrez descendants occupied the property until around 1900. Now state-owned, the casas are leased to businesses. (*—Historic American Buildings Survey*)

COLTON HALL (1847-49)

Pacific St.; 10-12 and 1-5 except Thanksgiving, Christmas and New Year's; free.
Built of limestone shale and adobe mortar, Colton Hall was planned as the town hall and public school. It takes its name from Rev. Walter Colton, a Navy chaplain who supervised its construction after being named Monterey's first mayor under the Americans. In 1849 California's first Constitutional Convention met in the beautifully proportioned second-floor assembly hall. Now operated as a museum. (*—Colton Hall Museum*)

» 161 «

THE PACIFIC HOUSE (1847)

Scott St. and Calle Principal; 9-5; 25 cents.

Probably no early California building had as many uses as the Pacific House, which in succession served as hotel, ship warehouse, courthouse, boardinghouse, newspaper, law offices and ballroom. Thomas Larkin was first owner of the two-storied, balconied adobe. David Jacks bought it in 1880, and in 1954 Miss Margaret Jacks presented it to the state. Today it houses a museum of California history and a collection of Indian artifacts. (—*Historic American Buildings Survey*)

STEVENSON HOUSE (1830s)

530 Houston St.; 9-5; 25 cents.

In 1879, in his 29th year, Robert Louis Stevenson lived and wrote in two rooms of this adobe house. Today it is a shrine for Stevensoniana: furniture, keepsakes, manuscripts and other personal possessions of the Scottish writer who came to California to marry an Oakland artist, Fanny Osbourne. The building's first owner was Rafael Gonzales, customs administrator, who used it for a warehouse. The state has owned and operated it since 1937. (—*California Dept. of Parks & Recreation*)

CASA AMESTI (1834, 1846)

516 Polk St.; open Fri. afternoon; free.

This adobe and wood house was built by José Amesti, a Spanish Basque who came to Monterey on a sailing ship in the 1820s and married into the prominent Vallejo family. It is an excellent example of the Monterey style, which combines New England influences with Spanish. The original one-story adobe was enlarged in 1846. A later owner, Mrs. Frances Elkins, restored the house and willed it to the National Trust for Historic Preservation. (—*Historic American Buildings Survey*)

HOUSE OF FOUR WINDS (About 1830)

540 Calle Principal.

This historic adobe got its name by being the first Monterey building to have a weather vane. American Consul Thomas Larkin built it for a residence; later Governor Juan Alvarado acquired it for a store. After Americanization, it served as the state's first Hall of Records and housed the office of the first county recorder. Its present owner is the Monterey Women's Club, which exhibits it during historic observances and on other occasions. (—*Historic American Buildings Survey*)

NEVADA CITY

THE RED CASTLE (1860)

109 Prospect Street.

A splendid example of the Gothic Revival style is this three-story brick house situated on the crest of Prospect Hill. John Williams, an early Nevada City trustee, built it for his son Lorin, a rising attorney in the thriving mining town. He hosted many a festive gathering there. The house, fallen into ruin, was purchased in 1963 by James Schaar, who restored it for use as a tourist home, furnishing it throughout with Victorian Era antiques. (*—Mills Photo Studio*)

NATIONAL HOTEL (1856)

Broad St.

Dominating downtown is California's oldest continuously operated hotel. Its ornate exterior remains unchanged from when the town was the hub of commerce for the Northern Mines. Its original bar, over which passed millions of dollars in gold dust, is still in use. The lobby (now dining room) served as headquarters for the stage lines and Wells Fargo. Public rooms contain many historical mementos; bedrooms are furnished with Victorian pieces. (*—Eastman's Studio*)

FIREHOUSE NO. 1 (1861)

Main St.; daily 11-5, June-Oct.; 50 cents.

The most photographed structure in the colorful Gold Rush town of Nevada City is this merry firehouse, once headquarters for the Nevada Hose Co., now a museum of the Nevada County Historical Society. When new, the red brick building wore a white Greek Revival façade which later gave way to a more fashionable Victorian front with bell tower. Hose carts first were pulled by men, later by horses borrowed from the town's express companies. (*—Eastman's Studio*)

NEWHALL

WILLIAM S. HART HOME (1926)

24151 Newhall Ave.; Tues.-Sun. 10-12:30 and
1-5 except Thanksgiving, Christmas, New Year's; free.

Overlooking Newhall from a hill is the 14-room Spanish-style ranch home of the pioneer of western films, William S. Hart. On display are the original furnishings and Hart's collection of paintings, historic weapons and movie props. Hart willed this ranch, where he lived 26 years, to Los Angeles County for use as a public park free to all.

DUNSMUIR HOUSE (1899)

2960 Peralta Oaks Ct. (off 106th Ave.);
Sun. 12-4; grounds 50 cents, mansion $1.

This majestic 17-room mansion with its soaring columns and classic pediment is one of the finest Greek Revival residences in the West. It was the home of Alexander Dunsmuir of the Vancouver mining empire and his wife Josephine, whose tragic romance inspired a motion picture. Owned by the City of Oakland, the house is operated by a preservation group which plans to increase the days of exhibit. (*—City of Oakland*)

VICTORIAN ROW (1850-1880)

400 Block of Ninth St.

This block, once the busy center of Oakland's commercial district, has remained miraculously unaltered and is popularly known as Victorian Row. Pictured is the Portland Hotel, formerly Henry House, built in 1877 by banker Ashmun Henry, which present owner James Wood is restoring. The Victorian Preservation Society is campaigning for the rehabilitation of all Victorian Row, which constitutes a veritable museum of 19th-century commercial design. (*—City of Oakland*)

MOSS COTTAGE (1864)

Broadway and MacArthur Blvd.; on request
weekdays, apply at adjacent recreation center.

Situated in Oakland's Mosswood Park, this house is a splendid example of Gothic architecture of French and English influence as adapted to wood frame. It was built by J. Mora Moss, who pioneered in Northern California with telegraphy, gas lighting, ice making and irrigation canals. The interior, also of Gothic design, was restored by Oakland clubwomen in the 1960s for use as a culture center. (*—Historic American Buildings Survey*)

BRET HARTE BOARDWALK (1860-1880)

500 block on Fifth St.

These delightful Victorian houses of Italianate design were restored in the 1960s by an Oakland investment corporation and converted into distinctive shops, galleries and restaurants. The block was so named because the popular author Bret Harte lived and wrote his colorful Gold Rush tales across the street in a cupola studio atop a lathe and plaster villa owned by his stepfather, Colonel Andres Williams, an early Oakland mayor. (*—Oakland Tribune*)

CAMERON-STANFORD MANSION (1871)

1426 Lakeside Dr.

President Rutherford B. Hayes attended a ball at this Italianate house when it was owned by Josiah Stanford, brother of Leland Stanford of railroad fame. Its builder was Will Cameron, who married Alice Marsh, daughter of pioneer Dr. John Marsh. From 1910 to 1969 the house accommodated the Oakland Museum. Still city-owned, it is being prepared for use as offices for cultural organizations with several rooms reserved for exhibit of period furnishings. (*—Drawing by Bruce Judd*)

JOAQUIN MILLER HOME, "THE ABBEY" (1886)

Joaquin Miller Rd.; open by appointment.

This quaint, peak-roofed dwelling, consisting of three one-room frame structures, was the home of Joaquin Miller (Cincinnatus Heine Miller), the famed Indiana-born "Poet of the Sierra." Here he entertained the San Francisco literati, erected strange monuments, planted exotic trees, and wrote most of his poems and plays. Six years after his death in 1913, the City of Oakland bought his estate and has since maintained it as a public park. (*—Oakland Tribune*)

OROVILLE

JUDGE C. F. LOTT MEMORIAL HOME (1856)

Sank Park, Montgomery St.; Fri.-Tues. 10-12 and 1-4, Wed. and Thurs. 1-4; 75 cents.

Built by Judge Lott, a 49er from New Jersey, this house is best known for the love story of his daughter Cornelia. Plain and afflicted with a nervous disorder, she lost her heart to handsome but poor Jesse Sank. The judge forbade them to marry but couldn't halt their clandestine romance. When the judge died at 94, Jesse claimed his 50-year-old bride. House has original furniture. (*—William Talbitzer*)

CHINESE TEMPLE (1863)

1500 Broderick St.; Fri.-Tues. 10-12 and 1-4, Wed. and Thurs. 1-4; 75 cents.

This Taoist temple was built to serve Oroville's Chinatown, which with its 10,000 residents was second only to San Francisco's. Considered the finest building of its kind in the country, it contains a dazzling array of shrines and artifacts. At the entrance is a two-ton brass incense burner said to have been a gift of Emperor Quong She. Now city-owned, the temple is all that's left of Chinatown. (*—Oroville Park Dept.*)

PACIFIC PALISADES

WILL ROGERS HOUSE (Early 1900s)

14253 Sunset Blvd.; daily 10-5 except Thanksgiving, Christmas and New Year's; 25 cents.

This house and surrounding ranch are maintained just as they were when the popular Oklahoma-born humorist, his wife and three children lived there. The house is an informal museum of Rogers relics, and a curator will tell you about the paintings, Navajo rugs, lariats and other mementos. Stable, corrals and riding ring are near the house. The state parks department has had jurisdiction since 1944. (—*Calif. Dept. of Parks & Recreation*)

PACIFICA

SANCHEZ ADOBE (1842-46)

Linda Mar Blvd.; Wed.-Sun. 10-12 and 1-4; free.

This Monterey-style adobe built on an 1839 Mexican land grant was long an important social center. Its master, Francisco Sanchez, *comandante* of the San Francisco Presidio and several times San Francisco mayor, entertained there Governor Alvarado, General Frémont and Hall McAllister. But it had become a lowly artichoke-packing shed in 1947 when San Mateo County bought it, restored it as a museum and assigned its care to the county parks department. (—*Historic American Buildings Survey*)

PASADENA

DAVID B. GAMBLE HOUSE (1908)

4 Westmoreland Pl.; Tues. and Thurs. 11-3:30 except major holidays; $1.

This is the most elaborate design of the noted architectural firm of Greene and Greene. The Greene brothers worked in a unique mixture of Mission, Oriental and Swiss Chalet forms, emphasizing the horizontal and designing the lighting fixtures, carpets and furniture to complement the composition. The Gamble family gave the house to the City of Pasadena and the University of Southern California. (—*U.S.C. School of Architecture and Fine Arts*)

RED BLUFF

WILLIAM B. IDE ADOBE (About 1850)

Adobe Rd.; daily 8-5; free.

This extensively restored adobe house was built by Massachusetts-born William B. Ide, president of the short-lived Bear Flag Republic, who later served as judge in Colusa County. The house contains a small museum. This state parks property, which includes a three-acre park, stands on the west bank of the Sacramento River at the point where the California-Oregon Trail crossed the river; a ferry operated there until a bridge opened in 1876. (—*California Dept. of Parks & Recreation*)

KELLY-GRIGGS HOUSE MUSEUM (1880)

311 Washington St.; Thurs.-Sun. 2-5 except Easter, Thanksgiving, Christmas, New Year's; donation.

A 49er from New Hampshire, Sidney A. Griggs built this Italianate house to cap his success as a sheep rancher. Later he married a beautiful widow, Melvina Montgomery, who lived into advanced old age until 1931; then the house was sold to the Kelly family. In 1966 a citizens' group formed to purchase and restore the house. Some rooms contain Victorian furniture; others are devoted to displays. (*—Kelly-Griggs House Museum Assn.*)

REDDING VICINITY

OLD SHASTA (1850s)

Highway 299, Shasta.

Old Shasta Courthouse, built in 1855, is one of a row of preserved buildings on Main Street of this town that in the 1850s was a booming center for mining camps, shipping out $5,000,000 a year in gold. Shasta was then called the headquarters of "Whoa Navigation" referring to the 2000 mules packing supplies to the diggings. Also standing is Masonic Hall, built in 1853, and on Shurtleff Hill an old mansion built by Dr. Ben Shurtleff. (*—California Dept. of Parks & Recreation*)

ROSAMOND VICINITY

BURTON'S TROPICO GOLD CAMP (1880-1900)

Rt. 1, Antelope Valley;
Oct.-June, Thurs.-Mon. 9:30-4; $1.

The atmosphere of a frontier gold camp of the late 1800s is preserved in this collection of 16 authentic buildings moved here from various Antelope Valley sites. Tour includes visits to a miner's cabin, miners' hall, assay office, general store, Indian hut and combined bath-barber-dentist office. There is also a museum exhibiting gold nuggets and other relics. An adjoining attraction is a gold mine that was productive into the 1950s. (*—Vanguard Photography*)

SACRAMENTO

SUTTER'S FORT STATE HISTORICAL MONUMENT (1839)

2701 L St.; daily 10-5 except Thanksgiving, Christmas, New Year's; 50 cents.

Sutter's Fort was built as a trading post and headquarters of John Sutter's 48,000-acre grant. The Swiss-born adventurer arrived in California in 1839 and prospered swiftly, only to lose most of his empire when gold seekers overran it. When restoration of the fort began in the 1890s, only the central structure was standing. The state parks department reconstructed the vanished buildings. (*—Tom Myers*)

OLD SACRAMENTO HISTORIC DISTRICT

Just west of central business district.

The Morse Building (1850s), once headquarters of Dr. John F. Morse, pioneer Sacramento businessman and public official, is among restorations in the continuing recreation of eight blocks of early Sacramento. Buildings constructed from 1850 to 1870 serve new private enterprises — shops, cafes and offices. The California Department of Parks and Recreation has restored several buildings connected with railroad history; one houses a museum. (*—Pacific Telephone and Telegraph Co.*)

CROCKER ART GALLERY (1871)

216 O St.; 10-5 except Mon., closed Aug.; free.

Judge E. B. Crocker, brother of the railroad mogul, Charles, built this fine classical building to house his art collection. The interior is exquisitely finished with parquet floors, paneled doors, and a symmetrical staircase made by German artisans. The judge filled it with choice works bought at bargain prices in France and Germany during the Franco-Prussian War. Crocker's widow gave the building and contents to the city for an art museum. (*—California State Library*)

STANFORD-LATHROP MEMORIAL HOME (1857, 1872)

800 N St.; by appointment.

The residence of two early governors, this house is outstanding for its fine detailing which combines Mannerist with mansard. With railroad riches Leland Stanford bought and enlarged it and while governor lavishly entertained there. Later Gov. F. F. Low occupied it. Stanford's widow gave the house to the Catholic diocese for a home for girls, which it remains. Lower rooms with original furnishings are used as a neighborhood culture center. (*—California State Library*)

ST. HELENA

RHINE HOUSE (1883)

Main St.; daily; free.

Frederick Beringer, one of the pioneer founders of Beringer Brothers Winery, built this 17-room house in exact duplication of his home on the Rhine River in Mainz, Germany. The leaded stained-glass picture windows and marble fireplaces were imported from Germany, as was the white oak for the beautifully carved paneling. Now used as a visitor center and wine-tasting room for the winery, the house contains many of its original furnishings. (*—Bancroft Library*)

SAN DIEGO

THOMAS WHALEY HOUSE (1856-57)
2482 San Diego Ave.; June-Sept., Wed.-Sun. 10-4:30, Oct.-May, Wed.-Sun. 12:30-4:30; 75 cents.

The first brick structure in San Diego County was built of bricks from Whaley's own kiln and plaster made from ground sea shells. Its white cedar woodwork, window glass and hardware came around Cape Horn. Whaley was a well-educated merchant; his home was a center of culture. The county court held sessions here for two decades. Restored in 1956, it is operated as a museum by the Historical Shrine Foundation. (*—Historic American Buildings Survey*)

DERBY-PENDLETON HOUSE (Reassembled 1852)
Next door to Whaley House and entered through it.

Built in Portland, Me., this house was disassembled and shipped to San Diego on order of Juan Bandini as a wedding gift for his daughter who had married an American soldier, Capt. Charles Johnson. In the mid-1850s it was occupied by Lt. George Derby, Army engineer who redirected the San Diego River. The third occupant was Capt. George Pendleton, who also took a Spanish bride. The house, now somewhat altered, contains furnishings of the 1860s. (*—Historic American Buildings Survey*)

SAN DIEGO VICINITY

HOTEL DEL CORONADO
1500 Orange Ave., Coronado; free tour 2 p.m. Sat.

Built in the elegant 1880s, the Hotel del Coronado is a Victorian architectural gem. The towered, red-roofed structure, one of America's largest wooden buildings, was one of the last of the old, opulent seaside hotels. Little changed today are the magnificent grand ballroom and Crown Dining Room which still attract top celebrities. Handsome furnishings include an ornate cast-iron elevator and an interior gazebo of carved mahogany. (*—Worden Collection, Wells Fargo Bank History Room*)

SAN FRANCISCO

GARDEN COURT OF SHERATON-PALACE HOTEL
Market and New Montgomery Sts.

Called "the most beautiful dining room in the world," the Garden Court has been designated an official San Francisco landmark. The original Palace Hotel, one of the wonders of America, was built around a palm-lined carriage court. After the earthquake, the hotel was rebuilt along the old lines, but the court became a dining room lit by an iridescent glass dome and flanked by Ionic columns. Top world figures have been entertained there. (*—Sheraton-Palace Hotel*)

FORT POINT NATIONAL HISTORIC SITE (1853-1861)

San Francisco Presidio, under southern end of Golden Gate Bridge; daily 10-5; free.

This massive brick, iron and granite structure stood sentry over the entrance to the Golden Gate during the Civil and Spanish-American wars, but it never fired a defensive shot before being abandoned in 1914. Its seven-foot-thick walls support four tiers of gun ports. Now under jurisdiction of the National Park Service, it contains exhibits of historic Army relics. (*—Historic American Buildings Survey*)

WHITTIER MANSION (1895-96)

2090 Jackson St.; Tues.-Sat. 10-4.

This four-level Richardsonian mansion of red sandstone was one of the first residences in California to be constructed of stone on a steel frame. Designed by Edward R. Swain, it was built for merchant William F. Whittier. Its spacious interior glistens with carved woodwork of mahogany and golden oak. The California Historical Society acquired the mansion in 1956 for its administrative headquarters, arts department and social rooms. (*—California Historical Society*)

SCHUBERT HALL (1905)

2099 Pacific Ave.; Tues.-Sat. 10-4.

This imposing baroque-style town house of wood and stucco has a formal side entrance, ornate grillwork and an elegantly spacious stair hall. It was formerly the home of John D. Spreckels, Jr., a wedding gift from his father of the pioneer sugar family. In 1961 the California Historical Society acquired it to house its collection of manuscripts, photographs, maps, rare books, genealogical reference works and exhibits of western printing. (*—California Historical Society*)

SAN JUAN BAUTISTA

CASTRO HOUSE (1840-41)

San Juan Bautista State Historic Park; daily 8-5 (8-6 from June to Aug.); 25 cents.

Facing the plaza of the old mission town is this adobe structure built by the flamboyant Mexican leader, Gen. José Castro, when he was northern prefect of California. The house later belonged to the Patrick Breen family, members of the ill-fated Donner Party of American immigrants. Other historic buildings around the plaza include the San Juan Bautista Mission, Plaza Hotel and Zanetta House. (*—Historic American Buildings Survey*)

SAN LORENZO

WILLIAM MEEK HOUSE (1869)

Hampton and Boston Rds.; daily 10-4 on request, apply to park groundsman to be admitted; free.
This splendid Italian Villa with several Second Empire features was built by pioneer fruit grower William Meek, who brought the first grafted fruit trees to California and developed the Royal Anne and Bing cherries. In the 1960s the house was slated for demolition, but a committee of citizens persuaded the Hayward Area Recreation and Park District to acquire the house and grounds for public use. (—Oakland Tribune)

SAN LUIS OBISPO

DALLIDET ADOBE (1853)

Pacific and Toro Sts.; May-Oct., Sun. 1-4:30; free.
Once surrounded by a vast vineyard, this adobe was built by the pioneer French vintner Pierre Hyppolite Dallidet. He married a Spanish belle and their children and grandchildren occupied the house for a full century. In 1953 their last living descendant, Paul Dallidet, willed it to the San Luis Obispo County Historical Society, which restored it for a house museum, furnishing it with original Dallidet furniture and other appropriate pieces. (—Loren Nicholson)

SAN RAFAEL

IRA COOK HOUSE (1879)

Boyd Park; Wed., Sat., Sun. 2-5; free.
This Gothic Revival house was built by Ira W. Cook, who came west after losing an arm in his Rochester, N.Y., stove factory. He was the grandfather of Mrs. John F. Boyd, who gave Boyd Park to San Rafael. The charming interior, which has Carrara marble fireplaces and molded ceilings, contains displays of historical exhibits including numerous photographs of Marin County residences. The house is operated by the Marin County Historical Society. (—Marin County Historical Society)

SANTA BARBARA

CASA DE LA GUERRA (1819-1826)

11 East de la Guerra St.; daily; free.
Built with Indian labor by Spanish-born Don José Antonio de la Guerra, *comandante* of the Santa Barbara Presidio, this big U-shaped adobe now houses a unique shopping center called El Paseo. Richard Henry Dana twice visited the casa and described a wedding fiesta he attended there in 1836 in his *Two Years Before the Mast*. In 1971 Mrs. Irene Fendon presented the El Paseo complex to the Santa Barbara Trust for Historic Preservation. (—Historic American Buildings Survey)

CASA DE COVARRUBIAS (1817)

715 Santa Barbara St.; open by appointment.

This L-shaped adobe was built by Don Domingo Carrillo, whose father José founded the noted Carrillo family in California. The 55-foot sala held the last meeting of congress under the Mexican flag. In 1853 the property was acquired by Don José Covarrubias, a native of France who had married Maria Carrillo. He became the first federal elector from California. The casa is now operated by Los Rancheros Visitadores, an equestrian organization. *(—Historic American Buildings Survey)*

SANTA ROSA

LUTHER BURBANK HOUSE AND GARDENS (1883)

Charles St. and Santa Rosa Ave.; daily; free.

On this site, acquired in 1878, the Massachusetts-born "plant wizard" conducted his hybridization experiments that resulted in scores of new plant varieties. Many of his creations may be viewed in the gardens adjoining the house. The house itself is not open, but an exhibit building contains Burbank mementos. He is buried on the grounds under a cedar tree of his own planting. The Santa Rosa parks department has jurisdiction. *(—John LeBaron)*

SARATOGA VICINITY

VILLA MONTALVO (1912)

Off State Rt. 9 just S. of Saratoga;
grounds daily 8-5, gallery (first floor) daily 1-4
except Mon.; weekdays free, week ends 25 cents.

This Italian Mediterranean villa with a Spanish flavor set amidst formal gardens was the summer estate of the late U. S. Senator James Phelan. When he died in 1930, the Irish-born San Franciscan willed Villa Montalvo to the San Francisco Art Association, which later assigned it to the Villa Montalvo Association for use as a culture center. *(—Bancroft Library)*

SPRING VALLEY

BANCROFT RANCHO HOUSE MUSEUM (1856)

9065 Memory Lane; Wed.-Sun. 1-4,
except Easter, Thanksgiving, Christmas; free.

The first house built by a white man in this area was built by Augustus S. Ensworth from adobe and timbers salvaged from a sailing ship. Its second owner was Rufus K. Porter, who named the town of Spring Valley in 1867. Porter sold to Hubert H. Bancroft, the San Francisco historian and publisher. The Spring Valley Historical Society now owns the house and operates it as a history museum. *(—Historic American Buildings Survey)*

SUSANVILLE

ROOP'S FORT (1854)

75 N. Weatherlow St.; Tues.-Sun. 10-4; free.

This log cabin which stands in the Susanville city park was built by Isaac N. Roop, pioneer gold prospector and founder of Lassen County, for use as a dwelling and store on the Nobles Pass Route. The shake-roofed cabin was dubbed Fort Defiance during the "sagebrush war" fought in 1863 between citizens of Plumas County and Lassen County to settle a jurisdictional dispute. The town of Susanville was named after Roop's only daughter. *(—Historic American Buildings Survey)*

TIBURON

DICKEY HOUSE (1874)

376 Tiburon Blvd.; bird sanctuary open 9-5 Fri.-Sun.

This diminutive Victorian gem with its scalloped shingles and steep mansard roof once stood on Strawberry Point, the home of pioneer Benjamin Lyford. In 1957 Mrs. Donald Dickey had it barged across Richardson Bay to Tiburon and restored as a memorial to her husband, naturalist-zoologist Donald R. Dickey. The house stands within the National Audubon Society's bird sanctuary and serves as headquarters of the Marin County chapter. *(—Anna-Jean Cole)*

VACAVILLE

PEÑA ADOBE (About 1843)

Highway 40 two mi. S.E. of Vacaville;
9-5 except Mon. and legal holidays; free.

Mission-trained Indians built this adobe ranch house for Juan Peña, who came with Juan Vaca from New Mexico in 1841 and received a land grant from General Vallejo. Two-foot-thick walls enclose three lower rooms and one above supported by hand-hewn redwood beams. Lower rooms with period furnishings and an attic display of Indian artifacts are exhibited by Vacaville parks department. *(—City of Vacaville)*

WEAVERVILLE

WEAVERVILLE JOSS HOUSE (About 1852)

Main St.; 10-5 except Thanksgiving, Christmas
and New Year's; 25 cents.

Built for 2500 Chinese then living in Weaverville, this Taoist temple is the oldest in the country, constructed exactly as those in China but made of wood instead of stone and tile. It was restored in the 1870s following a fire. Furnishings include carvings, gongs, panels and tapestries from China. In 1956 Moon Lee, temple trustee and grandson of one of the builders, presented it to the state. *(—Wells Fargo Bank History Room)*

NATIVE SONS' HALL (Late 1850s)
Main St.

This charming structure is one of three Weaverville buildings with outside spiral staircases leading from the sidewalks to the upstairs balconies. When erected during the booming gold-prospecting years, space was at a premium and each building had two owners, thus the outside access to the upper floor. The iron staircases were handmade by the town blacksmith. Many Weaverville buildings also have iron shutters, a fire-protection measure. (*—Wells Fargo Bank History Room*)

YOSEMITE NATIONAL PARK

PIONEER YOSEMITE HISTORY CENTER
Wawona; 9-6, June 15 - Sept. 15; free.

Rustic dwellings and utility buildings dating from the early days of the park have been moved from scattered locations and grouped into a village near the famous Victorian-era Wawona Hotel, which still stands. These include a wide variety of cabins, a Wells Fargo office, blacksmith shop, tack room and jail. There is also a covered bridge and the Yosemite Art Gallery with paintings and photographs by early Yosemite artists and contemporary works. (*—National Park Service*)

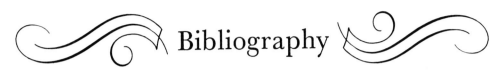

Bibliography

Bancroft, Hubert H. *California Pastoral*. San Francisco: The History Co., 1888.

Bauer, Helen. *California Rancho Days*. Garden City: Doubleday, 1953.

Beard, Joseph A. *Time's Wondrous Changes*. San Francisco: California Historical Society, 1962 .

Bowman, J. N. "The Peraltas and Their Houses." *California Historical Society Quarterly*, September, 1951.

Brackett, R. W. *The History of San Diego County Ranchos*. San Diego: Union Title Insurance Co., 1960.

Carlson, Oliver. *Hearst, Lord of San Simeon*. New York: Viking, 1936.

Carmer, Carl. "America's Victorian Homes." *The American Home*, March, 1964.

Carr, Harry. *Los Angeles, City of Dreams*. New York: Appleton-Century, 1935.

Cole, Martin. "Fact, Fiction and Supposition." *Journal of the West*, July, 1963.

Conmy, Peter T. *The Beginnings of Oakland, California*. Oakland Public Library, 1961.

Crane, Clare. "Jesse Shepard and the Villa Montezuma." *The Journal of San Diego History*, Summer, 1970.

Cullimore, Clarence. *Santa Barbara Adobes*. Santa Barbara Publishing Co., 1948.

Davis, William Heath. *Seventy-five Years in California*. San Francisco: John Howell, 1929.

Dillon, Richard. *Fool's Gold, A Biography of John Sutter*. New York: Coward-McCann, 1967.

Emparon, Madie Brown. *The Vallejos of California*. San Francisco: Gleeson Library Associates, 1968.

Ferrier, William W. *Berkeley California*. Berkeley: William Ferrier, 1933.

Fibel, Pearl R. *The Peraltas*. Oakland: Peralta Hospital, 1971.

Fletcher, Montelle R. "An Eveless Eden." *Sunset*, July, 1911.

Fryer, Roy M. "Pomona Valley before the Americans Came." *Journal of the Historical Society of Southern California*, December, 1939.

Garner, Bess A., and Post, Marian C. *The Story of the Adobe de Palomares*. Pomona First Federal Savings and Loan Assn., 1940.

Gebhard, D., and Von Breton, Harriette. *1868-1968 Architecture in California*. Santa Barbara: University of California, 1968.

Giffen, Helen S. *Casas and Courtyards*. Oakland: Biobooks, 1955.

Hammond, George P., ed. *Larkin Papers*. 10 Vols. Berkeley: University of California Press, 1951-1964.

Hawthorne, Hildegarde. *Romantic Cities of California*. New York: Appleton-Century, 1939.

Historic American Buildings Survey. Photograph-data Book Reports.

Honnold, Douglas. *Southern California Architecture 1769-1956*. New York: Reinhold Publishing Corp., 1956.

Hoover, Mildred; Rensch, H. E.; and Rensch, E. G. *Historic Spots in California*. Stanford University Press, 1966.

Hulanisky, F. J. *The History of Contra Costa County, California*. Berkeley: Elias Publishing Co., 1917.

Kirker, Harold. *California's Architectural Frontier*. San Marino: Huntington Library, 1960.

————. "California's Architecture in the Nineteenth Century: A Social History." PhD. thesis, University of California, Berkeley, June, 1957.

Krythe, Maymie. *Port Admiral*. San Francisco: California Historical Society, 1957.

Lewis, Oscar. *Fabulous San Simeon.* San Francisco: California Historical Society, 1958.

————. *Here Lived the Californians.* New York: Rinehart, 1957.

Los Angeles Historic-Cultural Landmarks. Los Angeles: Home Savings and Loan Association, 1968.

Melick, Weldon. "Sevenscore Gables." *Holiday,* February, 1947.

Muir, John. *The Mountains of California.* Garden City: Doubleday, 1961.

Murphy, Celeste G. *The People of the Pueblo.* Sonoma: W. L. and C. G. Murphy, 1935.

Murray, Ken. *The Golden Days of San Simeon.* Garden City: Doubleday, 1971.

Neasham, V. Aubrey. *Old Sacramento, A Reference Point in Time.* Sacramento Historic Landmarks Commission, 1965.

Nelson, Edna Du Pree. *The California Dons.* New York: Appleton-Century, 1962.

Newcomb, Rexford. *Spanish Colonial Architecture in the United States.* New York: J. J. Augustin, 1937.

North, Flora D. "She Built for the Ages." *Kappa Alpha Theta Journal,* Spring, 1967.

Oakland Tribune. "Oakland Centennial" section, May 1, 1952.

Otto, Von Geldren. *Recollections of the Late General Vallejo.* Sonoma, 1920s.

Peirson, Erna. "M. Theo Kearney, Fresno's Man of Mystery." *California Historian,* vol. 11, No. 3.

Pitt, Leonard. *The Decline of the Californios.* Berkeley: University of California Press, 1966.

Richey, Elinor. *The Ultimate Victorians.* Berkeley: Howell-North Books, 1970.

Robinson, W. W. *Los Angeles from the Days of the Pueblo.* San Francisco: California Historical Society, 1959.

————. *The Ranchos Become Cities.* Pasadena: San Pasqual Press, 1939.

Sanchez, Nellie Van de Grift. *Spanish Arcadia.* San Francisco: Powell Publishing Co., 1929.

Sargent, Shirley. "Past and Present in Our Valley." *California Historian,* June, 1971.

Smith, Sarah Bixby. *Adobe Days.* Los Angeles: Jake Zeitlin, 1931.

Smith, Suzy. *Prominent American Ghosts.* Cleveland: World Publishing Co., 1967.

Smythe, William E. *History of San Diego, 1542-1908.* San Diego: The History Co., 1908.

Stansell, Lois. "The Bidwell Letters." *Butte County Historical Society Quarterly,* Spring, 1972.

Swift, Hildegarde H. *From the Eagle's Wing.* New York: Morrow, 1962.

Thickens, Virginia E. "Pioneer Agricultural Colonies of Fresno County." *California Historical Society Quarterly,* vol. 25, pp. 169-77.

Thompson & West. *History of Sacramento County, California, 1880.* Berkeley: Howell-North Books, 1960.

Vail, Wesley D. *Victorians, An Account of Domestic Architecture in Victorian San Francisco.* San Francisco: W. D. Vail, 1964.

Van Dyke, T. S. *The City and County of San Diego.* San Diego: Leberthon and Taylor, 1888.

Vickery, Oliver. ". . . And he Named It Wilmington." Wilmington Chamber of Commerce Fact Book and Buyers' Guide, 1969.

Watkins, T. H., and Olmsted, Roger. *Here Today.* San Francisco: Chronicle Books, 1968.

Wells, Harry L., and Gilbert, Frank T. *History of Butte County.* San Francisco: Harry L. Wells, 1882; Howell-North Books, Berkeley, 1973.

Wolfe, Linne Marsh. *Son of the Wilderness.* New York: Knopf, 1945.

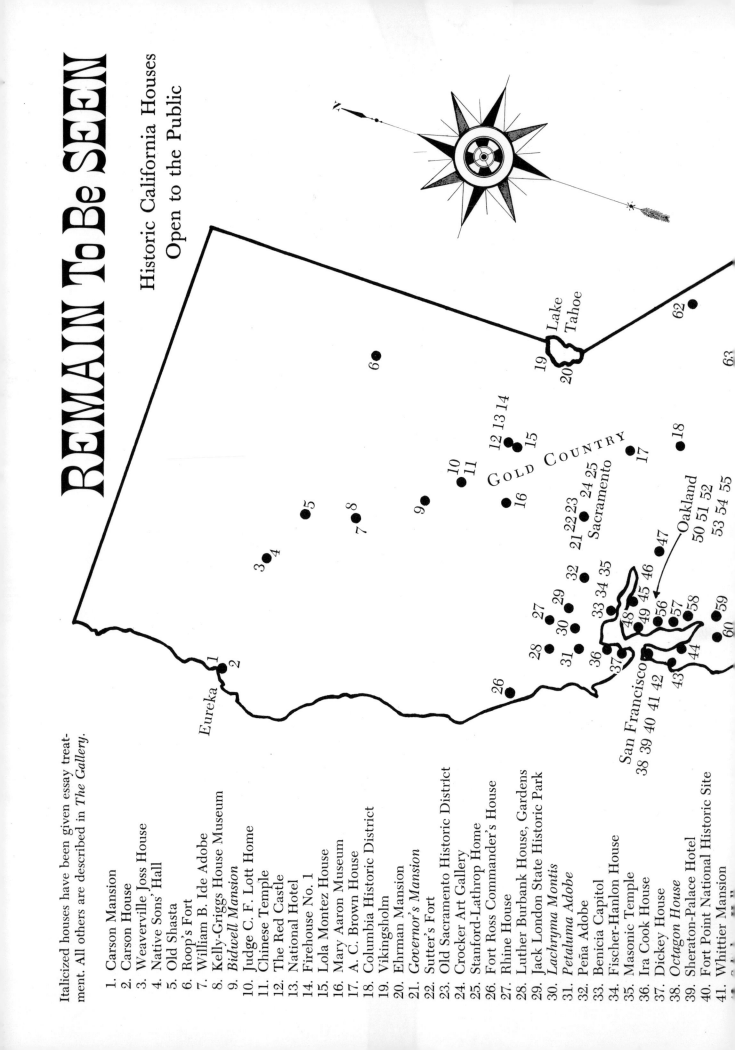

REMAIN To Be SEEN

Historic California Houses
Open to the Public

Italicized houses have been given essay treatment. All others are described in *The Gallery*.

1. Carson Mansion
2. Carson House
3. Weaverville Joss House
4. Native Sons' Hall
5. Old Shasta
6. Roop's Fort
7. William B. Ide Adobe
8. Kelly-Griggs House Museum
9. *Bidwell Mansion*
10. Judge C. F. Lott Home
11. Chinese Temple
12. The Red Castle
13. National Hotel
14. Firehouse No. 1
15. Lola Montez House
16. Mary Aaron Museum
17. A. C. Brown House
18. Columbia Historic District
19. Vikingsholm
20. Ehrman Mansion
21. *Governor's Mansion*
22. Sutter's Fort
23. Old Sacramento Historic District
24. Crocker Art Gallery
25. Stanford-Lathrop Home
26. Fort Ross Commander's House
27. Rhine House
28. Luther Burbank House, Gardens
29. Jack London State Historic Park
30. *Lachryma Montis*
31. *Petaluma Adobe*
32. Peña Adobe
33. Benicia Capitol
34. Fischer-Hanlon House
35. Masonic Temple
36. Ira Cook House
37. Dickey House
38. *Octagon House*
39. Sheraton-Palace Hotel
40. Fort Point National Historic Site
41. Whittier Mansion

Eureka

Lake Tahoe

GOLD COUNTRY

Sacramento

Oakland

San Francisco